THE 100X ENTREPRENEUR

STORIES OF EXTREME GROWTH

Mary J. Cronin and
David A. Reske

4QCatalyst

www.4qcatalyst.com

ISBN: 978-1-7379893-3-2 (paperback)
ISBN: 978-1-7379893-4-9 (ebook)

Cover design by Graphic Details

First edition

Contents

Introduction

What does it take to scale a startup 100 times in just a few years? What separates the entrepreneurs who achieve extraordinary growth from those who build solid but limited businesses? Is there any roadmap for founders who aspire to exponential growth?

To answer these questions, we talked with twenty 100X entrepreneurs. Some of these founders scaled their companies on the way to becoming industry leaders with billion-dollar valuations. Others grew more recently, rocketing to the top of the *Inc. 5000* and *Deloitte Fast 500* lists in the past few years. All of these entrepreneurs scaled their companies with vision, discipline, and fierce determination to build lasting value. In the process, they made tough decisions, overcame setbacks, and pivoted to the strategies that would fuel their rise. Their stories, and the strategies they adopted, form the heart of this book.

In these pages, you'll meet the founders of Wayfair, ButcherBox, CharterUP, OLIPOP, Carbliss, Harness, Odeko, Autosled, and many more extreme growth companies. You'll learn how these entrepreneurs validated product-market fit, motivated high-performance teams, navigated economic turbulence, and created digital and operational systems to support explosive growth. The growth stories they tell are candid, rich with insight, and packed with advice that you can apply at any stage of your business journey.

The 100X Mindset

The entrepreneurs featured in this book didn't follow a single playbook. Some launched direct-to-consumer brands. Others built enterprise tech platforms or reinvented legacy industries. Some raised large venture rounds. Others bootstrapped based on customer revenue, with profitability from day one. Regardless of their industry and prior experience, the entrepreneurs we studied share an exceptional entrepreneurial mindset that views problems as opportunities, obstacles as signals to adjust, not reasons to stop, and setbacks as a fast track to learning.

This mindset is manifested in our 100X stories, from beverage formulation to AI innovation, from building consumer brands and two-sided marketplaces to industry consolidation. The 100X entrepreneurs we interviewed knew their strengths, led with values, built complementary teams, and created systems that allowed their companies to scale fast, without breaking.

We also learned that 100X entrepreneurs share a number of interconnected principles that we call the Essential Elements for Extreme Growth. These elements are a critical foundation for every entrepreneur who aims to achieve scalability in tandem with long-term profitability. We've structured each company narrative to highlight the founder's key decision points and how the essential elements came together as an integrated strategy to drive growth.

As you read their stories, you'll see all the aspects of the 100X journey. You'll hear directly from founders in their own words, as they share their startup vision, early challenges, lessons learned, and next steps.

The Chapters Ahead

Mapping the Path from Startup to Scalability kicks off in Chapter 1 with the founders of CSN Stores (before it became Wayfair) and ButcherBox sharing how they navigated from vision to extreme growth by combining business innovation with core scalability strategies.

Chapter 2, **Essential Elements for Extreme Growth,** analyzes how founders in multiple industries adapt the essential 100X building blocks to achieve their goals, with a deep dive into the story of Amir Harris at CharterUP scaling his company's revenues 111,130% in just 3 years.

Chapter 3, **Building a Consumer Brand from Zero to 100X,** focuses on the cost-effective customer acquisition, loyalty and recurring revenue strategies that propelled OLIPOP, MUD/WTR, and Carbliss to scalable growth, and the missteps that almost derailed Songfinch.

In Chapter 4, the founders of Odeko, Relay, Autosled, and Harness describe how **Outsized Business ROI and Bottom-Line Impact** are essential to winning market share in the business services and enterprise software sectors.

Leveraging Data and AI to Outperform the Competition underpins the 100X trajectory of the data-forward and AI empowered business models implemented by the founders of Crisp, Rarebreed Veterinary Partners and ProxyPics described in Chapter 5.

Chapter 6 analyzes how mastering an often-overlooked essential element, **Hyper-Efficient Operations for Quality That Scales**, enabled the founders of Uwill, FlexCare Infusion Centers, and Oxygen8 to become industry-leading models while scaling revenues and customers.

As Chapter 7 illustrates, **Transformational Outcomes with Financial Discipline** underpin scalable growth across all industry sectors, from Upward Health's breakthrough innovations in patient health, to the outsized client value delivered at scale by Awestruck and WeCall.

In Chapter 8, **Is Your Company Ready to Scale?** we shift the spotlight over to you, with five essential questions every entrepreneur must ask before committing to a 100X trajectory. This concluding chapter is both a mirror and a roadmap that will challenge you to assess your current business with fierce honesty—and flag any areas you need to strengthen before accelerating to the next level of growth.

For the data-minded and the curious, we end with a bonus Appendix, **Insights from the *Inc 5000* and *Deloitte Fast 500* Leaderboard.** There we dive into key data sets from the top companies on the *Inc 5000* and Deloitte *Technology Fast 500* lists between 2022 and 2024 to analyze 135 companies that grew by at least 10,000% in a period of 3 years.

Why Read This Book

The entrepreneurial world celebrates success, but too often it glamorizes outcomes while glossing over the hard work it takes to get there. We decided to skip the stardust and write a book that told the truth—the complicated, deeply human truth—about the path to extreme growth. This book's 100X entrepreneur stories offer something rare: honest, first-person reflections on what it takes to ignite and manage scalable growth year after year.

We listened closely, asked tough questions, and took the time to recount each 100X story in the founder's voice– because we believe these details will put the reader inside the moments of hard choices and pivotal decisions that every entrepreneur faces. And because actionable insights are a lot more powerful than abstract theory when it comes to scaling a business.

At the same time, we analyzed how strategies for scalability and extreme growth are impacted by today's AI tools and competitive landscape. The result is a dynamic framework characterizing the Essential Elements of Extreme Growth needed for sustainable scalability and market leadership. We envision this framework as a high-value tool for entrepreneurs at every stage of growth and plan to expand it beyond the sample questions in Chapter 8.

Our hope is that this book and its 100X growth stories will inspire readers and empower more entrepreneurs to scale with confidence and wisdom. If you're dreaming of extreme growth, just starting your entrepreneurial journey, or ready for the next big leap – this book is for you.

1
Mapping the Path from Startup to Scalability

SOME STARTUPS FLASH BRIGHTLY and burn out. Others manage modest, steady expansion. Only a rare few achieve 100X growth—scaling revenue and operations more than one hundredfold within just a few years, often transforming industries in the process. This chapter tracks the path of two companies that bootstrapped their way to extreme growth: CSN Stores, an e-commerce pioneer that launched in 2002, and ButcherBox, a mission-driven healthy meat subscription service started in 2015.

Their stories are compelling for many reasons; 100X growth without external funding is the rarest achievement of all, yet the strategies that empowered such growth are available to every aspiring entrepreneur. We asked Niraj Shah, Steve Conine, and Mike Salguero to share how they did it, from their starting vision to unforeseen developments, pivots, and innovations on their way to industry leadership.

Niraj Shah and Steve Conine, cofounders of CSN Stores (now Wayfair), decided up front to invest in long-term value over e-commerce hype. Back in 2002, when venture capitalists had lost interest in online retail, these two entrepreneurs scaled their startup by launching dozens and eventually hundreds of niche online stores that sold everything from barstools to baby cribs. Their scalability strategy was to optimize each niche site's product-market fit, deliver stellar customer experience, and invest in innovative technology and asset-light logistics. By the time they consolidated under the Wayfair brand in 2011, they'd already built the backend muscle to become a dominant player in e-commerce, years ahead of competitors.

Mike Salguero's story at ButcherBox begins with a twist – his quest to find healthy, additive-free beef for his own family inspired him to offer this service to consumers nationwide. Resolved to forgo venture funding, Salguero launched ButcherBox via a Kickstarter campaign in 2015, and bootstrapped his startup to over $400 million in revenue within four years. Salguero prioritized customer trust, managing an outsourced supply chain, and financial discipline in every aspect of the company. He refused to sacrifice margins or values for the sake of growth—and ironically, that's what allowed him to scale faster.

These entrepreneurs implemented scalable strategies for companies they were building to last for decades. They validated market demand, set robust growth flywheels in motion, and insisted on disciplined cost management. They didn't chase 100X growth by raising millions in venture funding, or taking big risks. In fact, Shah, Conine, and Salguero scaled their startups successfully and minimized risk by prioritizing the essential elements of extreme growth from day one.

From CSN Stores to Wayfair

Wayfair went public on the New York Stock Exchange on October 1, 2014; one day later the company had a market value of approximately $3.1 billion. It was a dazzling milestone for the online retail venture that Niraj Shah and Steve Conine had cofounded in 2002 as CSN Stores. Even more impressive is the story of how Shah and Conine bootstrapped CSN Stores from a portfolio of niche online retail sites to achieve more than $500 million in annual sales in the years before Wayfair. The strategies that propelled CSN's extreme growth are foundational for today's 100X entrepreneurs.

At a time when e-commerce was still reeling from the dot.com crash of 2000, Shah and Conine re-wrote the playbook for online retail success. CSN Stores was profitable in its first year, and went on to set a blazing growth pace year after year, achieving $100 million in revenues by 2006 and $500 million in 2011 before rebranding as Wayfair. Knowing this track record, I asked Steve Conine and Niraj Shah to talk with me about CSN's early trajectory and reflect on the key strategies that powered their growth.

My first question for Steve Conine was what attracted him to online retail so soon after the dot.com crash had created widespread disillusionment with the sector.

Here's what he said,

> *We had already started and exited two enterprise-facing digital services companies during the Internet boom. I'd say our focus with those two startups was to go full out, make some money, and move on. By 2002, I was ready for something more long term. I kept thinking that Walmart was the biggest company in the world, and that retail was such a massive part of the economy. Yet there wasn't a lot of ambition or funding for entrepreneurs in online retail, which made it even more interesting. Many of the surviving e-commerce sites were making money, but they weren't set up for high growth. I felt if we worked hard and built great tech, we could turn CSN into a huge company.*
>
> *Niraj and I were aligned in taking the long view. We agreed that online retail had so much potential, and that we could grow an e-commerce company in a way that was fun. So, we decided to go for it and just keep doubling down to see how far we could take it.*

Where others saw a collapsed market that had wiped out thousands of online startups and trillions in venture investment, Steve Conine and Niraj Shah saw an exciting opportunity to put their expertise to work, solve the issues that were holding back e-commerce adoption, and build a profitable company designed for high growth and long-term success. The growth potential for online retail was certainly enormous. Back in 2002, all the U.S. e-commerce sites combined represented just a tiny fraction —about 1.5% —of the estimated $3.5 trillion in traditional US retail sales. Retail startups that figured out how to drive growth by attracting and converting more customers to buy online would generate hundreds of millions of dollars.

At the same time, the barriers to startup survival – much less profitable online growth — were formidable. Many consumers didn't trust unfamiliar, digital-only stores. E-commerce sites struggled to attract visitors and convert them into buyers. Over half of the visitors who put items into their shopping carts at online stores left without completing their purchase. Selling higher-priced physical products was especially fraught. Inventory, warehousing, and shipping costs were steep and so was the investment needed to build and maintain a secure and scalable e-commerce site. Profit margins ranged from slim to nonexistent. Small wonder that online retail was out of favor with investors and entrepreneurs.

These were the odds that Shah and Conine looked forward to beating with CSN Stores. They started by merging an ambitious long-term vision with a pragmatic and metrics-driven approach to launch. They focused on the essential elements of 100X scalability – validating product-market fit, cost-effective customer acquisition, creating an outstanding customer experience, profitable unit economics, a robust and scalable technical infrastructure that generated high-value data, and a lean, asset-light operational model. Even the name CSN Stores was pragmatic – the founders knew that many enterprise-focused companies in manufacturing, logistics and related sectors had similarly generic names. They decided that CSN (a combination of their initials) would be more credible to their future supply chain partners, and that advantage outweighed a clever name.

Niche Stores to Validate Product-Market Fit and Propel the Flywheel

Instead of going head-to-head with Amazon and well-established big-box retail brands, Shah and Conine also made a deliberate decision to build CSN as a collection of niche stores, each branded as a specific product category. The launch strategy was to pick a single product category – a moderate to high priced home item with established consumer demand and a limited selection available in physical and online stores. This niche store model allowed for validation of product-market fit on a rolling basis. Once consumer interest and willingness to buy online was confirmed for CSN's first store, the growth path was straightforward – keep adding product categories, each with its separately marketed niche store, while optimizing unit economics and cost-effective customer acquisition across the entire portfolio of sites.

The choice of RacksandStands.com as the first store to launch may seem odd, but in fact this product category checked all the boxes for CSN. The big box and specialty retailers who sold high end TVs and audio equipment didn't stock much of a selection of racks and stands. The consumers who were paying high prices for new home electronics wanted more choices; a larger or smaller size, or something that would match their décor. These consumers were often early e-commerce adopters who were comfortable searching for a better selection online. With a well-defined value proposition of better selection, competitive pricing, and the convenience of home delivery, CSN focused on reaching potential customers with targeted search marketing.

To outperform online stores that were selling similar products, CSN eliminated as many barriers to conversion as possible. The top reasons for shopping cart abandonment were already well-known: sites lacked any contact information or phone support to build customer trust; product listings didn't include important details; return policies were not clearly stated; and at the top of the list, encountering high shipping costs when an item was added to the shopping cart. The founders made two strategic decisions that significantly improved their conversion rates. The approximate cost of shipping was pre-calculated and bundled into the price of each item, to avoid surprises at checkout. From the customer's perspective they were getting free shipping. Even more central to the company's organizational culture, CSN established an in-house call center and located it in the middle of its operations. Each niche product store featured the company's phone number and an invitation to call with any questions. The two founders sat with the call center staff to learn what customers were asking about, and to model the priority of excellent customer service for everyone on the team.

Niraj Shah recalls how these decisions paid off when RacksandStands.com launched in summer 2002,

For any entrepreneur, when you start something, you're always optimistic about how much it can grow. But you don't really know. You just have to dive in and start working it and iterating. In our case, what iteration meant was adding products to the web store, so you're growing selection, and making sure that the products are priced competitively. At the same time, you need to attract customers by growing your advertising. For us, the advertising approach was very quantitative. We were always measuring the results to make sure the ads led to site visits and customer purchases, growing revenue. From the start, you are basically just trying to get that growth flywheel to work.

RacksandStands.com was the first site we launched. The nice thing is that we hit good product market fit right away. We were selling TV stands, speaker stands, and entertainment centers. We knew that there were a few other sites online that were doing that already and we could see from them what product selection and pricing would help give us an advantage. Once we had that in place, we focused on having the best customer service. Back in 2002, a lot of consumers would have questions about the product and wanted to talk with someone at the store before they made a decision. We realized that by making it really easy to call us, and making sure that CSN call staff were really helpful on the phone, we would have a much better chance of getting the order.

Putting all that together worked pretty well, to the degree where our sales at RacksandStands.com grew really quickly. At that point we knew there was a real product market fit. For that first year, we didn't spend a ton of time trying to project future revenue. We were just trying to drive the flywheel and keep turning it faster by adding more product stores.

RacksandStands.com and the niche store model hit an immediate chord with consumers; in just four months, CSN generated about $400,000 in sales. Seeing that success, Shah and Conine launched their second niche store in an adjacent product category, TV wall mounts. Next, they ventured into outdoor furniture with TeakWickerAndMore.com. From that focused start, CSN Stores set a fast pace proliferating sites for bar stools, beds, pet furniture, office desks, kitchen cookware, and dozens of other categories. By 2006, the company operated a web of interconnected storefronts covering furniture and home goods products. Each site was narrowly tailored – often using category-specific domain names like BarStools.com or Cookware.com – which helped attract organic search traffic and provided a better experience for shoppers seeking particular products. Behind the scenes, Shah and Conine managed this collection of sites as one integrated business and kept spinning the growth flywheel.

Cost-Effective Customer Acquisition with Data-Driven Marketing

The founders leveraged their expertise in data management and analytics to fine-tune CSN's customer acquisition strategy. They were early adopters of search advertising and SEO (search engine optimization), leveraging the fact that platforms like Google's AdWords were relatively inexpensive and underutilized at the time. Information-rich niche stores that were full of product keywords were an ideal match for the early search engine algorithms, often propelling CSN sites to the top of organic search results. This was especially valuable in the company's early years when so many shoppers turned to Google to look for specific products.

Crucially, they approached online advertising with quantitative and financial rigor: every dollar spent on Google AdWords or Yahoo's Overture platform was tracked against resulting clicks, conversions, and profit. Shah remembers that in those early days they "meticulously tracked advertising costs, keyword performance, and conversion rates, ensuring profitability on every sale." In other words, even as they pursued growth, each transaction had to pay off. This discipline of profitable unit economics became a cornerstone of their execution strategy.

Conine recalls that CSN was at the forefront of using analytics to guide online ad bidding. The team closely analyzed which search keywords led to sales and at what cost, then adjusted bids accordingly. That data-driven approach gave them an advantage, even as they avoided trying to "game the system,"

We were at the forefront of companies that were analytical about using Google and Google AdWords and other search engine ad platforms like Yahoo. They were all very immature platforms when we got started, so you didn't have to have a lot of sophistication to be a pretty advanced bidder. We figured out that by really watching bid levels, what traffic was, and what the yield on the traffic was, we could bid much more intelligently to get the most value from every ad.

To do that we looked at our internal analytics for CSN inbound traffic — where it came from, how we attribute credit for it, and how we use that data to decide how much we want to pay tomorrow. As we expanded our sites, people would assume we were an SEO play. But we didn't have any interest in playing SEO games – that wasn't a long-term growth plan. Our core strategy was always based on the analytics of advertising; how do you take advantage of the ad market that's emerging, and make the best decisions. CSN was part of a cohort of companies that came of age when online advertising was maturing, and we matured with it by using analytics and the systems we built. It gave us a kind of first mover advantage.

That said, operating so many content-rich retail sites with names matching specific product types (like strollers.com, barstools.com, bedroomFurniture.com, and ultimately over 200 more) gave CSN an edge in organic search rankings as well as in paid search marketing. Customers searching for a particular item would often find a CSN store at the top of their search result, and decide to take a look. Once those customers landed on the site, the company worked hard to convert them to become buyers – and often succeeded.

High Quality in a Lean Operation:
Vendor Relations and Drop Shipping

CSN Stores established lean operations, including an asset-light drop-shipping model with vendors and distributors. Customer orders were forwarded to a selected vendor, who would ship the product directly to the customer. CSN held very little stock – eliminating the high costs of purchasing and warehouse storage for expensive products. The company eventually operated small warehouses (in Massachusetts and Utah) to handle returns and a limited number of high-demand items that vendors couldn't ship quickly. Everything else, from couches to swing sets, went straight from supplier to the customer's door. This approach let CSN offer an "endless aisle" of products without tying up capital – they could list a manufacturer's entire catalog on their site, including multiple colors and configuration options, because they didn't have to pre-purchase the inventory. As Shah explained, "vendor integration and selection are key in our ability to not only serve the long tail of product selection in markets where carrying inventory is prohibitively expensive, but also maintain a high fill rate of orders while still shipping items quickly." Dropshipping allowed CSN to scale selection and volume fast, but it required carefully choosing vendors and integrating with their inventory systems to avoid stock-outs or delays.

Building relationships with the most reliable vendors fostered a collaborative path for CSN to determine which product categories to sell. Shah describes this as an iterative process,

> As we expanded, our suppliers noticed that we were selling more and more of their products — and that we provided really good customer service. That prompted more two-way conversations with suppliers about market demand and what other items they thought would sell well. Some vendors wanted us to offer their full line of products. Earning their trust was a big positive for us and we saw that deeper relationships with vendors opened another path to deciding on product niches. We started working our way

more deliberately through different categories of furniture, then moved
into home improvement, décor and home goods products. Even though we
also opened stores in some different categories during those years, we were
already on the path that led to us being primarily a home goods retailer.

The decision to deepen relationships with suppliers didn't just pave the way
for eventually branding as Wayfair—it helped CSN to increase profit margins
based on their rapidly growing volume of sales. The suppliers who benefited
from selling so many of their products through CSN were often willing to negotiate more favorable terms and volume discounts.

Scalable Unit Economics, Cash Flow, and
Revenue-Supported Expansion

Managing cash flow was a critical area where the CSN team demonstrated
their ability to maintain rapid growth while bootstrapping. The drop-ship,
pay-on-demand model not only saved inventory costs; it actually turned the
cash conversion cycle to CSN's advantage. Customers paid upfront on their
credit cards, and the card payments would settle to CSN in a couple of days.
Meanwhile, CSN typically had net 30-day payment terms with suppliers. In essence, customer purchases helped to finance the business. This positive cash
float grew alongside sales, providing working capital to fuel further expansion.

The collaborative relationships that CSN had established with vendors
became an asset in negotiating terms as their order volumes increased – not
just longer to pay, but also better wholesale pricing. Early on, as a small retailer, CSN paid standard prices. But as they proved they could move serious
volume, Shah and Conine went back to suppliers to secure volume discounts
and rebates. For example, they might tell a furniture manufacturer, *"We did*
$100,000 with you this year; if you can give us better pricing, we believe we can
do $250,000 next year." Often the vendor would hesitate to grant a big dis-
count on faith, so CSN crafted tiered rebate agreements – if they hit $150K,
$200K, $250K in sales, the supplier would retroactively increase the discount
percentage. In essence, CSN took on the risk of projected future growth in
exchange for improved margin on each product. This paid off handsomely.

Higher traffic led to more sales, which in turn gave them leverage to get
even better supplier pricing for the next cycle. It was a virtuous feedback loop
that their financially constrained competitors couldn't easily match.

As Niraj Shah describes the dynamic,

Our model was basically to manage sales growth and cash flow to self-fund our own working capital. That is how we bootstrapped, and we got to $500 million in sales before we took in capital and rebranded as Wayfair.

As we sold more, we would also push to get bigger volume discounts from our suppliers, because those discounts grew our margin. With better margin, we could bid a little more for our online ads to get a lot more customer traffic. CSN had predictably good conversion rates, because we focused on the call center and excellent customer service along with better selection and good pricing. That meant we could continually sell more products, which made the suppliers more willing to increase our discounts, and we used those volume-based discounts to get even better pricing. We weren't necessarily taking much profit out of the company along the way, but we knew that we always had a lot of profit coming due as we met our volume targets for higher discounts — accruing, if you will.

Building a System Architecture for Ten Years of Growth

As CTO, Steve Conine was responsible for the technology at the heart of all CSN operations. He designed the technical infrastructure that powered the company's web sites, order fulfillment, and analytics to handle high demand and rapid expansion. As Steve looks back on his CSN system architecture decisions, he remembers taking a 10-year view and planning for scalable growth from the very start even in the context of a lean budget,

I knew that for CSN we wanted a good central system of record database and so the core design of our site was around a database. I was very thoughtful about how I structured the database, and I actually ran some tests to benchmark the possibility of running a billion-dollar business on one or two SQL servers and thinking we could scale from zero to being that large. I also realized that the database would become a performance bottleneck, and so we were innovators in taking the load off the database as early adopters of Akamai to try and do edge caching with them. We were definitely pushing the tech envelope. Looking back, even knowing what I know now, there might be things I'd tweak, but there was a real advantage in the architecture we chose at the time.

Having a robust, scalable infrastructure gave CSN a competitive edge. While many rivals struggled to manage even a few thousand SKUs online, CSN's system could handle millions of product listings and updates in real time. By integrating directly with suppliers' inventory feeds, CSN could display up-to-the-minute stock information and send orders electronically – a seamless process that competitors found hard to replicate.

The company also developed sophisticated internal tools to manage its growing drop-ship operations. One tool, internally known as the "system weather report," monitored the entire order pipeline for glitches and delays – for instance, flagging if a given supplier was lagging in confirming shipments, or if a batch of orders was at risk of missing promised ship dates. This dashboard allowed the CSN team to proactively address fulfillment problems, often before customers noticed them. Over time, CSN amassed performance data on each partner and developed internal "trust factor" scores to identify any suppliers who were consistently lagging or providing inaccurate inventory data. Those insights informed which suppliers they would feature more prominently on the sites, and which vendors they needed to work with to improve performance.

In effect, CSN created its own early predictive analytics system to monitor shipment and delivery, managing the customer experience even though they didn't directly control fulfillment. This type of data and predictive capability supported reliable, predictable delivery schedules even as they scaled to hundreds of drop-ship vendors. It also differentiated them from the online vendors who, when faced with fulfillment issues, often resorted to curtailing their product assortment. In contrast, Shah and Conine "kept doubling down" on figuring out how to manage a distributed supplier network at scale. In turn, this capacity gave CSN the competitive advantage of a broader selection and better pricing for customers. By the time they were considering a rebrand, they had honed their drop-ship model enough in terms of consistency that they felt confident putting a single brand name on it.

Data Flywheel for Increasing Value

As the company grew, it continued to develop data analytics capabilities that were far in advance of most online retailers. CSN invested in building an internal analytics platform to pull data from every part of the business into a multi-dimensional cube, originally accessible via Excel pivot tables. This gave managers the power to slice and dice sales, traffic, and customer behavior data on the fly – a precursor to business intelligence dashboards. As Shah explains, the company's quantitative orientation set the stage for employing machine learning algorithms.

> *We're a very quantitative group, and one of the things we always did is to use all the data we collected to run the business better and better. Steve and I knew that one of the big benefits of running an e-commerce business is that you could really track what was happening in every niche store; you could track visitors and what products they looked at, what they bought, how they got to our site, and what marketing channels were sending the most profitable customers. We used all that data to analyze what worked well, what needed to be changed, and to optimize processes. That orientation really helped us a lot. Very early at CSN, we invested in building an analytics platform that allowed us to generate whatever reports we wanted.*
>
> *If you think about CSN in the first decade, we were using data science and machine learning to optimize everything in our store catalogs, using a pricing model that would meet our margin needs while maximizing demand and even taking competitor's pricing into account. We used algorithms and an AI model to determine which items to display first in responding to customer search, trying to personalize the display order based on their style and their preferences. That capability depends on a very big data science model, and we've had some of these working for a long time. At this point, we have algorithms and models all throughout the business and we'll continue to invest in advancing those with AI.*

This forward-looking culture of experimentation with technology ensured that as the company scaled, it stayed on the cutting edge of e-commerce tech and sophisticated retail analytics. Conine in particular championed constant innovation in the tech stack, earning Wayfair a reputation for being as much a technology company as a retailer. In short, the founders built not just a high-growth business, but one that was unusually analytical and innovative for the retail industry, setting it up to adapt and thrive in the years ahead.

Building a Customer-Focused Team and Culture

Both founders were also committed to building a company culture that was open, analytical, customer-focused, and geared for rapid growth. There were no private offices or rigid hierarchies; even as they grew to dozens and then hundreds of employees, the founders sat out in the open alongside everyone else. Conine likened the setup to a trading floor – a "relaxed, open-space environment" where staff members could easily walk up to him or Niraj with a question or a suggestion. This physical openness facilitated constant communication and a sense of shared mission. New hires quickly learned that CSN was a place where titles mattered less than results and information flowed freely. Shah and Conine set high performance standards and led by example. "Everyone worked around Niraj and I – we set the tone, we set the pace, we set the expectation for what people needed to get done," Conine says of the early culture.

> We focused on customers right from the start. Niraj and I both put on headsets and answered customer calls with everyone else. In our open office, the tech team sat right in the middle of where all the calls came in. Everyone knew what questions customers were asking, and what info they needed before deciding to buy. Sometimes those questions highlighted an issue on our site; maybe missing products, missing features, or something was down, so everyone was hearing about that. It naturally created this very customer-oriented group of developers and engineers who wanted to address every customer request quickly. As we scaled, sometimes that became too distracting and we needed to say, well, this is a 1 in 10,000 order problem, let's address it later.

Shah and Conine were very hands-on managers, personally ensuring that new team members, whether in engineering or customer support, got training in the company's systems and values. Even the customer service reps were taught basic SQL queries so they could pull data and understand the back-end of the store system – a reflection of how deeply data was ingrained in the culture. Engineers, for their part, spent time on the customer support phone lines. This created a team with a shared sense of purpose, centered on customer service.

Rebranding as Wayfair

By 2011, CSN Stores had become the largest online-only retailer of home goods, with over $1 billion in cumulative sales since its founding and roughly 250 websites, most known by their niche product name. Buyers who landed on one product store would have an excellent experience – but if they didn't realize they were buying from CSN Stores, there was little opportunity for converting that into recurring revenue or increased customer lifetime value.

Shah and Conine recognized this disconnect and tried to bridge the gap in 2009 by introducing a cross-site shopping cart and a universal "CSN Stores" header on all its sites. The company also ramped up email marketing to let customers know about other CSN websites and products that might interest them. These efforts helped them to almost double the repeat purchase rate. However, that repeat rate remained relatively low, and they suspected it had hit a ceiling within the CSN Stores structure. To truly unlock a customer's lifetime value, the company needed shoppers to shop with them for all their home needs.

Additionally, the economics of online advertising were changing. By 2010, the cost of customer acquisition through ads on Google and elsewhere had risen substantially. Acquiring customers profitably on the first order became more challenging every year. Shah and Conine could see that a different model was needed to turn satisfied customers into repeat buyers and grow their company to the next level. In the summer of 2011, the founders announced that CSN Stores would consolidate its hundreds of niche websites into one primary new brand: Wayfair. The tagline they chose – "a zillion things home" – emphasized the company's vast product selection and kicked off the process of branding Wayfair as the top online home store destination. Recognizing the need to fund the transition process and create consumer brand recognition for Wayfair, the founders raised $165 million in venture funding, their first-ever infusion of institutional capital.

Internally, the transition required a massive technical migration, but Conine's engineering team actually welcomed it. "From an engineering standpoint, having one site that everything's going to move to simplifies it a lot," he said of the consolidation. Maintaining hundreds of separate sites (each with slightly different features or designs) had been a burden; moving to a single platform allowed the tech team to focus on improving a single customer experience instead of hundreds.

In Wayfair's first year, the company surpassed $600 million in revenue – a significant leap from the $500 million high point reached by CSN Stores. Many consumers discovered Wayfair for the first time and were impressed by the one-stop-shop home goods experience. By 2012, Wayfair was routinely cited as one of the fastest-growing e-commerce companies in the U.S. and had cracked the top ranks of online home retailers. With momentum on its side, Wayfair continued to scale: by 2014, just three years post-rebrand, the company hit $1 billion in annual direct sales. Shah and Conine's long-held vision of building a truly enduring online retail company was coming to fruition.

The journey of CSN Stores, from a single niche website in 2002 to the Wayfair brand in 2011, offers an end-to-end roadmap for achieving extreme growth. Characteristically of Niraj Shah and Steve Conine, the takeaway is both pragmatic and inspirational: commit to a long-term scalability plan, work hard and smart, measure everything, iterate, innovate – and have fun along the way.

ButcherBox

Can you become a 100X entrepreneur by planning a side hustle or a lifestyle business with plenty of time to pursue other life goals? Absolutely! As long as you start with an entrepreneurial mindset, a scalable business model, and the agility to adapt when market demand takes off like a rocket instead of the motor scooter you envisioned. That's what Mike Salguero told us happened when he launched ButcherBox.

Salguero's path to ButcherBox was paved with hard-learned lessons from his six years as cofounder and CEO of CustomMade, an online marketplace that connected artisans with consumers for custom-made products. Salguero's summary of that experience packs a world of regrets into a few sentences,

> *My first company was a venture-backed business. We raised about $30 million of financing to support this online marketplace that matched up artisans and consumers. But the company never generated the revenue we had projected. Basically, we couldn't keep it going; in the end I felt that we had let everyone down and lost everyone's money.*

After CustomMade, Mike Salguero vowed he would never again rely on venture capital as a growth engine. Even so, his disillusionment with venture funding didn't shut down his inner entrepreneurial drive. It just transformed his goals for balancing work, life, and creating value through business into something besides making as much money as possible.

At the same time as figuring out his next business opportunity, Salguero was working on a family challenge. His wife had a thyroid condition that made access to grass-fed beef with no antibiotic or added hormones important for her diet. Mike believed this diet would be healthier for the whole family. But finding a local source for high-quality, sustainably raised meat proved surprisingly difficult. That problem became an "aha moment" for Salguero, shaping his mission for ButcherBox. As he recalls,

> *I had no idea where to find this type of grass-fed beef. Eventually, I ended up buying it directly from a farmer. But unfortunately for me, farmers generally sell beef in quarter shares or half shares of the entire animal. That's a lot of meat! I ended up giving away what we couldn't use to my friends. Then one of my friends said, this would be so much easier if you just delivered a box to my house every month. Yeah, I thought, who wouldn't like that?*
>
> *I had already been trying to figure out what type of product would fit a subscription business mode for my side hustle. I knew monthly subscriptions had great potential for recurring revenue and compounding over time. And here was the idea – sell subscriptions to grass-fed beef.*

It turns out that the first steps Mike took to launch his planned lifestyle business were very similar to the early pages of the playbook for building a scalable, profitable venture. Both start with validating market demand, attracting customers, and honing a lean, asset-light operations model.

Salguero was convinced that grass-fed, additive free meat would appeal to health-minded consumers and be good for the environment. He had already decided that a subscription business model matched his personal goals. The next three steps were more daunting — he needed to validate market demand in a way that would jump-start consumer interest; he had to figure out how to set up an asset-light model for delivering boxes of grass-fed beef to monthly subscribers; and as a bootstrapped company, he had to ensure that his business could generate profitable revenues from the beginning.

Market validation and revenue generation are the proof points where a founder's vision meets reality – and where that vision frequently falters. In Mike's case, it was a chance to put all the lessons he had learned in his previous startup to good use.

Lean Operations Design from an Industry Expert

To operate ButcherBox as a lifestyle business, Mike had decided that everything he could outsource to reliable, high-quality partners would be handled remotely, from the farmers raising sustainable meat to companies that specialized in butchering, cutting, picking, freezing, packing, and shipping that meat to households throughout the U.S. This partnership model was the only way that Salguero figured he could manage all the logistics necessary for order fulfillment without investing in extensive infrastructure, or becoming consumed by the demands of a complex supply chain. However, Salguero didn't have personal expertise in any of the supply chain components that ButcherBox needed. He wasn't even sure what companies would be the best partners, or how to establish a reliable, high-quality end-to-end chain from farms to a subscriber's front door.

Instead of trying to figure out every aspect of the business himself, Salguero took what he called a "who not what" approach. This approach let ButcherBox tap into top level expertise from industry veterans that a small startup wouldn't be able to recruit into full time positions. Mike reached out to Ron Eike, the retired head of operations at Omaha Steaks, then the largest shipper of boxed, frozen meat in the country. Eike responded positively to Salguero's request that he become an early-stage advisor; he even agreed to take equity in ButcherBox rather than charging his normal consulting rate. Eike's expertise and nationwide network were essential for designing a seamless supply chain and bringing the best partners on board to tee up a ButcherBox launch. Even customer support was outsourced. Salguero's logic was that a specialist call center could handle inquiries more efficiently, and that he would hold that partner accountable through strict service-level agreements. The only operational area ButcherBox kept fully in-house was overseeing food safety and quality control, since the brand's reputation would rise or fall based on consumer trust in its products. Sourcing sustainably raised meat from trusted farmers became a core competency for the company.

Even though Salguero was still thinking of ButcherBox as a small lifestyle business, his decision to work with experienced national partners all along the chain metaphorically saved his startup's bacon when consumer demand for ButcherBox subscriptions took off faster than anyone had anticipated. Over the long term, the outsourced supply chain gave the company the agility to weather periods of market volatility and rapid growth. Without the burden of fixed costs, ButcherBox could scale operations up or down as demand fluctuated.

Before managing rapid growth became an issue, even before deciding to commit to a full business launch, Salguero still had to validate that strong market demand for monthly delivery of grass-fed beef actually existed. He took on this essential step with a characteristic focus on getting the most value possible at the lowest cost.

A Tiger by the Tail: From Kickstarter to 100X Growth

To test customer demand, Salguero turned to Kickstarter, seeing it as a cost-effective market awareness builder as well as a test of consumer interest,

> *I started with Kickstarter because I thought it would be a cheap way to get the word out about our business, and also the most direct way to test the market and the demand level. The other option was to launch a website and buy inventory, but then what if nobody is interested in buying it? I'd be stuck with all this inventory. Kickstarter was the easy and cheap way to see if anyone wanted this product.*

Aware of crowdsourcing best practices, Salguero set a campaign fund-raising target of just $25,000. He knew that quickly exceeding this modest goal would trigger the platform's algorithms to feature his campaign more prominently to create a positive spiral of increased visibility. He contacted friends, colleagues and supporters in advance, asking them to place orders on the opening day of the campaign. As the pre-orders started to roll in, ButcherBox promoted the campaign and its healthy meat subscriptions over social media with engaging videos that encouraged viral sharing.

This strategy paid off dramatically. Within 24 hours, ButcherBox doubled its original goal, reaching $50,000 in pre-orders. It ended the 30-day campaign with over $200,000 in orders from around the U.S. Even more significant for the company's future growth, 40% of those who contributed to the Kickstarter campaign eventually became monthly subscribers, establishing the foundation of recurring revenue that Salguero had envisioned as his growth engine.

It was a decisive moment of market validation. Clearly, ButcherBox had the potential to become a lot bigger than a side gig. As Mike put it, "we had a tiger by the tail." Rather than trying to cram this beast back into a smaller cage, he committed to bootstrapping his emerging venture to grow faster and bigger than anticipated so that ButcherBox could meet a groundswell of customer demand,

> We way oversold what we had expected. I guess then I realized we had a tiger by its tail. One that was much, much bigger than I had imagined. Maybe because I had young kids at the same time that this business was starting, and as a parent I had realized that you really can't control what your kid wants to be. Anyway, I had the same feeling about ButcherBox; the little company I had intended to build was so small compared to what ButcherBox actually wanted to be. And I felt it was important for me and eventually the whole team to help ButcherBox get big enough to make a real difference in the world. Then the main question became, OK, how do we do that?

After bringing in about $300,000 in revenues in 2015, including the Kickstarter orders, ButcherBox flexed its growth muscles and demonstrated that what it wanted to become was indeed really, really big. The company reached $5 million in revenues in its first full year of operation, as the subscription model gained traction beyond the crowdfunding base. From there, revenue growth accelerated each year, to about $30 million in year 2, then $100 million in year 3, with another giant leap to $220 million by year 4. By its fifth anniversary ButcherBox was generating over $400 million in annual sales – truly extreme growth for a company built on bootstrapping.

Let's revisit the question that Mike Salguero asked himself after his Kickstarter campaign launched a growth tiger. How did he and his team do that?

Disciplined Growth with Profits from Every Box

The one compass point that didn't shift was Mike's determination to bootstrap his company instead of raising venture capital. Embracing rapid growth meant sharpening the focus on lean operations, with disciplined financial management of cash flow and profit margins. As Salguero recalls,

> *We were doggedly focused on being box one profitable. Everyone in the company knew the mechanics of the margin that we made for every box. If we could make $20 on delivering that first box, and the marketing team would acquire a subscription customer for $20, then the next month and as long as that subscriber stays with us, we're making pure profit. That focus forced us to be a lot more operationally disciplined. For example, we had to negotiate all our costs. Still to this day, we negotiate everything. I like to say that if we had started by raising money, we'd probably be out of business right now, like all of the meal delivery startups that had so much venture backing before they crashed.*

ButcherBox's business was designed around subscriptions because that model supported compounding revenue growth and rewarded customer retention. Unlike many meat providers who specialized in one-time or gift purchases at the time, Salguero recognized the potential of a recurring revenue model in an industry not traditionally structured this way.

As subscription demand skyrocketed, the company expanded in ways that further increased operational efficiency and helped to drive down costs. For example, when ButcherBox started shipping significant volumes to west coast customers, the company opened a regional logistics facility to cut down on expensive cross-country shipment. This decision reduced shipping time, increased customer satisfaction, and bumped profit per box from $20 to about $25. As growth continued, ButcherBox leveraged its bulk buying power to reduce costs and further streamlined operations to push the profit per box even higher without sacrificing quality. In turn, the positive cash flow enabled Salguero's vision of self-funding ButcherBox's accelerating growth.

Cost-Effective Customer Acquisition and Retention

Rather than spreading its early marketing efforts across multiple channels, Salguero adopted a lean and cost-effective customer acquisition strategy, telling us that, "Companies really only need one marketing trick to get to around $50 million in revenues." For ButcherBox, that "one trick" was partnering with paleo nutritionists, bloggers, and influencers in the health and wellness space, and recruiting the leading influencers to promote subscription sales. These partnerships provided access to audiences already interested in high-protein diets and sustainable food sources, creating a direct channel to reach the demographic most likely to subscribe to ButcherBox.

This influencer marketing became a key driver of ButcherBox's rapid growth during its first several years. In 2015, influencer marketing wasn't the ubiquitous, pricey channel it is today. In fact, it was an underutilized strategy, especially for food subscriptions. Salguero knew there were numerous bloggers and social media figures who passionately advocated for grass-fed beef and sustainable farming. These content creators had large, loyal followings but often lacked ways to monetize their popularity. Since ButcherBox didn't want to spend their cash on high up-front advertising fees, the marketing team developed an innovative affiliate model that rewarded influencers over the long term. ButcherBox paid referral fees on every box sale attributed to the influencer— not just on the first box, but for the lifetime of the customer. In other words, if an influencer's referral maintained their subscription for multiple years, that influencer earned a fee on every single box. This approach was compelling; it attracted influencers and even better, it convinced many of them to be long-term evangelists.

The influencer strategy had major advantages for ButcherBox. It conserved cash at a time when the company had little to spare. Importantly, it aligned incentives – influencers only got paid when they delivered paying customers, so the company's marketing spend directly correlated to sales. An unexpected bonus was that the extended referral fee created a cadre of loyal social media influencers. Since promoting a rival brand could reduce residuals from ButcherBox, many referral partners stuck exclusively with ButcherBox, giving the company a quasi-exclusive stable of advocates without requiring extra exclusivity incentives. Salguero notes that influencer marketing gave them a strong presence in different channels and kept early marketing costs low while reaching the consumers who were most likely to become subscribers. Most impressively, this cost-effective customer acquisition strategy did indeed propel ButcherBox revenue growth to reach that $50 million milestone.

Once it had crossed that milestone, ButcherBox expanded beyond the influencer strategy to budget for paid advertising campaigns. The company's first forays into Facebook and Google ads, armed with some viral content, delivered its message to a much broader audience, helping drive revenue into the hundreds of millions. By its fourth year of operation, ButcherBox had reached the kind of subscriber count and brand awareness that put it on the map nationally. Their subscriber list had expanded to include busy families, health-conscious consumers, and customers across many demographics who valued healthy, grass-fed meat.

Customer retention is vital for a successful subscription business model – if too many customers cancel, the recurring revenue advantage quickly evaporates. As revenues soared, Salguero focused team attention on improving customer satisfaction and lifetime customer value. By the numbers, ButcherBox's retention is quite strong for its category. The average lifetime of a subscriber is about 12 months, and many customers stay for several years, indicating a cadre of very loyal meat lovers who have stayed with the company from the start. This retention profile, combined with robust margins, means ButcherBox today can afford to invest more to acquire a new customer than they were able to do in the early years.

Nonetheless, ButcherBox still prioritizes cost-effective strategies to acquire and keep customers in a maturing market. Salguero notes that customer-to-customer referral marketing – incentivizing their satisfied customers to refer friends for a small reward – is a lever they haven't fully pulled yet. The company is also mining its rich historical subscriber data to re-engage lapsed customers ("farming vs. hunting," as Salguero puts it). They know 1.5 million households have tried ButcherBox. Convincing even a fraction of these customers to resubscribe could boost growth without heavy marketing spend. These strategies show that achieving hundreds of millions in annual revenue hasn't eroded ButcherBox's financial discipline. Salguero still insists that marketing creativity, leveraging data, and innovative, customer-centric thinking are superior to growth-at-all-cost strategies.

Tracking the Metrics That Matter

When it comes to analytics, Salguero focuses on fundamentals – the metrics that track how effectively the business makes money and keeps customers happy. He highlights that ButcherBox's key performance indicator, above all, is still "dollars per box" – essentially the profit on each order. Prioritizing positive unit economics has guided ButcherBox since day one and is baked into how the company evaluates success. Salguero is proud of this metric – it's a tangible outcome of relentless optimization in sourcing, logistics, and pricing. It's not a static data point: the team continues to seek ways to squeeze out more efficiency, whether through better packing methods, bulk purchasing, or leaner packaging. Dollars per box is still the north star for tracking ButcherBox performance.

Of course, profit means nothing without customers to serve, so the other metrics that dominate Salguero's dashboard are all about customer growth, satisfaction, and retention. Subscription sign-ups reflect the success of marketing efforts and overall demand, while churn is a barometer of customer satisfaction and continued product-market fit.

Cash position is a metric Salguero always keeps in view, as an essential element of financial discipline. Running out of cash is the death knell for any business, and with no cushion of venture funding, ButcherBox initially had to manage its working capital tightly. Salguero believes that this attention to cash inspired many of ButcherBox's smartest moves in financing and operations. For instance, he arranged favorable payment terms with suppliers so that they often sell through inventory before they have to pay for it – a favorable cash conversion cycle. Early on, their processor had agreed to invoice them net 30 but often didn't actually send out invoices for 60 or even 90 days, which effectively functioned as an interest-free loan. Later, ButcherBox negotiated an agreement where a distributor financed inventory up front, and ButcherBox paid the distributor a week after each unit sold. This took inventory completely off ButcherBox's balance sheet and freed up even more cash for growth.

Salguero's view is that many entrepreneurs "don't focus on [cash cycle] early enough," which means they end up in a crunch. He was determined not to fall into that trap, so metrics like inventory turnover, accounts payable days, and accounts receivable have been carefully managed. Tellingly, cash wasn't just a finance team concern; it was a company-wide concern, reinforced by making the cash position a visible week-to-week metric.

These and other core ButcherBox metrics are much the same in 2025 as they were back in 2015: new sign-ups, churn rate, cost to acquire a customer, lifetime value, profit per box, and cash flow. As the company and its employee group have grown over the years, ButcherBox has added metrics around employee satisfaction, internal process efficiency, and other measures of a dynamic company culture. Even so, when it comes to steering the financial and growth ship, those original KPIs remain front and center.

Salguero shares ButcherBox's key metrics with all employees, believing that everyone – from marketing to ops to finance – should be informed and aligned on the actual numbers that equal success. When every team member knows that sign-ups, churn, profit per box, and cash are the company's lifeblood, they can connect their day-to-day decisions to those outcomes. The operations folks know that sourcing a slightly less expensive beef supplier is great, but not if it hurts quality and thus affects churn. The metric-driven culture, reflected in Salguero's dashboard of KPIs, creates a common language and clear priorities. As he put it, sometimes companies drown in numbers that don't matter; ButcherBox chose a handful that did matter and tracked them consistently, year in and year out. That discipline has been key to staying financially healthy over time.

Alongside traditional data analytics, ButcherBox is enthusiastically embracing artificial intelligence to further sharpen its operations. Salguero's view is that business is entering an era where AI can augment customer services as well as make operational roles more productive. One of the first areas where AI has been deployed is in improving the customer experience by implementing more personalized support services.

Envisioning a Future with Growth and Impact

Mike Salguero brings our conversation back to his belief that ButcherBox's business success is grounded in its mission to make a difference in the world. His original value proposition for ButcherBox was to deliver 100% grass-fed beef with no additives. Not only was this a product that customers valued; increasing the supply of humanely raised, healthy beef had a broader positive impact by supporting sustainable livestock farming and reducing negative environmental effects.

When ButcherBox launched, grass-fed beef represented only about 1% of the total U.S. beef supply. Early on, it wasn't clear if there would be enough supply to meet skyrocketing customer demand, or if suppliers would work with a tiny startup. Salguero navigated this risk by forming relationships with a network of small farms and cooperatives who raised cattle to grass-fed standards. The company's commitment to buying only humanely raised, hormone- and antibiotic-free meat was a differentiator that won it customer loyalty. Today, ButcherBox's quality standards and mission have become a point of pride, a cornerstone of company culture and employee engagement.

In 2021, ButcherBox cemented its commitment to making a difference in the world by becoming a Certified B Corp, meeting high standards for social and environmental performance.

Mike Salguero emphasizes that the growth ButcherBox has achieved is based on core values shared by everyone in the company, and by their supply chain partners and customers. His vision of how ButcherBox will make a difference in the world continues to expand as he looks forward more growth and more impact in the years ahead,

> *A lot of great people want to work for a company that they believe in. People spend more time at work than anywhere else, and spending that time doing something meaningful is really important. At this point, the only companies I would ever want to run are ones that are mission focused and are making a difference in the world. At ButcherBox, I'd like to hit a billion dollars in revenue. I'd like to break into food service and retail. ButcherBox is now a brand that people recognize and it can grow into more areas, with partnerships and possibly acquisitions. We're looking to be around for the long term, and we will continue to do well by doing good.*

◆ ◆ ◆

CSN Stores and ButcherBox mapped a direct path to 100X growth, from entrepreneurial vision, well-planned execution, and validated product-market fit, to customer acquisition at scale, hyper-efficient operations, asset-light business models with disciplined unit economics, and mastery of the metrics that drive growth flywheels. As you will read in the following chapters, 100X growth strategies are adaptable to many different founder goals, business models, and industry sectors. No matter which path they chose, however, the founders whose companies succeed over time center their strategies on these essential scalability elements.

2
Essential Elements for Extreme Growth

EVERY ENTREPRENEUR DEFINES their startup vision and the problems they plan to solve in a deeply personal way. Any founder ambitious to scale their company will be more likely to succeed if they adopt well-established strategies for product development, customer acquisition, operational efficiency, financial management, and the many other tasks required to move from vision to company launch to profitability.

The entrepreneurs who achieve 100X growth take this process to the next level with an integrated set of strategic building blocks we call the Essential Elements for Extreme Growth. When tailored to a company's mission and market, seamlessly integrated, and connected to multiple growth flywheels, these elements power rapid and sustainable expansion.

The Essential Elements include three prerequisites for scalability – an entrepreneurial mindset that embraces challenges as opportunities, a business idea that addresses billion-dollar problems with high-value solutions, and a validated product-market fit. Even this high bar is just the starting point.

As founders set their sights on higher growth targets, they must complement cost-effective customer acquisition strategies with increasing customer lifetime value, create multiple revenue streams with strong unit economics, and build or outsource hyper-efficient operational systems that can scale while maintaining top quality. They leverage data and AI for internal optimization, rapid innovation, and differentiating their products and services, all while delivering increasing value to customers and outperforming competitors. Disciplined financial management ensures profitability and keeps expansion sustainable, while a values-driven culture ensures that team members and ecosystem partners are aligned, motivated, and performing at the highest level.

These building blocks are not unique to 100X entrepreneurs; in fact, one or more of them are foundational for any profitable enterprise. What enables scalability is adapting and integrating the essential elements to create a multiplier effect that drives all of the company's growth flywheels. The best way to appreciate the power of this multiplier effect is seeing it in action.

The growth story of Armir Harris, founder and CEO of CharterUP, allows us to do just that. From his earliest days bootstrapping a capital-light logistics company to transforming a fragmented $30 billion industry, Harris has strategically built these essential growth elements into every aspect of his company. His story is a blueprint for transforming vision and ambition into operational excellence, rapid market capture, and scalable growth.

CharterUP

When I email Armir Harris to introduce myself and request an interview, he responds in less than an hour. Here's what he says,

> Thank you for reaching out and for your interest. Yes, we can definitely connect. I'm currently at the Emergency Management Center in Florida, overseeing a large-scale evacuation and disaster recovery operation due to the hurricane. Depending on the extent of the damage, I may be here through part of next week as well...Weekends or Wednesday through Friday after 6 p.m. ET work best for me.

Before we even talk, I've learned a lot about the work ethic, leadership style, and boundless, super-focused drive that characterize Harris. He is on the front lines, putting people first, and still finding time to do more. That's the same drive behind CharterUP's achieving 111,130% revenue growth over 3 years to rank as the #2 fastest-growing private company in America. It's propelling Harris's determination to "create a model for accountability and transparency that has never existed in the charter bus industry." Lots of entrepreneurs aspire to lead transformative ventures. Most of them fail. Armir Harris is one of the very few who has managed to transform a $30 billion industry while achieving extreme growth and profitability.

The CharterUP story that Harris shares during our meeting starts with working in the family business, a commitment to lift his family out of poverty, and launching Shofur, his first startup, with $800 in savings. Here's how Harris tells it,

So, we're immigrants in my family, and my parents had a very modest limousine, black car service company based in Charlotte, NC. They didn't speak English very well, so I would do everything I could to help them out, from dispatching to reservations to a little bit of their online marketing and even taxes, from when I was only 16. In 2012 the Democratic National Committee came to Charlotte. At the last minute the convention organizers needed 60 buses and they called my family business.

I made a split-second decision on that call to say we could provide the buses. I didn't know if I could or if I couldn't, but I felt, hey, this is too big of an opportunity to turn down. I said yes, hung up the phone, quickly became my own lawyer to draft up a contract, then got to work finding enough buses. The contract was for several hundred thousand dollars, and when that amount landed in the family business bank account, it was more money than we had ever earned at one time.

Fast forward to 2013, when I started my own company, Shofur, to become the front-end booking engine for other vehicle drivers. I wanted a capital-light business model that I could self-fund without a lot of risk. My primary goal at that point was to get my family out of poverty. Shofur became cash flow positive with a few million a year in revenues and I owned 100% of it. I grew Shofur until 2017 and at that point I'd reached my personal, family goal. In the process, as I started to scale the business and spend more time in the charter vehicle industry, I realized that there were much broader industry problems that nobody had solved, and even bigger opportunities.

That's when my goals evolved and I had the vision of creating a platform, a fully integrated, real-time marketplace, that would transform industry dynamics and significantly improve the customer experience. I launched the initial booking platform as a kind of skunkworks inside Shofur around 2018 and soon conversions more than tripled from the legacy business model. Those proof points were enough for me to fully commit myself to CharterUP.

That split second decision Harris made in 2012 to say "yes" to opportunity, and then pull out all the stops to deliver, reflects the essence of the entrepreneurial mindset. Using Shofur's startup success to launch a more ambitious, transformative venture epitomizes his drive to solve problems at scale. Harris had experienced the frustrations and limitations inherent in an industry with thousands of local companies operating independently. Where others saw barriers, he envisioned a digital platform that would transform the charter experience. And he was determined that CharterUP would lead the way.

Ramping Up a Two-Sided Marketplace

Out of the gate, CharterUP faced the perennial two-sided marketplace dilemma: it needed to attract paying customers while also signing up bus operators. Harris and a subset of the Shofur team had validated customer demand on both sides through its pilot program in Atlanta. With the launch of CharterUP, Harris focused on expanding operations and populating both sides of his platform. On the supply side, he persuaded local bus companies to join the marketplace, often leveraging his industry connections from years in the transportation business. The promise to operators was compelling: CharterUP would bring them incremental business at no upfront cost. This free-to-join model, combined with evidence of demand from early adopters, helped CharterUP sign up a critical mass of operator partners to populate the platform.

CharterUP's consumer-facing promise was to "provide a group transportation experience that's transparent, safe, and good for the planet" while enabling customers to "charter a bus in 60 seconds." Such a dramatic improvement over the traditional multi-day booking process, together with enthusiastic user reviews helped to generate word of mouth awareness. CharterUP leveraged cost-effective digital marketing instead of expensive ad blitzes to attract consumer interest and jump start charter booking.

CharterUP connected its customers with a network that quickly expanded to include hundreds of operating partners controlling over 5,000 vehicles available to charter. Unlike the industry's traditional brokers who just matched customers with operators, CharterUP had developed a proprietary system to deliver real-time availability information, dynamic pricing, instant booking, and live trip tracking. Its system aggregated real-time data from hundreds of operators, processing over 20,000 qualified leads monthly, and maintaining 24/7 customer support while ensuring backup coverage through its extensive operator network.

However advanced the platform, Harris understood that technology alone wouldn't guarantee success. CharterUP needed to demonstrate that its marketplace could seamlessly address the needs of both customers and operators. It's no surprise that when I asked Harris what key metrics he ranked highest for CharterUP, he put sales and customer acquisition at number one (including metrics for lead generation, conversion rates, and the cost of customer acquisition). As Harris notes,

> *Sales and customer acquisition is number one. I think you know this common saying – sales cures all. We don't take any lead for granted. We're highly focused on conversions, in particular inbound conversions, because those customers have higher intent. We also focus on cost of sales, cost of the sales team and marketing as a percentage of overall sales. That has always been very, very important.*

Once CharterUP ramped up to a critical mass of customers and charter providers to utilize the marketplace, the growth flywheel began to spin. The customer experience was a quantum leap in speed and convenience, further enhanced with access to operator ratings, customer reviews, safety records, and real-time vehicle tracking. Once a charter is booked, customers are offered live tracking of the arrival time of their rides, bringing an Uber-like sense of control to charter trips. In Harris's words, CharterUP became an "information factory for the customer," displaying each bus operator's years in business, safety record, fleet size, on-time performance and more. This data gave early customers the confidence to press that "book online" button.

Since the marketplace is solving a giant headache for customers, CharterUP can set price points that are attractive to both sides of the market without positioning itself as the lowest-price option. Saving time and ensuring excellent quality are high-value attractions for corporate customers as well as individual consumers. The platform now handles everything from corporate shuttles to private events, sports teams, school trips, and government transportation needs. Corporate shuttle demand has increased 283% year-over-year, as CharterUP has become the #1 shuttle choice for Fortune 500 companies including Amazon, Apple, Google, Microsoft, and Delta airlines.

The transport providers that join the marketplace reap the benefits attracting corporate and group clients and national customers they could never reach on their own. Based on his industry experience, Harris knew that small providers didn't have the budget to invest in sales and marketing or advanced dispatch systems. CharterUP offered to handle marketing for them – for example, by aggregating local SEO traffic instead of each operator needing to spend thousands on separate ads.

CharterUP ensured quality service by requiring each partner vehicle to install GPS tracking and integrate with CharterUP's software, enabling real-time availability management and efficient dispatch. This was initially a tough sell to some old-school operators. But Harris knew that operating partner buy-in to upgraded tech was key to maintaining customer satisfaction and measuring service performance,

> One of our goals is to really improve the service level of bus operators and bus companies. Previously there was no platform ensuring accountability in this industry. Now we keep track of everything. What percentage of time does a particular bus arrive on time, or what percentage of all the vehicles in that company, or how reliably is a particular driver on time? If they arrive late, is it by five minutes, 10 minutes, 30 minutes? Are there any no-shows? We keep track of all this, and maintaining SLAs is very important to us. We want to have at least 98% on time arrival for all of our bookings.

As Harris notes, performance tracking and accountability levels were unprecedented in the charter bus industry. Delivering it wasn't just a priority operations goal inside CharterUP – it was an important reason for customers to trust their transportation needs to the company.

As the marketplace took off in 2019, CharterUP expanded its team and began rolling out services to new cities. As CharterUP landed major corporate shuttle contracts and large-group clients, revenue was starting to scale. The company was poised to become a national platform.

2020: Crisis as Opportunity

Then in March 2020 the brake lights came on. The COVID-19 pandemic wiped out demand for group travel virtually overnight. At one point in spring 2020, the overall U.S. motorcoach business was down 98% year-over-year. CharterUP's revenue dropped in parallel, bookings sputtered out, and Harris was forced to furlough 75% of his staff to conserve resources. This crisis could have led CharterUP to shut down, but instead it became a defining inflection point that steeled the company and prepared it for faster, more profitable future growth.

Rather than give up, Harris doubled down on technology during the enforced pandemic slow down. With a skeleton crew of engineers and product managers, CharterUP spent 2020 optimizing every aspect of its platform – from bolstering inventory management tools for operators to fine-tuning SEO and digital marketing in preparation for the return of group travel. CharterUP was still in bootstrapped mode, but Harris didn't hesitate to invest his own money in accelerated platform and product development.

During 2020 the team optimized the platform to handle everything from small wedding groups to emergency evacuations, anticipating that flexibility and response time would be key for post-pandemic customers. With equal foresight, Harris also productized the operations software component of the platform to create a new offering, "CharterUP for Operators." This was a software suite that bus companies could purchase to manage bookings, fleet data, and more. Such a heavy investment in new product development during the downturn was a bold bet by Harris which paid off spectacularly.

By late 2020, charter demand was ramping back up, but few transportation providers were ready. The downturn had thinned out weaker competitors: an estimated 20% of small bus companies went out of business by early 2021. Harris's strategy to enhance the platform's self-service capabilities and to productize software services for its operator partners proved to be prescient. When pent-up demand for group travel exploded in 2021, CharterUP was arguably the best-prepared in the industry to capture it, in large part because of the investment made in enhancing the technology platform that underpinned all of its marketplace features.

Scaling High-Quality Services with Operational Efficiency

Platform enhancements implemented during the pandemic set the stage for CharterUP's "high-tech, lean-touch" model of expansion – relying on technology and process automation to minimize the cost of sales and operations as volume grew.

By making the booking process as frictionless as possible online, CharterUP converted many customers without any human sales interaction. Customers could come to the website, enter trip details, see multiple quotes, and book. This product-led growth approach meant CharterUP didn't need to spend as heavily on paid advertising or hire as many sales reps to cold-call clients; the platform's stellar performance became a selling point. As the marketplace reputation for quality service spread, more corporate procurement departments and event planners started coming directly to CharterUP after hearing about the positive experiences of their peers.

As corporate and consumer demand and bookings accelerated, favorable industry word-of-mouth about the platform's advanced features also helped the company's relatively small business development team to attract new operator partners. In fact, CharterUP was soon in a position to selectively partner with operators who met the company's quality service metrics. Thanks to strong inbound interest fueled by its digital presence and brand credibility, CharterUP could scale nationally while maintaining a low customer acquisition cost.

CharterUP's operational system uses algorithms to automate the process of matching customer requests with operator supply, seamlessly pairing customer trip requests with appropriate operators based on location, capacity, and performance metrics. The system even facilitates instant online quotes, booking, and payment. Once transport is booked, live tracking and communication tools allow one operations manager at CharterUP to oversee many simultaneous trips – they can monitor bus locations, delays, and issues in real time and proactively alert customers if needed, rather than fielding constant status calls. The company also uses data analytics to optimize operations: for instance, by analyzing past trips, CharterUP can intelligently route buses to minimize deadhead (empty) miles or suggest optimal departure times to clients, improving reliability and reducing costs.

On the other side of the platform, CharterUP's Operator Portal software streamlines the interface with bus companies. This portal gives operators a dashboard to accept or decline trip requests, manage their fleet availability, and input driver details, all in one place. By integrating so tightly with operators, CharterUP minimizes the back-and-forth that typically bogs down charter bookings. CharterUP's central team doesn't have to manually call or email each operator for every booking – the portal handles confirmations and logistics digitally. This scalable design allowed CharterUP to handle a 10x increase in trip volume from 2020 to 2023 without a comparable increase in ops staff. In fact, CharterUP's headcount has roughly quadrupled since 2017, a period during which its business by revenue grew over 1,100-fold. Such non-linear scaling of people vs. revenue is a hallmark of scalable 100X operations.

Maintaining high customer satisfaction during rapid expansion was another key focus. CharterUP recognized that trust and reliability are paramount in group transportation – one badly handled trip could cost future business. To ensure high quality as it scaled, CharterUP implemented strict performance standards and feedback loops. All bus operators in the network are continuously rated on metrics like on-time performance and vehicle quality; poor performers can be downgraded or removed, while top performers get more trip opportunities, and can even be "promoted" within search results. This built-in accountability motivates operators to uphold high service levels, which in turn keeps customers happy.

Once a booking is confirmed, the CharterUP platform automatically provides customers with advance information about driver contact, pickup instructions, real-time bus ETA, and more. During large-scale events or complex multi-bus jobs, CharterUP often assigns an on-site coordinator or sets up a dedicated support line – a relatively small investment that yields outsized client satisfaction for big accounts. Even as it grew, the company didn't abandon the personal touch where it mattered: Harris's own presence in Florida overseeing the hurricane emergency evacuations in fall 2024 was one of many occasions where he took part in front-line operations. CharterUP's ops team developed a reputation for responsiveness and problem-solving, which secured repeat business. By 2024, CharterUP had facilitated over 100,000 client trips cumulatively, and its overall customer rating stood impressively high (ResellerRatings shows 9.45/10 from verified reviews). Such satisfaction is both a result of and a reason for its scale – happy customers become return customers and even evangelists.

Leveraging Data and AI

To keep accelerating this internal efficiency- customer satisfaction flywheel, Harris and the CharterUP team are actively leveraging AI capabilities in today's platform, and thinking ahead about how AI can do even more to enhance user satisfaction, operational efficiencies, and sales volume in the years ahead.

One of CharterUP's strongest tech differentiators is its emphasis on real-time data. All charter buses in the network are equipped with tracking devices and connected to the platform, feeding it a constant stream of live location and performance data. This data not only provides transparency (customers can track their bus on a live map, for example); it also serves as fuel for AI-driven optimization. For instance, the platform can use historical and real-time traffic data to adjust recommended departure times or to flag a planned itinerary where the timing seems too tight. AI-tools can monitor the performance of pricing algorithms – analyzing which quotes convert into bookings, at what prices, and for what trip profiles, then adjusting future price suggestions for optimal consumer and bus provider outcomes. AI also helps make smarter matches on the marketplace, by learning each operator's patterns (e.g. which routes they favor, their reliability, their cost structures), allowing CharterUP to rank the best operator options for a given trip.

CharterUP's AI efforts extend to real-time customer service as well, incorporating AI behind the scenes to make split-second decisions that previously would have required human intervention. The company has experimented with substituting AI for human team members to handle reservation changes. Internally, AI is used to forecast demand in various markets, allowing CharterUP to proactively recruit more operators or vehicles in areas where bookings are trending up. This continuous innovation cadence keeps CharterUP well ahead of less technically advanced competitors.

Harris is a proponent of AI as long as it reliably delivers a quality experience along with operational efficiency,

> I'm generally very positive on AI implementation to improve customer service and operations functions. Previously, if a customer wanted to make a change to their reservation, they would have to call in and talk with a service agent. We used to dedicate a whole team to managing that kind of person-to-person interaction. We had other people monitoring real time vehicle deployment and arrival times. As we grew, it became impossible for one person or even a team of people to monitor all these data points and then to alert the operating company about issues. Deploying AI agents in our system to monitor all of this activity in real time and manage alerts is the key to improving services and keeping costs under control.

Diversified Revenue, Profitability, and
Disciplined Financial Management

CharterUP's early growth was driven by a straightforward commission-based revenue model, based on taking a percentage of each transaction booked through their marketplace. Harris quickly identified more profitable revenue opportunities, and invested in new product development to diversify the company's revenue streams. He describes this evolution as an essential element of growth, and explains the three major sources of the company's current revenue,

I generally think you've got to evolve to keep growing, and so I've pivoted the business model many times. To be a successful business, you really have to listen to the data and listen to the market. Initially, when I launched this business, it was primarily around individuals and small customers chartering a bus –consumer event charters, maybe your local high school or university would need buses. Then I realized there was this whole other, bigger opportunity providing enterprise shuttles for corporate employees, work crew shuttles, airport shuttles and so on. These are multi-year, multimillion dollar contracts. To keep growing, we expanded into all sorts of shuttles on top of providing the original charters.

Then it became clear that the platform software we were giving to bus companies for free had a load of added value. Bus companies were using our software to run their entire business, including the business outside of our platform. That's when we decided to monetize our software and add more features to create our SaaS product. We launched a mobile app for all their drivers. We launched a payment system, so now we get a transaction fee for all the payments we handle, on top of our SaaS revenue. Today, our current business model has expanded to three components. The original charter model—essentially B2C for low-frequency events, like a wedding or a Bar Mitzvah or a birthday party. Hopefully a given customer isn't getting married every year, right? But even in that model we have some high frequency customers like universities or athletic teams or regular event organizers.

The second component of our business is the shuttles, which generate high recurring revenue. Same with the third component of our business, which provides a predictable monthly SaaS revenue stream. Then extras

like getting basis points from every single payment transaction that runs on our platform.

When we started CharterUP in 2018 we had a little bit over $100,000 in revenue. Today (in 2024) we're run rating at over $250 million of revenue. Our goal is that the business is going to compound at anywhere between 40 to 50% for the next few years.

In response to my question about profitability, Harris confirms that CharterUP has been profitable since inception, except for one quarter during the COVID-19 pandemic. He expands on this by emphasizing the importance of profitability as a key discipline for most startup ventures, even well-funded companies that have set their sights on achieving market domination and extreme growth,

In my view, unless you are sending a rocket into space or building a self-driving car, there's rarely a reason for companies to be cash flow negative over long periods of time. I'm very mindful of the need for profitability. The benefit is that maintaining positive EBITDA keeps you highly disciplined. CharterUP has been profitable from the start. We had only one unprofitable quarter, during the pandemic when group travel bookings went way, way down. Outside of that, we have always been profitable. My philosophy on EBITDA and cash management in general, is to start with positive working capital dynamics and grow from there. In our case, where the customers are paying us ahead of time, and we're typically not paying the bus operators until the services are rendered, that positive dynamic is foundational. In fact, we are flexible if the bus operators are long-term partners and they ask to be paid before the trip is rendered. But then we typically add an additional commission in exchange for taking a little more risk. That becomes another revenue line—it's very small, but it's there.

On the other hand, I know that many founders of high-growth VC-funded companies have this view that, hey, there has to be an eventual path to profit but for now the focus is growth. Well, some businesses have succeeded with that attitude, but many have failed, because that's a very slippery slope. Once a founder embraces negative EBITDA, negative economics, it's really easy to lie to yourself and say, I know how to get out of this, and eventually turn a profit. In fact, I think it's pretty difficult to change that mindset. You can't just flip that profit switch on. So I believe in having positive economics and the discipline that comes with it.

At the same time, we're growing very fast, and my primary focus is growth. I generally think that one point of growth is more valuable at one point of EBITDA, and I know that growth markets typically reward that as well. But only as long as every single cost line, the cost of sales, cost of marketing, cost of technology, all demonstrate efficiencies that are trending and improving over time.

CharterUP's diversified revenue model, disciplined cash flow management and focus on profitability have been central to the company's rapid growth. There's no arguing with the revenue numbers that the company has achieved with Harris's disciplined financial management.

This emphasis on positive economics attracted significant investor attention, allowing Harris to select a funding partner who would add experience in scaling technology platforms and managing rapid growth, as well as dollars to accelerate expansion. CharterUP received a $60 million Series A funding round in October 2022 led by Tritium Partners, a Texas-based private equity firm managing over $1.2 billion in assets. Tritium Partners specifically cited CharterUP's capital efficiency focus and balanced approach to growth and profitability as key factors in their investment decision. CharterUP used the funds to enter markets faster than organic growth alone would allow – expanding into Los Angeles, San Francisco, Houston, Dallas, Miami, New York and beyond with enhanced on-the-ground presence. This marked an inflection from rapid growth to hypergrowth, as CharterUP's already strong revenue curve accelerated.

Leadership, Company Culture, and Impact

Harris's leadership style combines the determination shaped by his refugee experience with a clear-eyed understanding of how to scale technology-powered businesses. His management emphasizes setting "relentlessly high standards for yourself and people around you" while prioritizing "execution over strategy." CharterUP's core company values reflect Harris's leadership and growth philosophy. These values include: **Commitment to Excellence; Customer Focus; Taking Ownership; Invent and Innovate;** and **Built for Speed.**

Harris has been clear from the start that he expects employees to fully commit to the company's ambitious goals,

Company culture and internal alignment is really important. All the external threats, competitors and market dynamics are out of your control, even though you still have to keep on fighting them to keep growing. To win, you really need to get your internal culture right. Because if the team is driving together, things are just moving faster. It's much easier when everyone is aligned, and rowing in the same direction. CharterUP needs to hire people who want to work really hard and who will buy in and thrive in this high-growth environment. I'm very transparent about that expectation in the interview process. Basically, I say, listen, we want to win in this market, and so we prioritize hard work and we prioritize speed. When people ask me, who's your biggest competitor, I always say, time is our biggest competitor. To win against time, we need to make sure we have a culture of hard work and a culture of urgency.

It's a challenge to maintain the urgency and accountability of a small startup team now that CharterUP has over 300 employees. One solution Harris has embraced is a rigorous and transparent hiring process. He believes in hands-on management, sometimes dropping in on team meetings unannounced, and he has learned to scale the feedback process by switching from one-on-one meetings to pulling together an entire department as needed for a brief feedback and problem-solving meeting.

One of the most powerful messages that Harris shares with his team is that entrepreneurs thrive on challenges — the tougher the better. He coaches CharterUP teams to enjoy overcoming the business challenges they are bound to encounter. That's a hard lesson to teach, but if anyone can transmit resilience in the face of obstacles and a love of problem solving, it's likely to be Harris,

I think maybe my upbringing has wired me this way, but I really look forward to challenges. I thrive in challenges. As strange as that may sound, I think you've got to love challenges and obstacles and learn how to break through every single wall you encounter. Breaking through walls is one of the biggest things that I try to teach the team. When you have a very difficult problem to solve, don't think first about hiring a consultant or finding someone else to solve the problem. Own it. Whenever we've got a tough challenge at CharterUP and someone says, we need to hire an expert to solve this, I just like, shake my head, no...., we've got to solve this ourselves.

CharterUP's Next Chapter

CharterUP's growth story demonstrates how technology-enabled innovation can transform an entire industry when guided by deep domain expertise and unwavering commitment to customer value. CharterUP's success in modernizing the charter bus industry is a model for disrupting other fragmented, technology-lagging sectors through marketplace platforms that create transparency, efficiency, and accountability, combined with determined leadership.

Harris's leadership philosophy offers insights for other entrepreneurs seeking to build technology companies that scale rapidly while maintaining strong culture and values. His emphasis on execution over strategy, personal discipline, and overcoming obstacles provides a practical framework for navigating the challenges of high-growth company building.

When I ask him to summarize CharterUP's growth targets for the next three years, Harris confirms that he is aiming at compounding growth and revenues at around 50% annually. Then he smiles a bit ruefully, and adds that he sees a downside to pinning the company's potential future growth to today's targets. Not because he's worried about meeting them, but because even these ambitious targets may turn out to be too conservative and end up limiting CharterUP's potential,

I'll tell you this about growth targets, even though the growth fund that invested in us is probably going to hate me for saying it. I see growth targets as just a formality because in some ways, you may end up capping your growth by sticking to them. I think that early on, CharterUP didn't need formal growth targets. Actually, it was better not to have them. If I had set rational growth targets in the beginning, we would have never imagined growing this company by over 100,000%. So, even though we do now set these targets by department, my personal philosophy is to give it your absolute best and don't live with regrets.

I'm very optimistic about the future of CharterUP, and typically I've had somewhat of a sixth sense for anticipating step function growth opportunities. I do think there are step function opportunities ahead for CharterUP, opportunities that we'll be able to execute on. And I believe these are going to accelerate our growth even faster.

Stay tuned. The next chapter of the CharterUP story may be even more exciting than the extreme growth that Armir Harris has already achieved.

◆ ◆ ◆

While the Essential Elements are powerful building blocks for 100X growth, there's no one-size-fits-all instruction manual. You have already seen how the CSN Stores and ButcherBox founders adapted these elements to their startup vision and business models. Armir Harris deployed the same scalability elements at CharterUP to power multiple growth flywheels for a two-sided marketplace and advanced tech platform. In the chapters ahead, you will meet entrepreneurs who adapt these building blocks to different industry sectors, market challenges, and solutions.

It's clear that entrepreneurs don't achieve extreme growth by copying some other startup's playbook—they build a growth strategy to achieve their vision of transforming an industry, solving a specific problem, making someone's life better; all while building a profitable business. They take different paths, while implementing strategies that are grounded in the same essential elements. These core principles apply whether you're in consumer goods, business services, healthcare, logistics, fintech, or software and whether you are well-positioned to attract venture capital or determined to bootstrap your business from cash flow.

The coming chapters will go deeper into how each of these elements is executed across different business models and sectors. From consumer brands to AI-powered platforms to healthcare and logistics services, you'll see the essential 100X elements at work—and gain insights in applying each element in your own entrepreneurial journey.

3
Building a Consumer Brand from Zero to 100X

LAUNCHING A NEW CONSUMER BRAND in the U.S. market is like entering NASCAR driving a souped-up Ford F-150. The arena is crowded, the competition well-financed, and the dominant brands have already won consumer loyalty, shelf space, and mindshare. Nowhere is this more evident than in the beverage industry, where Coca-Cola, PepsiCo, Keurig Dr. Pepper and other giants dominate retail placement and advertising bandwidth. For startups, building brand awareness and ramping up sales in such a crowded space is notoriously difficult and expensive. The costs of marketing, distribution, and retail access often exceed a fledgling company's financial runway. Against these odds, only a rare few consumer-facing startups manage to survive – and fewer still go from zero to 100X growth by building not just a brand, but a movement.

This chapter highlights three beverage startups—OLIPOP, MUD\WTR, and Carbliss—that defied those odds and scaled rapidly by building brands that deliver value, inspire customer love, and generate profits. That is, they offered clear, differentiating value propositions—something consumers could feel good about drinking—and coupled it with a product experience that people genuinely resonate with and want to share. From the healthy, functional soda Ben Goodwin and David Lester have leveraged to make OLIPOP a profitable 100X unicorn, to the caffeine-light ritual of powdered mushrooms promoted by Shane Heath at MUD\WTR, to the no-carb cocktails-in-a-can business built from scratch by Adam and Amanda Kroener at Carbliss, each founder brought a deep personal commitment to their product.

Taste, health, and lifestyle alignment are central to the value of these brands. But the extreme growth only happened when that value proposition was paired with operational efficiency, financial discipline, and cost-efficient marketing strategies that cultivated enthusiastic customer evangelists. OLIPOP's nostalgic flavors and vibrant social media storytelling earned it a cult following and coast-to-coast retail distribution. MUD\WTR's creative founder voice built a lifestyle brand that resonated deeply with wellness-focused consumers, turning customers into loyal subscribers and vocal advocates. Carbliss focused on a hyper-local "backyard-to-backyard" sales model, saturating regional markets with committed sales reps before expanding outward. Their approaches differed, but each founder proved that even in one of the most competitive sectors imaginable, it's possible to win by building a product people genuinely love—and by growing a brand with scalability in mind.

John Williamson, the founder of Songfinch, learned this lesson the hard way. His personalized music startup began with a visionary idea and significant venture funding, but it nearly collapsed under the weight of its own marketing missteps. Songfinch focused too much on what it produced—custom songs—and not nearly enough why buyers would love them, so revenue stalled. It wasn't until Williamson pivoted the brand messaging to emphasize emotional impact that Songfinch finally achieved breakout growth. His story underscores the essential principle behind each of the successes in this chapter: founders who deliver both lasting value and genuine emotional resonance have the power to create a community that keeps scaling.

OLIPOP

Ben Goodwin, OLIPOP's Co-Founder, CEO & Formulator, emphasizes early in our conversation that making authentically healthy soda is ingrained in his vision of building a deeply responsible 100X business,

> *I want OLIPOP to prove that you can build a massively successful company in a really healthy way, without cutting corners, without misleading consumers, and without sacrificing integrity.*

Coming from someone else, this might sound grandiose. But Goodwin's vision is the real deal. Long before co-founding OLIPOP, he had embarked on the quest to create a health-forward, gut-friendly soda alternative. Ben spent years experimenting with different ingredients, doubtless consuming quantities of not-so-great tasting trial batches in the process. Each time, he emerged more determined than ever to create the ideal formula. "I grew up drinking soda, it's one of the most ubiquitous American beverages of all time," Goodwin relates. "I thought, if you really want to create a healthy product that's accessible and can break through at mass scale, soda is the perfect vehicle."

The foundation for OLIPOP's success was built from all those cycles of experimentation, Goodwin's extraordinary commitment, and prior startup setbacks honed into a breakthrough growth strategy in one of the world's most competitive consumer industries.

Prelude: Cofounder Chemistry Seeking Market Demand

Before OLIPOP, there was Obi, a startup launched in 2013 to sell a different healthy beverage formulated by Goodwin. Obi was a fermented functional soda, loaded with probiotics that were extremely gut-friendly. Buoyed by the drink's nutritional benefits, Goodwin went looking for a business-oriented cofounder to help him bring it to market. He met with David Lester, who had stepped off the corporate ladder after a 10-year career at Diageo and moved to San Francisco to explore entrepreneurial opportunities. Despite their very different backgrounds, Lester and Goodwin hit it off at their first meeting. A few weeks later, they agreed to partner to launch Obi. Obi's healthy ingredients won shelf space in some California health food stores; however, it soon became clear that the beverage's appeal was limited to a niche market that valued wellness over taste. After a frustrating three years, the cofounders sold Obi in 2016 and walked away from their first venture with a number of hard-won lessons to digest.

Despite Obi's commercial failure, their joint struggle to build market demand was an enlightening trial by fire. Lester had internalized the challenges of building a new brand from scratch. Goodwin had decided that the future formula for a popular healthy soda would not be based on probiotics.

Reinventing Soda with Healthy Ingredients and Great Taste

Armed with a beverage formulation that combined essential health benefits with a much more appealing taste profile, in 2018 Ben Goodwin and David Lester were ready to take another swing at reinventing soda.

Unlike Obi's fermented probiotics (which required refrigeration and had a somewhat vinegary taste), the key ingredients in OLIPOP soda featured prebiotics and plant fiber – essentially feeding the gut's existing beneficial bacteria. Goodwin had also realized this new product had to taste much more like mainstream soda. As he explains, "We have always been rooted in our mission to positively impact consumers' health at scale... At the same time – it's important that you create a product that delivers a taste that is absolutely delicious,"

That commitment to being delicious in a familiar, soda-like way shaped OLIPOP's marketing strategy from day one. Even though the new product's name was grounded in the world of botanicals and gut microbiomes ("Oli" in OLIPOP stands for oligosaccharides, which are a type of prebiotic fiber that is a key ingredient in all of the OLIPOP flavors), Lester firmly steered his marketing team away from focusing their messaging on such arcane details. Great taste, with low sugar and high fiber, were the key selling points for most consumers. As Lester recalled in a 2023 podcast interview,

> *"My mantra from the outset was that we've got to behave like a soda. So it's about refreshment, it's about fun. I actually banned our marketing team from talking about functional health benefits. ... Even now, I would guess that 80 percent of our customer base does not know what a prebiotic is, and under 5 percent would be able to accurately describe what it does for our bodies. ... People buy certain brands because of the way those products make them feel, and we wanted to position ourselves emotionally within this space to really go toe to toe with the likes of Coke and Pepsi."*

Positioning their startup to take on soda's biggest brands was a long-term goal. During the company's first year, the cofounders focused on simply winning local shelf space for OLIPOP. They started by selling into 40 independent natural food stores and local co-ops around Northern California. In classic startup mode, they handled any and all tasks that needed doing, including delivering cartons of OLIPOP in person. This hands-on approach gave Goodwin and Lester a better insight into consumer reaction by facilitating candid feedback from store managers. Hearing that buyers were enthusiastic about OLIPOP and seeing retail restocking orders arrive validated that this time around they had a winning taste formula. Their in-store launch strategy paid off financially too, generating over $800,000 in revenues for OLIPOP by the end of their first year.

This early validation was exciting, but OLIPOP was in a marathon, not a sprint. Despite years of declining sales and health-conscious critics, the American soda market remains stubbornly top-heavy. The industry's leading brands aggressively defend their retail advantage. Achieving long-term traction in the shadow of such well-established soda companies would require compelling brand messaging, scalable production and distribution strategies, and managing rapid growth on a startup budget.

As it turned out, OLIPOP's launch was well timed. The decline of traditional soda popularity was accelerating, and market interest in alternative soda options was on the rise. OLIPOP's positioning as a great-tasting soda with health benefits resonated with an increasing number of consumers looking to enjoy their favorite classic soda flavors without guilt. The fact that OLIPOP had only 2 to 5 grams of sugar (compared with about 40 grams of sugar in traditional soda) was a solid selling point. OLIPOP's growing selection of nostalgic, great-tasting flavors like Classic Cola, Ginger Lemon, Strawberry Vanilla, and Root Beer appealed to soda drinkers of all ages, and kept customers coming back for more.

In 2020, OLIPOP signed a major deal with Sprouts Farmers Market to carry their soda in all 300 stores across the country. For the first time, OLIPOP had coast-to-coast presence. In 2021, Whole Foods Market approved OLIPOP for national distribution across the U.S. Gaining Whole Foods shelf space signaled to consumers that OLIPOP met strict ingredient standards and served as a gateway to more mainstream chains. Retail store placement was on a roll, and poised to accelerate.

Historically, a new beverage brand aiming for shelf space in the largest national retail stores would hit a wall at this point in its expansion. The slotting fees and promotional allowances required to get on the shelves of big supermarket chains often add up to millions of dollars, and are payable in advance of actual sales revenue. Startups typically don't have that kind of cash in hand and OLIPOP was no exception.

OLIPOP's brand messaging and timing provided a way forward. Alarmed by the downturn of in-store sales during the pandemic, retailers were seeking popular new products to attract in-person shoppers. Supermarket operators had also learned that customers who gravitated toward emerging, better-for-you brands tended to spend more overall per store visit. To attract these high-value customers, chains started allocating shelf space to trendy new brands and offering reduced or even zero slotting fees, essentially betting that the draw of in-demand items would outweigh the lost slotting revenue. OLIPOP was exactly the kind of product that benefited from this shift. By 2021, their brand had achieved significant social media popularity and a loyal following of Millennials and Gen-Z shoppers, giving them real leverage in negotiations with the large retail stores they approached.

OLIPOP quickly parlayed its leverage into more deals with major chains. In 2022, Target began carrying OLIPOP nationally, followed by Kroger, Albertsons/Safeway, and Wegmans, among others. OLIPOP even gained place-ment in Walmart's beverage aisle, a massive milestone that opened over 4,000 additional retail doors. By early 2024, OLIPOP reported being in over 30,000 retail locations in the U.S, a number that included not just supermarkets but also Sam's Club and convenience stores. In a few short years, OLIPOP went from a local niche product to virtually ubiquitous retail availability – a rare feat for a nontraditional beverage brand without a big corporate parent.

To understand the drivers that propelled OLIPOP onto so many store shelves, let's take a closer look at how the company's social media, digital marketing, and direct-to-consumer sales strategies were designed to work to-gether to accelerate adoption and build market demand–while keeping down the cost of customer acquisition.

Creating a Winning Marketing Mix

OLIPOP's early marketing strategy included leveraging social media influenc-ers and celebrity partnerships that aligned with the brand's vision, creating viral narratives around nostalgia, joy, and special moments with family and friends (while sharing an OLIPOP, of course). Rather than expensive ad cam-paigns, OLIPOP invested in partnering with health-conscious celebrities and athletes who became authentic spokespersons for OLIPOP's value proposi-tion. An unexpected benefit was that many of these celebrity promoters, in-cluding NFL quarterback Patrick Mahomes and actor Mindy Kaling, became OLIPOP investors.

OLIPOP's small internal marketing team also mastered the art of creat-ing their own viral content. They hopped on memes, and secured product placements: a can of OLIPOP makes a cameo in a 2022 Nicki Minaj and Ice Spice music video, a result of savvy cultural scouting. These organic and paid efforts built OLIPOP's social media presence to cult status, yielding an estimated $100 million in earned media value in 2023, all without paying the astronomical cost of a single Super Bowl ad.

In May 2023, the company launched its first major ad campaign, *"Real Love Makes Us,"* starring pop star Camila Cabello. The campaign's video spots showed Cabello in candid scenes with her family and friends – sharing meals, dancing in the kitchen, cuddling her dog – always with OLIPOP somewhere in the scene. The message: OLIPOP is part of the little moments that bring people together. By tying OLIPOP to feelings of love and togetherness, the brand tapped into emotional nostalgia while also subtly encouraging consumers to "share a soda" without guilt. The ads ran on streaming platforms like Hulu and Peacock as well as on social channels. This digital-focused media strategy was a great fit with OLIPOP's target demographic of online-native consumers. In the background, the marketing team measured the impact of every marketing dollar, carefully tracking engagement and brand lift. Eventually, Cabello also became an investor.

Even as the digital buzz grew, OLIPOP didn't neglect marketing collaborations with bricks and mortar stores. The OLIPOP marketing team worked to set up classic in-store samplings in health food stores and groceries in 2019–2020, letting shoppers taste the product and learn about its benefits on the spot. These grass-roots efforts helped build localized word-of-mouth, but they were labor-intensive and expensive.

As OLIPOP scored shelf space in more and more retail stores, the team shifted to more scalable marketing tactics like branded shelf placements, end-cap displays, and retailer-specific promotions (e.g. special pricing for loyalty card members). For instance, when launching in Sprouts Farmers Market stores, OLIPOP coordinated with Sprouts to set up eye-catching displays and used geo-targeted Facebook ads to announce *"New OLIPOP flavors now at Sprouts"* in those neighborhoods. By marrying their digital ads with physical availability and selected discounting, they moved their engaged online shoppers into nearby stores.

By 2023, OLIPOP's marketing strategy was firing on all cylinders: the company had a viral social media presence, targeted influencer partners who closely aligned with its brand message, community-building content, and data-driven ad spending that could be dialed up or down on short notice.

Cracking the Code on Direct-to-Consumer Sales

OLIPOP didn't initially focus on direct-to-consumer (D2C) sales. They didn't even have a D2C subscription model in their first year. But the founders quickly recognized the enormous potential of a strong direct-to-consumer channel to build on the growing popularity of OLIPOP's brand and its digital marketing success. In another instance of planning coinciding with an unexpected opportunity, when the COVID-19 pandemic forced a shift from in-store shopping to online retail in 2020, OLIPOP was ready to put the pedal to the floor to generate online sales and subscriptions. Before 2020, e-commerce had accounted for less than 5% of OLIPOP sales. By the end of that year, online sales had shot up to about 30% of revenue, locking in a scalable sales platform that featured both cost-effective customer acquisition and profitable subscription revenue.

OLIPOP designed an innovative text message marketing program to deliver more value directly to its online subscribers at the same time as ramping up recurring revenues. They launched a "subscribe and save" option, encouraging customers to sign up for monthly shipments at a discount by emphasizing the subscription option at checkout and adding a dedicated landing page. These simple steps resulted in the number of subscriptions skyrocketing from 500 to over 5,000 within months. With this foundation in place, OLIPOP shaped its subscriber base into a community of engaged product evangelists, giving them early access to new flavor launches and encouraging them to share their reactions on social media. To keep engagement high, the company sent insider updates and behind the scenes photos directly from company team members, asking for suggestions and feedback in addition to offering regular discounts and coupons.

One resounding proof point of engagement was OLIPOP's launch of a limited-edition Blackberry Vanilla flavor. They sent a text announcement to subscribers as soon as the new flavor went live and it notched up about $15,000 in online sales within 15 minutes. Based on extraordinary subscriber uptake, OLIPOP sold more Blackberry Vanilla soda in two weeks than some of its older flavors had sold all year. The 80% open rates and 40% click-to-purchase rates on their text message campaign far exceeded typical email marketing performance. OLIPOP had succeeded in creating a loyal D2C community that generated immediate revenue. Even more, these subscribers created a buzz about new flavors on social media that was strong enough to drive measurable spikes in retail store demand.

This active and engaged subscriber community also gave OLIPOP valuable first-party customer data and a vibrant feedback loop. It allowed them to experiment with offers and test creative marketing ideas in a controlled way. For instance, they could A/B test different landing pages or run limited flash sales to gauge price sensitivity – insights they wouldn't easily get from a distributor selling to grocery stores. By 2022, online sales generated nearly half of OLIPOP's business. Through their online store, they could see which flavors were repeat favorites, what bundle configurations worked best, and even which geographies had clusters of customers who were particularly partial to new flavors and most active promoting them on social media. This data has been invaluable for long-term growth planning, creating a virtuous cycle of subscribers' early adoption of new flavors that generates social media buzz, spills over into retail demand, and gives OLIPOP a leg up in expanding its in-store footprint in new geographic locations.

A Flywheel Effect for Omnichannel Growth

Today, OLIPOP benefits from a scalable omnichannel strategy where online and offline sales reinforce each other. Some OLIPOP customers first try out a new flavor by purchasing a single can in their local grocery store. If they love the taste they will switch to the company's website for a 12-pack subscription. On the other hand, some new buyers may be moved by a Facebook or Instagram ad to order a sampler pack online, and then become retail buyers because they find their favorite flavor on the shelf in a nearby Kroger. With $500 million in annual sales, OLIPOP can afford to operate a truly channel-agnostic approach and sell their products wherever their customers want to buy them – from grocery, big box, and convenience stores to sports venues and Amazon.

OLIPOP has put its omnichannel flywheel effect to good use in promoting retail store demand for its products. They localize their digital ads specifically around stores to promote in-stock flavors, as a highly scalable sales driver. For example, when OLIPOP rolled out a new flavor chain-wide in Sprouts, they geofenced Facebook ads to target consumers near each Sprouts location, boosting their new offering. These ads were cheaper than online conversion ads and reached millions of impressions – a much more efficient and cost-effective strategy than hiring reps for store demos, or traditional advertising.

The company's skill in digital and mobile marketing gives it an edge over less savvy competitors. For example, instead of waiting for consumers in a new region to discover OLIPOP on the shelves of their local grocery chain, they actively drive local awareness online, something many beverage startups cannot do effectively. Execution in retail – from maintaining strong fill rates and on-time deliveries to fostering retailer relationships – is a core competency and competitive advantage for OLIPOP.

By 2025, OLIPOP had achieved a national distribution footprint that earlier soda brands took decades of work and enormous capital to achieve. That said, OLIPOP now faces competition not just from incumbent soda brands, but a raft of other "better-for-you" soda startups, including newer companies inspired by OLIPOP's success and new product lines launched by the biggest brands in the industry. This means that OLIPOP must be prepared to defend its hard-won shelf space, even though its early mover advantage and impressive velocity have given it a head start.

Operations Behind the Bubbles

Handling the explosive growth of OLIPOP requires scalable operations management behind the scenes. One key operational choice OLIPOP made early was to outsource production to experienced co-packers rather than build its own manufacturing plant. This allowed them to scale output quickly by adding shifts or additional co-packing facilities as needed, without bearing the full capital expense of factories.

Internally, OLIPOP operates as a fully remote company, which is somewhat unusual for a manufacturing-oriented business. They make it work to the company's advantage by leveraging digital collaboration tools and recruiting experienced sales and ops managers around the country to oversee different regions. By prioritizing and supporting their people, the founders have fostered the high levels of energy and commitment needed to manage breakneck growth with a lean headcount.

Financial Management for Sustainability and Profit

OLIPOP's financial story is as remarkable as its sales growth. Consumer packaged goods startups often burn cash for years in pursuit of scale, but OLIPOP charted a more disciplined, sustainable path. As of 2024, the company had achieved something rare: it was profitable while doubling revenue year-over-year. For Goodwin and Lester, the focus on profitability was a deliberate strategy from the beginning. In an industry where "unicorn" beverage brands often sacrifice margins for growth, OLIPOP's balanced approach sets it apart.

In the early days, OLIPOP was funded by the founders' own money (including $100,000 from the Obi sale) and a $2.5 million seed round in 2019. With that capital, they demonstrated the brand's product-market fit and built the initial team. As revenues started climbing, they raised a Series A round, and then a Series B of $39.7 million in 2022. The Series B brought in high-profile individual investors including Gwyneth Paltrow, Mindy Kaling, and the Jonas Brothers – celebrity cash that also doubled as marketing clout. By January 2023, total funding reached about $55 million. Unlike many startups that burn through venture capital quickly, OLIPOP used its funds efficiently to fuel expansion while moving toward breakeven. The company crossed $73 million in revenue in 2022, a 223% jump from the prior year. Yet even as it doubled sales again in 2023 to roughly $200 million, it managed to improve unit economics enough to break into the black.

A pillar of this financial discipline is Goodwin and Lester's philosophy of "not compromising on top or bottom line." They priced OLIPOP as a premium product to ensure healthy gross margins. Gross margin on beverages can be quite high if volume grows rapidly, and OLIPOP's ingredients, while health-minded, aren't prohibitively expensive at scale. Fiber and botanical extracts cost more than corn syrup, but the premium pricing offsets that. The company also benefited from the slotting fee waivers discussed earlier, saving millions in expenses that typically hit a new brand's P&L when entering big retail. Additionally, their savvy use of digital marketing meant that customer acquisition costs were managed by focusing on channels with measurable ROI and turning off campaigns that weren't performing. This prevented wasteful burn and allowed them to selectively ramp up the most effective marketing campaigns.

By maintaining relatively lean operations, with remote teams and outsourced production eliminating the fixed overhead costs of factories and corporate campuses, OLIPOP can channel funds primarily into growth initiatives – production, distribution, and marketing – rather than spending heavily on fixed administrative costs.

The company's fundraising also never got ahead of actual business growth. In February 2025, OLIPOP closed a $50 million Series C at a $1.85 billion valuation. This unicorn status came on the heels of hitting over $400 million in sales in 2024. In contrast, most beverage startups operate at a loss until they either plateau or get acquired. OLIPOP proves that visionary management, 100x growth, financial discipline, purpose and profitability can go hand in hand.

Even more impressively, OLIPOP achieved this rapid growth while attaining B Corp certification, signaling to investors and consumers alike that it aims to grow responsibly, balancing profit with social good while achieving the founders' vision of creating a new market-dominant soda brand, one healthy sip at a time.

MUD/WTR

Meet Shane Heath, an artist, senior designer of web and mobile apps, lifelong mushroom enthusiast, mental health advocate, founder and CEO of the improbably named MUD/WTR. When asked about his founding inspiration, Shane talks about the importance of morning rituals, balanced nutrition, and creative design. Soon it becomes clear how all of the ingredients of Heath's life came together to turn his vision for a healthy coffee alternative into an extraordinary 100X growth story.

Here's how Shane describes the first "aha moment" that launched his startup:

> I didn't set out to start a food and beverage business. I'd been working in the tech industry as a designer for long enough to have bought into the hustle culture and I just thought that caffeine would allow me to do more and do it faster. Everyone on the team had a 'sleep when you're dead' mentality... But a couple years into that lifestyle, I started to feel overly stressed out and anxious. I wasn't sleeping well... my initial instinct was like, oh, something's wrong with me. Maybe I need to go to the psychiatrist and get on anxiety meds or something. But the more I explored what could be causing the problem, I realized it was my caffeine intake.
>
> I wanted to feel better and perform better–to feel more creative, and rely on my body's natural processes. At the same time, I loved waking up and sipping on something warm, with a robust flavor profile. I thought,

aha, what if my morning ritual could be more than just a vessel for high doses of caffeine? I started playing around, mixing these different ingredients into a mug and taking it with me to work.

Shane experimented with a homemade mix of cacao, tea, spices and a variety of powdered functional mushrooms. Once he had perfected the balance of ingredients that energized him and tasted like morning, he shared it with curious colleagues and friends who wanted a taste. When they asked what the drink was called, he jokingly told them it was "mud."

Then came his second "aha moment" – the conviction that a morning coffee alternative had real business potential. Even though he couldn't afford to quit his fulltime job, Shane took the leap to pilot test his vision online.

I knew that 90% of the population drinks coffee and believed many of them could benefit from drinking less caffeine. My new morning drink helped me feel better, so I was my own case study on the benefits of switching from coffee to Mud. I already knew how to build brands with ecommerce funnels to sell products, and I loved doing that. Launching a company combined the skill sets I had acquired over the years with my personal passion to work on something that could make the world a better place. Over a weekend in May 2018, I basically designed the MUD/WTR brand, and it's very much what you see on the website today. Designing it was a very intuitive process; almost like an extension of myself, my passions, my purpose.

Once the site was live, I put out an Instagram post without telling anyone close to me. I wanted to see if any strangers would order it, and not just my mother. My first post said, 'I'm not mad at coffee. I'm just disappointed'.

Within a couple months, I was shipping out hundreds of orders a week. I would just mix up product at night, and then I would ship products out on my lunch break. It was a very humble beginning, like building the wings on a plane while I was still trying to figure everything out. Ever since, it's been a very wild ride. I've grown MUD/WTR into a mid-eight-figure a year business, a brand with subscription sales that's now on the shelves of Target and Sprouts, and in hundreds of cafes across the country.

The wild ride that took MUD/WTR to #29 among the fastest growing companies on the *Inc 5000* list in 2022 involved a lot of bumps, and an early stage Catch-22. From his previous startup experience, Shane knew that a founder's total commitment and demonstrated product-market fit were prerequisites for investor funding. But he didn't have the money to cover launch expenses, or even to pay his rent without working his current job. To keep startup costs to a minimum, he leveraged social media to attract customers, then mixed, packaged, and shipped his product well into the night. He reached out to early customers via email to ask what had convinced them to buy, what they liked about MUD/WTR, and whether they would recommend it. He wanted to generate orders, demonstrate customer loyalty, and build a base of testimonials before approaching investors. It was a smart strategy – and a recipe for burnout. As the orders grew from 300 to 500 to over 1,000 a month, Shane was working around the clock; he had reached a critical decision point.

> *Five months in, I was at this tough crossroads. I had a close friend named Paul DeJoe and he'd been kind of watching me grow this thing. I remember calling him one night, literally like in tears, because keeping up with all the work was exciting, fun, crazy, and just exhausting. I told Paul, 'I don't know if I can do this anymore.' Then he said, 'Shane, I've seen the growth that's happening here. This is something extremely special. I'm going to write you a check for $25,000 so you can quit your job. We are going to raise funds, and we're going to do this.'*

True to his words, Paul DeJoe joined MUD/WTR as a cofounder, helping to land around $1.1 million in seed funding, and focusing on the company's finance and operations. By the following year, MUD/WTR's extreme growth phase was underway. Revenues grew over 400% in its first full year of operation, and 300% in its second. MUD/WTR wasn't yet a household name, but it was on the way to becoming a habit-forming, and loyalty-inducing brand.

Changing Minds and Morning Rituals

From the outset, MUD/WTR's marketing has been anything but ordinary –anchored in authenticity and reinvention of ritual, it relied on a bold brand voice to cut through the digital marketing clutter. Heath made a very deliberate choice to turn his informal joke about drinking "mud" into a brand name that would evoke strong emotions. He wanted to break through consumer indifference to ensure a "scroll-stopping" reaction, regardless of whether that reaction was initially positive, negative, or just curious.

> *Your biggest challenge in creating a new brand is not the competition – it's consumer indifference. You need a strategy to stand out, especially on social media with its short attention spans. Why should people pay attention to you? I felt that naming a drink after mud, that's polarizing. People won't be indifferent, and I think that can be an advantage if you play into it. Because polarity is a beautiful storytelling opportunity. Our name helps create initial curiosity, contradictory ideas, reasons for people to pay attention, followed up with moments to tell stories. We wanted to trigger people who had never considered coffee in a negative light to think again.*

This emphasis on standing out became MUD/WTR's leading wedge in breaking into an oversaturated beverage market. The brand had an edgy, irreverent personality that felt more like a lifestyle movement than a health mandate. One of MUD/WTR's first viral ads was shot with Shane's iPhone and captioned, *"We're not mad at coffee, just disappointed."* The ad didn't go into any details beyond poking fun at coffee – but it generated roughly $4 million in sales during the company's first year. As Paul DeJoe later observed, *"that ad worked… because it was provocative enough to get people to stop and click."* Attracting a social media following allowed MUD/WTR to acquire early customers cost-effectively.

Rather than demonizing coffee, MUD/WTR tapped into what people loved about it, including their wake up ritual. Another early message *"your new morning ritual,"* emphasized *adding* something beneficial rather than scolding consumers for drinking so much coffee. This resonated with habitual coffee drinkers who were open to a healthier alternative.

As MUD/WTR grew, its marketing evolved from scrappy hand-held videos to polished multimedia campaigns, and leveraged brand storytelling to build a community around its mission of "healthy minds through healthy habits." MUD/WTR launched an information-rich content platform, podcast, and quarterly print magazine called *Trends w/ Benefits*. With curated articles on topics like sleep, nutrition, meditation, and psychedelics, MUD/WTR became a thought leader in the wellness space. This content-driven approach educated consumers about healthy habits and strengthened their emotional connection to the brand.

Under Shane's leadership, the company prioritized a "test-and-learn" mentality online, constantly iterating creative content. Social media ads are carefully targeted to fit stages of the customer journey: some snappy and attention-grabbing for newcomers (as with the "not mad, just disappointed" ad), others educational for retargeting, all aiming to convert curious skeptics into subscribers. The "Change Your Mind" advertising campaign in early 2023 followed a single protagonist through a day, using choreographed dancers to symbolize how making different choices (like swapping coffee for MUD) leads to a healthier mental state. This long-form video garnered over 20 million direct views and coverage in *Advertising Age*, cementing MUD/WTR's reputation as a leading brand storyteller in wellness. It also fueled sales volume and product extension launches. MUD/WTR used the campaign to introduce three new blend flavors (matcha, turmeric, and an evening relax blend), and within months those new products made up about 15% of the company's revenue.

MUD/WTR continues to diversify its marketing and advertising mix to build its social following and customer community. When it invests in podcast advertising, the company focuses on niche shows that align with its health-minded demographic, for example by sponsoring podcasts where listeners seek advice about improving daily routines. This strategy speaks to MUD/WTR's disciplined customer acquisition approach – rather than scattering expensive, one-off ads widely, they double down where they can see direct results. The same discipline characterizes the growth of MUD/WTR's affiliate and ambassador community. Unusually, the company took a "less is more" philosophy to affiliates, hand-picking a core group of partners who truly align with the brand's ethos. This community-driven word-of-mouth marketing helped affiliate sales to surge 280% in one year.

Building on a Creative Founder's Superpower

Of course, every consumer product company relies on marketing and advertising to reach and retain customers. Typically, however, winning brand recognition and loyalty for an unknown, category-busting new product typically takes deep pockets and multiple advertising campaigns over a long period of time. The adoption velocity and depth of consumer loyalty that MUD/WTR achieved through cost-effective creative marketing rests in large part on Shane Heath's ability to convey his vision and the benefits of Mud using his design skills and creative instincts.

In our conversation, Shane notes that relatively few designers and creatives become CEOs, even though his experience demonstrates that a creative background is a definite asset in designing authenticity and soul into a new consumer brand,

> *I'm definitely a unique CEO in that my background is in design, and you don't often see a creative becoming a high-growth CEO. Personally, I would love to encourage that career path. I think having a CEO with a creative design background in a CPG business is kind of akin to someone with a technology background becoming the CEO of a tech firm. There are so many advantages.*
>
> *From the start of MUD/WTR, my primary focus was on our brand, on how we express ourselves, how we differentiate ourselves through our message, conveying what we stand for. That has to come across in a variety of ways — in our organic content and our ads, from the product aesthetic, just how it looks, to the standards that we hold our products to. I wrote almost all of our copy early on; for our ads, our social copy, and our email copy. I was able to create a brand that on the outside looked elevated, premium (and it was). Then once you purchased it, it would feel very human, very authentic, like it has a soul. I was striving to build all that into all of our brand messaging. And from the start, I got feedback from a lot of customers that this feeling of humanity, of having a soul, was what they loved about us and what differentiated us from other companies.*

Extreme Growth with a Classic Ecommerce Model

MUD/WTR's early customer acquisition and sales strategy was focused heavily on direct-to-consumer (D2C) channels and subscription revenue, allowing the company to rapidly grow a loyal customer base from scratch. By selling primarily through its own website and mobile app, MUD/WTR controlled the customer experience, collected regular feedback, and could analyze key customer purchase data, all of which proved invaluable in iterating on product-market fit.

Several factors drove the company's explosive online sales growth. First, its digital advertising efficiency attracted interested consumers into the top of the funnel. Many were intrigued by the company's social media presence and the ads that spoke to a growing desire for healthy rituals and energy-boosts with less caffeine. MUD/WTR's ability to convert those prospects into subscribers was aided by smart onboarding: a visually attractive "Starter Kit" offer lowered the barrier to purchase by bundling everything needed to enjoy Mud (product, a beverage frother, even an elegant, full color Guidebook). To promote long-term customer relationships with recurring revenues, the site prominently featured discount-priced subscriptions with a money-back guarantee, described as a "100% happiness guarantee." It committed MUD/WTR to issuing a no-hassle refund. These options fostered trust and made new users more comfortable signing up for a subscription. The company's humorous FAQ – for instance, clarifying that its mushrooms are "magic… but not that kind of magic" (i.e. non-psychoactive) – also helped address skepticism among the fence-sitters and moved them to give the product a try.

After that first purchase, strong customer retention and enthusiastic word-of-mouth amplified sales. Many people who incorporated MUD/WTR into their routine and experienced their own benefits posted reviews about "sustained energy without jitters" or praising the "unique, earthy flavor" and became brand evangelists. The company has collected nearly 40,000 five-star reviews online – a compelling level of social support. In parallel, the growth of an online MUD/WTR community makes customers feel like part of a movement. The community anchor, along with responsive customer service and an expanded product line, has resulted in a low churn rate that supports strong recurring revenue.

More existing customers subscribing to MUD/WTR products designed for consumption throughout their day (morning, afternoon, and night), has increased the company's wallet share and overall customer lifetime value, while also attracting new customers seeking the benefits of matcha or a calming bedtime drink. MUD/WTR's high-end pricing and premium positioning is another strong foundation for increasing customer LTV. Drinking MUD is roughly 8 times more expensive per cup than brewing your own generic drip coffee at home, a price point based on ingredient quality (100% organic, with many exotic botanicals) plus the healthy lifestyle and wellness value proposition. MUD/WTR has essentially pioneered a new premium functional beverage category, and enthusiasts are willing to pay for the benefits it offers.

MUD/WTR's direct to consumer sales engine – dominated by direct online subscriptions – has been remarkably efficient and scalable. By owning the customer relationship end-to-end, the company has nurtured a faithful following and demonstrated how tapping into a deep consumer need – the desire for energy and wellness without burnout – can scale quickly and achieve rapid revenue growth. For Shane Heath, the next step was to expand his company's reach through traditional retail channels and a presence on ecommerce platforms such as Amazon.

Omnichannel Aspirations: The Leap to Retail Distribution

After establishing a loyal customer base through online sales and subscriptions, MUD/WTR's next step was onto retail shelves and global online shopping carts. To kickstart its retail expansion, the company showcased its product at industry trade shows and started with introducing its products in small, local health food locations before expanding on the shelves of wellness-friendly national retail stores.

MUD/WTR's first national retail partner was Sprouts Farmers Market, a grocery chain known for natural and organic products. Being on Sprouts shelves around the country gave MUD/WTR a credible brick-and-mortar presence in the wellness aisle. Its next step was winning shelf placement in some Whole Foods Market regions and other health food chains.

At the end of 2023, MUD/WTR landed a breakthrough agreement with Target to sell its full product line in more than 500 Target stores nationwide. Target positioned the company's product in its health and wellness aisles, effectively betting on the appeal of the emerging "coffee alternative" segment. The brand's distinctive packaging, with minimalist black tins and pouches, helped it stand out on retail shelves. MUD/WTR also created lower-priced 12-serving trial packs to win over new retail customers.

As of 2025 MUD/WTR has achieved a notable retail footprint, and retail revenues now complement its still-growing online sales channel, creating a synergistic sales flywheel –store presence increases brand exposure, driving more people to subscribe online, while the large subscriber base helps drive adoption by more physical stores. For a product originally mixed at home by Shane Heath, shelf space in the aisles of big box retailers marks a significant market demand milestone.

MUD/WTR's channel strategy has been multifaceted: using every relevant platform to reach consumers (the brand's own site, Amazon, social media, podcast networks, retail stores, and even a branded café); partnering with like-minded brands and influencers to amplify the message; and relying on key service providers to ensure high-quality execution. This expansive approach has empowered MUD/WTR to accelerate its growth trajectory. Instead of limiting its identity to providing a coffee alternative, the MUD/WTR brand is now integrated into diverse touchpoints of a consumer's life, from scrolling on social media, to listening to a podcast, to shopping at Target, to attending a meditation class at the company's branded Santa Monica cafe and community gathering spot. Few beverage startups manage to create such a holistic ecosystem of partnerships and channels so quickly.

Scaling Operations with Aligned Company Culture and Team Benefits

Behind the marketing buzz and booming sales, MUD/WTR's internal operations and logistics had to scale aggressively to keep the wings on this high-flying airplane. In the early days, operations were extremely lean. A now iconic part of the founding story is that Shane Heath literally hand-mixed early batches of Mud powder himself, sourcing ingredients in small quantities to fulfill orders while keeping costs low. After he joined up as cofounder, Paul DeJoe also took part in late-night shifts, helping Shane with preparing and shipping orders. This willingness of the founders to wear every hat – product development, fulfillment, customer service, finance – set the tone for MUD/WTR's operations culture: no task was too small if it served customers well and helped the company grow.

As orders ramped up and hundreds per week turned into thousands per week, the company partnered with a co-manufacturer facility in Southern California to handle blending and packaging the powders. According to MUD/WTR, "All of our mushrooms are American-grown... we work with a producer in California." By insisting on USDA-organic ingredients and domestic mushroom sourcing, MUD/WTR ensures consistency and quality control – which is crucial for both compliance (organic certification, Prop 65 in California, etc.) and brand trust.

Internally, MUD/WTR has managed to scale with a company culture that balances employee productivity with wellness and stress reduction. Shane Heath's personal experience with burnout has shaped his leadership style and support for policies like every other Friday off for employees and an annual paid wellness retreat. This balanced culture is rare for a hyper-growth startup, but entirely in keeping with Shane's founding vision and wellness values. While growing revenues and achieving profitability, he has ensured that success at MUD/WTR doesn't require regular infusions of caffeine.

In an era where consumers and employees care about corporate values, MUD/WTR's mission to improve wellness and mental health, and its open support for causes like psychedelic research resonate strongly. It is environmentally friendly; compared to ready-to-drink coffees, MUD/WTR's powder means less packaging waste and shipping weight per serving. The brand's encouragement of mindfulness and moderation reinforces a broader societal interest in personal wellness. All this strengthens brand affinity and encourages customers to feel they're part of a larger movement.

Essential Ingredients for MUD/WTR Growth

MUD/WTR's financial story also features balance – rapid growth of orders, customer subscriptions and market expansion have been balanced by disciplined financial management and strategic use of outside investment. While MUD/WTR has raised an estimated $60 million in external funding so far, the company has not engaged in the cash-burning, top-line growth strategies common to many venture-backed consumer brands. Heath prioritizes cash flow management and financial discipline with capital-efficient marketing, customer acquisition, and operations. Overall, MUD/WTR's financial profile can be summarized as rapidly growing top-line, healthy gross margins, strong but efficient reinvestment in growth, relatively modest outside funding with creative financing to bridge working capital, and an eye toward long-term value.

Having achieved a large recurring revenue base before the arrival of the inevitable crowd of "coffee alternative" competitors, MUD/WTR has established brand recognition, SEO dominance, multichannel retail placement, and a passionate customer community. Its brand carries a cachet that emphasizes wellness without being preachy. Customers wear its merch, share their morning ritual stories, swap recipes for Mud smoothies, and participate in MUD/WTR's online and offline discussions about wellness. This level of customer love bodes well for long-term loyalty, strengthening MUD/WTR's potential to become a high-value, enduring lifestyle brand.

Shane Heath set MUD/WTR on the path to extreme growth and profitability by blending visionary branding with disciplined and fine-tuned execution.

His early decisions – from a provocative brand name, to a product with purpose, to creative marketing messages – now define the company's DNA. Beyond its financial success, MUD/WTR's leadership team has shown that a company can invest in employee wellness, community health, and social impact while still aggressively driving growth. That balance is arguably one of MUD/WTR's major strengths heading into the future.

Carbliss

In the highly competitive ready-to-drink (RTD) cocktail market, few companies come close to matching the extreme growth rate of Carbliss. Founded in 2019 by Adam and Amanda Kroener, this Wisconsin-based company has catapulted from mixing their own no-carb cocktails at home into a national beverage phenomenon, achieving extraordinary 27,127% growth over three years and earning recognition as the #7 fastest-growing private company in America according to *Inc. Magazine's* 2024 rankings, and the #1 food and beverage growth company nationally.

Talking with Adam Kroener makes it abundantly clear that his company has forged a surprising, inspiring, and often downright contrarian path to 100X growth. Like Carbliss itself, the Kroener's story combines classic ingredients into an invigorating entrepreneurial cocktail.

Adam kicks off our conversation with a founding anecdote that he has shared widely on social media. It goes like this,

> *So, Amanda and I were doing keto -a low carb, low sugar diet. I tried some of the low-carb cocktails that were available back in 2018, and they were high in carbonation and low in flavor. I started making a vodka lemonade drink at home that didn't have any carbs or sugar, just for myself. When I got sick of carrying all my own ingredients around to mix it up, I went out and bought $500 worth of low carb drink products, just to see if there was anything that tasted like what I was making. Nothing I bought tasted even close to what I was making at home.*
>
> *And then I started saying to my wife, you know, somebody should put this in a can. Soon, that turned into, **we** should put this in a can. And when Amanda asked me, what's your plan? I said, 'Well, I'm going to put this drink in a can. Then, I'm going to sell the shit out of it.' She looked at*

*me and said, 'No, what's your **business plan**?' To which I said, 'I just told you – that's my plan!"*

It's a great anecdote. What happened next demonstrates that the Kroener's decision to start Carbliss wasn't based on impulse or overconfidence. As co-founders, Adam's career in corporate sales and operations is well balanced by Amanda's financial expertise and corporate experience as a CFO and Vice President of Finance. No surprise that she asked Adam for a lot more details about everything from the manufacturing costs and distribution logistics for this new cocktail in a can, to how he planned to convince enough customers to try and buy an unfamiliar beverage, to how much money it would take to get this startup off the ground. As Adam recalls, those pointed questions were the genesis of their first real business plan.

The critical steps before finalizing their new business idea involved answering the questions that Amanda had posed; testing the market demand, manufacturing a sample batch of Carbliss; and carefully calculating their startup costs.

The Kroener's approach to validating market demand and launching the business was notably grassroots and unconventional. Adam conducted informal market research by talking with hundreds of local Wisconsin residents about why they were drinking low or no-carb cocktails, and what they thought about the taste. He knew full well that his informal survey wasn't statistically valid, but his face-to-face discussions with unsatisfied consumers confirmed his instincts that there was a market gap waiting to be filled.

I asked about 300 people in bars and restaurants, what are you drinking and why did you pick it? The main answer was, "It's low carb, it's low sugar, or low calorie." Then I would follow up with the question, "Do you like the taste?" And the best answer was, "Meh, it's okay."

Imagine serving your guests a grilled steak, and nobody saying that the steak was juicy and moist and the flavor was amazing. All they could say was, yeah, that was definitely a low carb meal. That's not a compliment, right? At that point, I didn't follow up with a more elaborate study. I didn't go to business school. I just bet on the positive reaction to what I was describing – a great tasting zero-carb cocktail in a can. And we used that reaction to decide that we were ready to go ahead and start a business.

The next step was to manufacture and sell their product, with the goal of bootstrapping the business with their own savings until it generated enough revenue to at least cover costs. As Adam recalls, the transition from manufacturing and distribution agreements to a predictable volume of sales turned out to be the bumpiest part of the launch.

> *I had found a place that would make my little sample product into a scalable batch, and that cost us $2,500 and so that was really the first indicator of, you know, can I get money from my wife to be able to bet on this?*
>
> *It took us about a year to get it onto store shelves. Finally, we got cans of Carbliss on the shelf about August of 2019. We found out that when you are running a new company, a lot of your biggest challenges hit in the first year, year and a half. During that period, we had operational challenges up the wazoo. If I was not still working full time and Amanda wasn't working full time, we would have gone out of business about three times.*

Launching with high hopes, confronting unexpected roadblocks, and watching your savings get swallowed up by mounting startup costs is a true test by fire for any founder. Remarkably, Adam and Amanda had not only invested up front in the Carbliss launch, they had budgeted enough of their savings to cover several loss-making years. In fact, they were so committed to bootstrapping that when an angel investor first offered to invest a million in seed funding for Carbliss, the Kroener's turned the offer down.

Adam describes the process of confronting the financial realities of supply chain, distribution, and restocking costs, and realizing the importance of full-time founder attention. That led to their learning the true value of fundraising, and Adam reengaged the angel investor, who became their first and only investor. As it turned out, that first million in angel funding was enough to launch Carbliss into its revenue growth stage.

> *In our original financial calculations, I was just trying to figure out how much we needed to make our money back. We had agreed to put in around $100 grand of our own to start the business. And I did some math based on knowing that there are 72 counties in Wisconsin, so if Carbliss could sell X amount of cases per county, with a conservative gross profit projection, we could afford to manufacture, distribute, and sell that many cases.*

After that, even if we decided not to manufacture any more, we would not lose any more money. But, you know, those early projections didn't really reflect a ton of foresight, because I quickly learned that when reorders come in, you obviously have to pay for more product, and then your potential losses start to become bigger and bigger. Working out the details of this kind of business is a really fun math problem. Anyway, originally, I was just trying to figure out, can I just bootstrap this business and not lose my butt?

When we got the angel investment at the beginning of 2021, that was the catalyst for me to quit my corporate job – even though that meant taking about a 75% cut in pay. I had been making about a quarter million dollars a year, but I only paid myself about $60 grand to manage Carbliss full time. I put together an updated financial plan that projected that after five years, Carbliss would be generating $78 million in annual revenue, based on having distribution in 36 states. In that plan, I projected we would still be losing about half a million dollars at the tail end of 2026. Well, as it happened, much sooner than anyone expected, we're already drastically profitable. We are actually doing better financially in EBITDA percentage than a lot of our publicly traded counterparts. At the end of 2024, we will be selling in 13 states, and we hit just under $100 million in revenues. Even though at the start a lot of people told us that we had a very aggressive growth plan– and very little chance of making it work –in fact we have been beating that plan by leaps and bounds.

The Backyard-to-Backyard Distribution Strategy

Carbliss operates on a business-to-business-to-consumer model, selling premium ready-to-drink cocktails through the three-tier distribution system mandated by alcohol beverage regulations in the United States. Those regulations dictate that the company's distribution chain and primary revenue comes from selling its canned cocktails to distributors, who then sell to retailers, ultimately reaching consumers through various retail channels including grocery stores, liquor stores, and on-premise establishments like bars and restaurants.

The Carbliss product portfolio initially centered on vodka-based fruit flavors, with Black Raspberry emerging as the most popular variety, alongside Cranberry, Pineapple, Lemon Lime, and Peach offerings. The company has expanded into a classic cocktail collection, as well as offering a margarita variety pack. All products maintain the Carbliss core value proposition of great taste with zero carbohydrates, zero sugar, 100 calories, and gluten-free formulation at 5% alcohol by volume.

In the early days, Adam and Amanda literally built brand awareness one location at a time. They would mix cocktails for friends and at local gatherings, creating evangelists out of early tasters. This approach soon evolved into what Adam Kroener calls the "bar to bar, backyard to backyard" campaign. "Our sales plan at retail was to build backyard to backyard," Adam notes, emphasizing deep local penetration before any splashy national advertising. In practice, this meant focusing on one community, one city at a time, and ensuring Carbliss became a local favorite before moving to the next. An illustrative early move was seeding the product in Wisconsin bars and liquor stores through personal relationships and in-store tastings. By convincing one friend, one bartender, and one neighborhood store after another, the founders created organic market demand. Consumers who tried Carbliss at a friend's barbecue or a sampling event often became loyal customers – and sometimes vocal advocates.

This cost-effective, viral customer acquisition strategy relied on extensive sampling programs rather than traditional advertising. Adam and Amanda initially conducted sampling personally, driving hours to events and selling four cases for $40 profit, not counting their own time and travel costs. Amanda questioned the economics; Adam viewed it as an investment in future growth, "that's 24 four packs, which now are going to sit on people's shelves... They're going to give it to their friends. They're going to try it. And I'm betting that the $40 we made today on those cases of Carbliss will become $400, and then $4,000 and maybe even become $400,000 over time.

This locally-intensive approach directly contradicts conventional wisdom about scaling beverage companies and represents a fundamental philosophical difference from venture-backed Ready-to-Drink competitors. The Kroeners had learned a lesson from following the standard national playbook for expansion in the early days of their company, and deliberately took a different path. Adam recalls listening to consultants who urged them to expand as quickly as possible, "They said, 'Adam and Amanda, you have to go to Florida, Texas, California, Chicago, New York — those places have to be your focus because that is where all the population is.' We thought, 'well, they are the professionals' and we tried that approach. Adam learned that these initial attempts at wide geographic distribution failed because "nobody knew who we were, and we didn't know how to support the brand yet at that time." This experience reinforced their commitment to the narrow-and-deep approach.

The decision to stick to a locally-grounded strategy was inspired in part by the expansion methodology of Craig Culver, the founder of Culver's restaurant chain. Adam explains, "Craig came up with the backyard-to-backyard concept — where they didn't expand 45 minutes from their last store. They compounded that for so many years, that the word of mouth became large enough that now they can drop a Culver's in Florida or Texas or Arizona and people know who they are."

When they do enter new states, Carbliss typically launches in 3-12 counties at a time rather than taking on the entire state or its biggest population centers. Then they work to achieve complete market saturation in those counties before expanding into the rest of the state. As the business scales, the launch plans scale. The timeline for achieving saturation ranges from two weeks to two years depending on market characteristics. As Adam notes, even though Carbliss is going against conventional wisdom with their expansion strategy, the results have paid off in multiple ways,

As I see it, there are 3 expansion models out there: the most popular one is hub and spoke; number two is narrow and deep, which we describe as patiently aggressive, and number three is casting a wide net hoping to get distribution in big volume stores (wide and shallow rather than narrow and deep). For us, the narrow and deep plus patiently aggressive are really working in tandem.

Most brands in our space, at this point, are going national, meaning they're being distributed in 46 plus states. For Carbliss, narrow and deep means that rather than activating a bunch of states, or even an entire state at once, we target specific areas and saturate those before expanding. For example, when we started distributing in Kansas, we launched in just seven counties. Kansas will be done by the end of 2025. During that time period, most of the competing brands would already have launched seven states at a time. And the other brands in our space would probably have just one sales person for maybe four states; a local rep for Kansas, Iowa, Nebraska. Instead, Carbliss will have four sales people for one state.

So as we grow, that allows us to keep going deeper, and we don't move on until we've hit our goals and our metrics in one spot. So that's how narrow and deep, patiently aggressive characterizes our strategy. Even knowing that most people in our position would be going national already, we are patient. Sometimes it is really, really hard knowing that people in Florida will love this liquid, Boston will love this liquid, to sit back and just say, OK, if we pushed into more territory, we could probably be a half a billion-dollar company next year. Let's do it! The reason we have adopted the deep and patient approach is we want to be a personable brand, and we want the Carbliss brand to be around for 30 or 40 years. I don't think you can do that and scale nationally tomorrow.

So then that last piece of distribution is hub and spoke. Chicago is typically a hub location in this approach. But here's why narrow and deep and patient aggressive is working so well for Carbliss. We just launched Chicago last week, and the Chicago metro area is the last piece of Illinois where we launched. Most brands would go into Chicago first, and say, let's see if we can make it. Then we can go national. But then they're drowning in the wave of competition, because everybody is thinking the same way.

On the contrary, Carbliss started outside the Chicago area. We launched first to the rest of the state, and we created a pent-up demand. Suddenly, all the Chicagoans who are used to getting everything first travel around in Wisconsin or go down south in their own state, or 20 miles west in their own state, they're trying our cocktails and saying, this Carbliss stuff is amazing. Where can I get it in Chicago? And we start getting this feeding frenzy where they're asking their local Chicago bars and retail to stock Carbliss. So now, when we launch in Chicago, 80% of the people that our reps meet with will be saying, yes, we've already heard about Carbliss. Go ahead, bring it in. In this world of alcoholic beverage distribution, a lot of people in these big cities "welcome" new brands with their hand out, as in, give me that illegal money, rather than with a handshake. The beautiful part about how we have managed growth is we have gotten a lot of genuine handshake welcomes. And that's because their customers have already been asking for Carbliss.

The strategy requires intensive local presence and support since Carbliss assigns four sales representatives to single states. As Adam notes, this resource-intensive approach enables deeper market penetration and stronger retailer relationships. Once Carbliss enters a city, the sales reps have had time to develop grassroots campaigns that will get consumer attention. For example, in 2024 Carbliss literally wrapped a Chicago Brown Line train in Carbliss branding, turning heads in the city's crowded transit system. Commuters and tourists alike were invited to "celebrate Chicago in Carbliss style" as a Carbliss-branded train crisscrossed the city. This kind of high-visibility, localized advertising, essentially a moving billboard, helps to announce Carbliss's arrival in new urban markets in an unconventional way.

A deep and patient expansion strategy doesn't reflect any lack of extreme growth ambition. Adam is well aware of the new market opportunities still waiting to be tapped in the next few years,

> *Right now, I calculate that Carbliss is being sold to about 20-25% of the nation's population today… My basic entrepreneur math is you multiply that, or you divide that by 20 for every 1% of the population, and multiply by 100, as we should be able to accomplish very easily with just this product lineup, then we should be able to flirt with a billion dollars in revenue.*

This basic math assumes linear scalability across the untapped U.S. markets, which may prove too optimistic given varying regional preferences and fast-changing competitive landscapes. However, the company's success in diverse markets from Wisconsin to Kansas to Texas is a reasonable foundation for expected continued revenue growth as Carbliss works to penetrate more states in the next several years.

Even here, in making a well-grounded projection of the enormous growth potential ahead of Carbliss, Adam pauses to remind me (and himself) that the billion-dollar figure may be a distraction. It's certainly not an all-or-nothing goal.

> *So going back – we smashed our five-year goals, I am very excited to be in a position to have a business that we built in five years, that 90% of business owners would be so jealous to have. But I don't want to get too big for my britches, right? We are focusing on just doing the right things to keep winning and growing by keeping on track, rather than going after the shiny new toy. That being said, in the next three years I think a fairly conservative revenue number would be around $300 million.*

That's a conservative projection that leads naturally into the next strategy that underpins Carbliss success – disciplined financial management.

Financial Discipline on the Path to Profitability

The company's focused, patient market expansion strategy has a parallel in Carbliss's disciplined financial management and initially conservative growth projections. Here's how Adam recalls the balance of revenue and expenses in the company's first 5 years,

> *In our first partial year, 2019, we did around $80,000 in revenue, and we lost money. 2020 was our first full year. But we had four months of no revenue, going back to some of those operational challenges that I was talking about. So that year, we did $280,000 and lost 70K. In year three, 2021, when we got the angel investment and I quit my job to work fulltime at Carbliss, we did $1.5 million in revenue and we lost $350,000. And THEN, March of 2022 became my favorite month ever. That's when we had our first profitable month at Carbliss and the revenue took off. For the rest of 2022, our only non-profitable months were May, because we ran out of inventory, and then December, because we didn't know soon enough that distributors would kind of pull back at year end to do inventory counts. Outside of that, every month has been profitable. Starting in 2022, every year has been profitable. We had just under $56 million in 2023, and for 2024, we almost hit $100 million in revenue.*

One of the company's many impressive achievements is their gross margin optimization. The founders began operations with an unimpressive 18% gross margin, learned fast, and systematically improved company performance to approximately 61% gross margin by 2024. This leap resulted from tighter supply chain management and volume-driven purchasing power negotiations rather than price increases.

Carbliss has instituted cash flow management strategies designed to be cash-efficient and leverage high market demand. Most of their suppliers operate on net 30-45-day payment terms (compared to industry standard net 10-15 days), while most distributors pay on net 15 terms. This structure allows Carbliss to collect revenue from distributors before paying suppliers, providing crucial working capital during growth phases. Without this, many distributors would've had to wait years more to bring Carbliss to their market.

Adam explained the strategic importance of this approach: "we take a longer time to pay all of our vendors...when we're in an inventory crunch, we're making money like, it's nobody [else's business]; cash is building up. If we can't make product fast enough, because I'm paying them in 45 days to make it, I could almost have it resold two or three times."

Even after reaching the point when explosive revenue growth attracted investor interest, the Kroener's have deliberately avoided raising venture capital funding to expand even faster. The angel investor who provided crucial support in the company's early growth phase continued to support Carbliss by serving as the guarantor of $2 million in readily accessible capital until in 2024, Bank of America doubled the company's line of credit based on business cash flow performance, removing the need for personal guarantees from the angel investor

> Our angel investor, two or three times put his assets on the line, put cash in. The first time, he put $2 million of cash in the bank just for us to draw off, and he didn't ask for anything else more. Who does that? This guy's an angel like in the term. Finally, after being profitable for two and a half years, in April 2024 Bank of America took a leap and offered us a substantial line of credit. I never expected a big bank to double our line of credit, based on the cash flow of the business. Without our angel investor and Bank of America, we couldn't have done what we are doing. They truly believed in the vision, and we are forever grateful for that.

Now that the company is consistently profitable and cash-flow positive, this bank credit line is providing enough flexibility to support the preferred patient expansion strategy that has worked so well for Carbliss.

Metrics That Matter for Carbliss

Carbliss has developed a metrics framework that prioritizes actual market performance over traditional shipment-based measurements. This approach reflects a clear-eyed understanding of beverage industry dynamics and consumer behavior patterns, and the lessons that the Kroeners learned on the front lines from the bumps they encountered in early years of operation. As

Adam notes, the number one item they track is sales and revenue. Their other top performance metrics include:

Depletions vs. Shipments: The company focuses on depletions (distributor sales to retailers) rather than shipments (company sales to distributors). Adam learned this lesson early when a distributor purchased a $70,000 truckload and never reordered. Rebuys, especially the frequency of distributor reorders, serves as a key indicator of product velocity and market acceptance.

Distribution Penetration: The company measures penetration as the percentage of available retail accounts actually carrying Carbliss products within each market. Sales teams are held accountable for distribution metrics rather than case volume targets, reflecting the philosophy that "for example, if you have 10 accounts, we expect you to sell into at least eight of them, and then we bet on our team and our model to create that continued revenue generation."

Cost of Goods Detail: Carbliss maintains granular cost tracking down to individual ingredients. Adam explains: "I know that my citric acid, which goes into almost every beverage, might be $0.025, in one can, and it might be $0.018 in another can, based on the formula." This level of detail enables precise margin optimization and informed purchasing decisions.

Performance vs. Actual Financials: The company maintains dual financial tracking systems: "performance financials" based on distributor sales to retailers, and "actual financials" based on cash receipts. While actual financials determine cash flow management, performance financials indicate true business health and market acceptance.

Data Analytics and AI Integration

Carbliss's approach to data analytics and artificial intelligence reflects an open, exploratory philosophy, emphasizing human judgment while investigating technological capabilities. The company currently uses AI primarily for learning and experimentation rather than decision-making. As Adam explains: "I'm not relying on AI at this time, in that I'm not using it to make decisions, I'm using it to learn and play."

Specific applications include:

Forecasting Experiments: Historical sales data and market variables are input into AI models to test predictive accuracy against traditional forecasting methods. The company tracks AI performance without relying on outputs for actual planning decisions.

Administrative Tasks: AI assists with job description generation and product ideation, representing lower-risk applications that supplement human creativity.

Operational Analysis: Given the company's history of forecasting challenges ("we have failed to forecast well almost every single year"), AI represents a potential solution for demand planning in high-growth environments.

This test-and-evaluate AI adoption strategy reflects broader company philosophy emphasizing proven fundamentals over technological novelty. Adam noted: "It's not embedded in our business. It's not making decisions. It's not part of any language model. We're using it as a let's feel this out. Let's see what it can do." As AI capabilities evolve and prove their value in controlled testing, integration may expand into demand planning, inventory optimization, and sales and marketing applications. However, the company prioritizes human relationships and decision-making, viewing AI as a supplementary tool rather than a replacement for core business functions.

Company Culture and Leadership

It's clear from listening to Adam describe how all his team members contribute to the company's success, that the company's culture matters a lot to him and Amanda. Throughout our conversation Adam reflects a sense of shared purpose and having each other's back. That's due in no small part to the Kroener's genuine care for the people they work with. This culture extends to employees, customers, suppliers, and distribution partners, creating sustainable competitive advantages that technology or capital cannot easily replicate.

Describing his leadership strategy, Adam emphasizes empowerment over control, reflecting his belief that to "hire an amazing team and get out of their way" produces superior results. It manifests in minimal bureaucracy and maximum individual responsibility, with the expectation that employees will function as "contributing adults" who are independent problem solvers rather than rule-followers.

The company explicitly avoids corporate hierarchies, instead asking employees to "be a contributing adult, and if you do that, we treat you with respect." This approach creates both opportunities and challenges, as many employees arrive expecting traditional corporate frameworks and require time to adapt to entrepreneurial expectations. The company's investment in intangibles like culture, relationships, and employee experience has generated significant returns in terms of loyalty, word-of-mouth marketing, and operational effectiveness.

A signature Carbliss benefit is grounded in the Kroener's conviction that hiring the right people often means that employees will be super engaged in their work, to the point where they won't be able to wind down and enjoy a vacation break. Instead of exploiting that level of dedication, Adam has "put my money where my mouth is" and from the start, he has budgeted $5,000 each year for each employee to get away for a week. The company partners with travel agencies to facilitate the program, and employees can use their $5K for any vacation purpose, from all-inclusive trips to family Disney excursions. It's part of what Adam calls a policy of "building all these weird and intangible things into the business" in addition to the company's stellar list of standard employee benefits and regular touch points where the entire company travels to activate new markets together, combining business development with team building. These events include sales training, market activation, and team dinners, creating shared experiences and mutual understanding across departments.

At the beginning, we had a commission-based structure. To work as a team and have people help each other, we quickly had to switch to a structure where we paid people a higher salary and then had their bonus be directional based on what we wanted for corporate initiatives, rather than being completely commission-based. We bet on people, gave them the intangibles to make their work successful. And I think that is the biggest thing that we're seeing come back in spades. If we want somebody off the team, we let them go. We have only had one person quit. That person is a testament to the strength of our culture. We told them, you will need to travel and work from the office 3 days a week. They said, "I can do that." They found after a few short months that they wanted to work from home and not travel so they found a role outside of the company that had those things in place.

It goes back to my fear of corporatization. To be able to grow this fast, you need to have a great product. You need to have great execution. We have a different liquid than ANYTHING in the market. We work to be the best supplier, and make our supply chain the most money. We also have a team who care about being the best, who deliver because of their passion. And that matters. Quite frankly, if the Carbliss team were a bunch of arrogant asses, our distributors would feel that. Our retailers would feel that. And I think the team we have is a big part of why we win.

Staying the Course

Carbliss demonstrates how first-time founders can build a 100X business from scratch with a disciplined focus on essential growth elements, and lots of heart. The company's remarkable growth trajectory from homemade brew to a consumer-favorite brand underscores that well-reasoned contrarian strategies can succeed in highly competitive markets without massive infusions of venture capital.

The "backyard-to-backyard" expansion path challenges conventional wisdom about scaling consumer product companies, proving that depth of market penetration can create deeper customer loyalty than geographic breadth. This approach, combined with an uncompromising focus on product quality and customer experience, has enabled Carbliss to compete effectively against industry giants with substantially greater marketing budgets and distribution leverage.

Notably, Carbliss achieved rapid growth in tandem with profitability and a distinctive company culture, demonstrating that entrepreneurs need not choose between scale and sustainability. The company's financial discipline and strategic independence provide a foundation for long-term success that venture capital-backed competitors may struggle to replicate.

As Carbliss continues expanding toward its goal of national distribution, the company's experience offers valuable lessons for entrepreneurs seeking to build lasting businesses in competitive markets. The emphasis on product excellence, relationship building, and strategic patience provides a blueprint for growth that transcends industry-specific applications.

The founders' commitment to Carbliss still being "around for 30 or 40 years" rather than seeking quick expansion as a hot brand for 6 months, then being nonexistent a year later, is the long-term perspective that has informed every strategic decision. This approach has created a business positioned for continued, profitable growth while maintaining the entrepreneurial spirit and cultural values that enabled its initial success.

Songfinch

Every entrepreneur has a compelling startup story to tell. It turns out that John Williamson, cofounder and CEO of Songfinch, has a handful. He starts our conversation by reflecting on the interconnected entrepreneurial ventures that preceded his decade-long journey with Songfinch,

> I've been through a ton of ups and downs, a lot of building something up and feeling like you're getting towards the top of the mountain, then realizing that maybe I had climbed the wrong mountain and that it's time to reset and start over with a new company. That's been my experience of entrepreneurship over the years.
>
> Songfinch is actually startup number five for me. It seems like I have a kind of primal need to build and create new companies. It's just a deep part of who I am. For years now, I've been building and operating companies, mainly in the music industry, usually at the crossroads of music and technology.

One of his earlier "crossroads" startups was Music Dealers, a two-sided B2B music marketplace that Williamson cofounded in 2008. His vision for Music Dealers was to create a platform that would connect independent musicians with opportunities to license their music to corporate customers around the world. Leveraging his experience in the music industry, Williamson and his founding team succeeded in growing this new venture into the biggest pre-cleared library of music in the world. As Williamson recalls with pride, "We had licensed music from about 30,000 artists from 150 countries, and our clients included a big chunk of the Fortune 500 list, companies ranging from

Coke to Microsoft to Airbnb." Within a few years, the company's marketplace had become a significant source of new revenue for indie musicians, who benefited from licensing their songs for use in TV shows, marketing, commercials, video games, and more.

Music Dealers was successful enough that one of their largest clients acquired a significant stake in 2011. It was a financial win, but the deal required the founding team to switch gears from building a startup to managing a very small part of a giant global corporation. As Williamson diplomatically puts it,

> *I came to understand the positives and negatives of taking the company that you started and built with a strong vision, selling it to your biggest client, and finding out the client didn't necessarily have the same goals or vision for the business that you had founded.*

He parted ways with that venture in 2013, looking for a new entrepreneurial mountain to climb.

> *I was pretty disenchanted with the music business in general at that point. And I figured, hey, all the things I've learned from these music startups should translate to other ventures. So now I'm going to move away from the music industry. One business I launched with cofounders was an incubator/accelerator and coworking space in Chicago. Our goal was to support very early stage, pre seed companies in different industries. We looked for really great people who had startup ideas for everything from a fantasy sports company to a restaurant application. Basically, anything except music.*

The Startup Allure of Songfinch

Despite his "anything except music" vow, Williamson's deep roots in the music industry were still alive and well. The idea for Songfinch first sprouted when he was best man at his brother's wedding. Instead of just giving a traditional toast, Williamson decided to contract for an original song to celebrate the newly married couple's story with lots of insider references to how they met and fell in love. That song became an emotional high point at the wedding reception, and John loved watching the wedding party and guests transition from a bit of confusion about the unfamiliar tune to a mix of laughter and tears. That emotional impact started him thinking about another new venture — a business that matched consumers with custom-created original songs.

That sprout took several more years to become a full-fledged business idea. John was well aware that his prior success had been in B2B businesses, not in consumer markets. But the pull of the music industry, memories of that joy-inducing wedding song, combined with the challenge of attempting something completely new, eventually became too strong to resist,

> *By 2016 I was ready to say, let's actually try this, let's make it go. After a few years hiatus from the industry, it felt like time for me and my co-founders to come back to what we were really comfortable with. And a direct-to-consumer music venture based on creating something that didn't really exist felt like an exciting new challenge.*

Searching for Consumer Demand and Product Market Fit

John Williamson envisioned a win-win marketplace model in which participating musicians would be compensated for writing bespoke original songs that consumers could gift to loved ones to celebrate a special occasion. Songfinch would match musicians with buyer requests; the musician would write the song and deliver it though a digital platform.

When the company launched in 2016, however, Songfinch struggled to attract buyers for personalized songs. Many consumers feel a need for music composed just for them. Others were reluctant to pay a premium for a song by an unfamiliar artist. It didn't help that Songfinch's early ads highlighted specific use cases "The perfect gift for an anniversary!" which positioned custom-written songs music as a convenient digital gift solution than a way to create powerful emotions. The few orders Songfinch received were almost all for birthdays and anniversaries.

Even though Songfinch had raised $750,000 in angel funding to support its launch, the lack of product/market fit soon became painfully clear. Early orders trickled in based on paid marketing campaigns, but the order volume remained stubbornly low. Williamson recalls that in its first full year of operation, Songfinch generated about $150,000 in revenue. By 2019, revenues had increased only minimally to a discouraging $180,000.

In retrospect, Williamson acknowledges that he hadn't anticipated the challenges of convincing customers to buy an untested product at the premium price of $199 per song. It was tempting to just shut the company down. But even on the brink of failure, he held on to his vision and pushed his founding team for one last effort to break through and reach potential buyers,

> We had to admit that no one seemed to understand what we were trying to sell. As hard as we tried to connect with customers, our message just didn't grab them. It felt like the market demand was never going to pop. Looking back, I should have closed Songfinch down a dozen times. Why keep a business going without any growth, and without ever figuring out how to reach more customers? What kept me going was seeing how an original, personal song did impact the customers who ordered one. It was such an absolutely beautiful, powerful experience that we were able to create. Despite the metrics being so bad, I kept feeling that this business had so much potential for good. If only I could do this at scale, it would be like a good karma flywheel. But after the first few years, the founding team needed to start working on other things, just to support themselves. Some of us started a new agency business that was doing really well, generating a few million dollars a year. I kept Songfinch open but honestly, by the end of 2019 our platform was just running in the background.
>
> In January 2020, we decided to invest our last $30,000 to try and reinvent the Songfinch marketing message. Finally, after all this time, we let go of focusing on delivering music as our product. Instead, we created a new advertising campaign that was all about the emotive experience and the memories the song could create. We developed a new ad campaign that featured people laughing and crying and hugging over music. We hoped that by showing how music could create such powerful moments, potential customers would envision themselves sharing an emotional moment with someone they loved, and give Songfinch a try.

Challenges of Pivoting to Meet Explosive Demand

Songfinch launched its last-hope marketing campaign on Facebook ahead of Valentine's Day 2020. The results were immediate and explosive. That February, the company generated more orders and more revenue than it had attracted in the whole of 2019. Along with shaking his head over how long it had taken to find a compelling value proposition, John remembers his exhilaration at this turning point. By shifting from marketing the product (a custom song) to the outcome (the recipient's emotional reaction), Songfinch could appeal to a much larger audience.

However, this sudden uptick in market demand came with a new set of challenges. Orders surged so fast that Songfinch's remaining staff couldn't fulfill them all. Exploding order volume was a positive long-term growth indicator, but it created a massive short-term headache. The company had to temporarily pull back advertising despite soaring demand because they lacked the operational capacity to deliver so many songs on time. This highlighted a critical area that required much more attention: Songfinch needed operational efficiency to manage growth.

When orders had slowed to a trickle, the company had cut staffing and relied on a manual fulfillment system. Even in those low-volume days, staff would sometimes have to scramble to find a suitable songwriter from their artist pool to match up with a specific song request. With torrents of song orders arriving, upgrading the platform became an urgent priority.

Williamson hired staff to rebuild capacity and develop a more functional online platform where customers and artists could be matched, and deliveries could be managed without manual bottlenecks. By 2022, much of the song fulfillment process had been streamlined and accelerated. This operational scaling was a vital pivot that enabled Songfinch to convert its wave of popularity into continued revenue growth, and avert the danger of collapsing under the weight of its own success.

Having demonstrated product/market fit, and landed a new VC investment, Songfinch doubled down on driving its top line growth. Elated at seeing how targeted ads could generate demand, Williamson embraced paid advertising as the company's primary growth engine. The company leaned into a "growth at all costs" mindset – spending heavily on marketing to acquire customers and capture market share. Through 2022, Songfinch operated like a deep-pocketed, high-growth tech startup, willing to spend heavily on marketing to seize the moment. The company's burn rate increased as it poured millions into social media ads highlighting emotion-filled song moments. This helped to catapult revenue from just $1.45 million in 2020 to $5.5 million in 2021 and $36 million in 2022. Unfortunately, betting the house on paid ads as a customer acquisition strategy had a major downside: the cost of customer acquisition far outpaced each customer's lifetime value.

By 2023, macroeconomic shifts and a cooling funding environment required a second pivot as Williamson sought to rein in customer acquisition costs. The marketing team optimized targeting and creative to get more ROI from each ad dollar, and promotions were more carefully managed to preserve margins. New marketing campaigns were measured by strict return-on-ad-spend goals rather than pure growth numbers. Despite these adjustments, performance marketing remained a cornerstone of Songfinch's strategy. As Williamson describes it, the company was shifting its focus to "efficiency and long-term impact" without abandoning the aggressive marketing that scored it the #11 spot on the *Inc 5000* list of fastest growing companies in 2023.

At the end of 2024, Songfinch had a growing revenue base, venture capital still in reserve, and improved margins. It had survived scraping by on a shoe-string, followed by investing heavily in a venture-funded growth surge, and Williamson was focused on reducing his company's reliance on high-priced advertising, implementing more scalable customer acquisition strategies, and improving operational efficiency. He hopes to achieve profitability in the coming year. It's an ambitious goal. A breakthrough distribution partnership and an emphasis on technology-driven scalability should help Williamson to make it a reality.

Expanding Customer Reach

Early in 2025, American Greetings and Songfinch announced a partnership to embed custom songs into digital greeting cards, marrying Songfinch's personalized music with American Greetings' vast user base of e-card senders. American Greetings online customers can now add a Songfinch custom song to their e-card purchases, simply by entering a few key details. The custom song is delivered to the recipient along with the card, situating Songfinch at the point-of-sale for a broad range of digital gifting occasions – birthdays, anniversaries, Mother's Day, Valentine's Day, and more. Williamson is eyeing more partnerships with companies in other gift-giving verticals, leveraging the company's technology innovations to create profitable product extensions with expanded market reach.

Digital Platform Technology, Instant Songs, and AI Behind the Scenes

The updated Songfinch platform includes a guided customer interface (sometimes called the "Song Builder") where buyers answer prompts about the recipient, occasion, preferred music style, and share personal stories or "must-have details" for the song. Songfinch's system uses this input to match the customer with the best available musician for the job, based on genre, mood, and vibe. The matching that was initially handled by a human music supervisor is now managed largely by algorithms that filter and recommend artists from Songfinch's curated musician cohort. Customers still have the option to browse and choose a specific artist themselves, or they can let the platform automatically assign one.

On the musician side, artists can accept song commissions, communicate with the client (if needed for clarification), and upload the finished track. Moreover, the platform gives artists visibility into their earnings, lets them manage their workload, and even retain the master and publishing rights to the songs they create. That means artists could (with the client's permission) potentially re-use portions of the music or release it on streaming platforms, and it encourages them to produce high-quality work they're proud of.

Songfinch can now handle thousands of orders concurrently without a linear increase in staff. The company has delivered over 400,000 original songs on the platform since its launch. Behind the scenes, Songfinch's platform also collects data on customer satisfaction, genre preferences, artist turnaround times, and more to improve recommendation algorithms and identify top-performing artists. All these elements – a smooth digital customer experience, algorithmic matching, automated workflows, create a competitive advantage for Songfinch. The technology not only enables operational scale, it also reinforces the company's brand promise of delivering "studio-quality songs" efficiently and reliably.

Williamson emphasizes that he believes in " a future where artists are forever the centerpiece of the creation – the output is always crafted and created by real artists." This commitment to human-authored music will remain at the center of Songfinch's music catalog. In the face of ever-evolving technology, however, it seems inevitable that a mix of premium original songs and lower priced options like the products created for American Greetings will be essential for long-term profitability and scalable revenue growth at Songfinch.

Songfinch is exploring the potentially lucrative middle ground between high-priced and personalized original music and expanded use of a proprietary technology it has developed to aggregate and re-mix all the hand-crafted songs in its continuously expanding music library. In 2024, it launched an "Instant Song" option that leverages this music library to create semi-custom tracks generated by combining pre-written musical templates with the Instant Song customer inputs. These Instant Songs use human vocals recorded in the templates and maintain a "human touch," relying on technology to enable re-mixing at speed and scale. The Instant Song product is an innovative step to attract budget-conscious customers and serve last-minute gift-givers.

Opportunities and Challenges Ahead

Songfinch launched in 2016 as a pioneer in the custom song market but instead of benefiting from first-mover advantage, it faced a challenge convincing consumers to pay for custom-composed songs. The company's pivot to marketing the emotional impact of music saved Songfinch from shutting down in 2019, and set the stage for extreme revenue growth powered by a heavy investment in performance marketing. Today, after almost a decade in the music gifting business, Songfinch is surrounded by competitors and still striving to achieve profitability and sustainable growth.

One of the company's bedrock strengths is its carefully curated community of talented musicians. Musicians genuinely value Songfinch because it offers them the rare opportunity to earn a living wage through their craft. Over the years, Songfinch has paid out close to $40 million to the artists on its platform, and it boasts a 95% artist retention rate. This "artist-first" company culture not only ensures a high-quality talent pool but also turns some artists into evangelists for the service. However, if emerging AI-based song vendors convince consumers that personalized music generated entirely by AI tools is comparable in value to human creativity, this Songfinch advantage could evaporate.

That puts more pressure on the company's technology and data to support its future growth. Williamson is leading Songfinch in this direction, without abandoning the company's founding value proposition. The custom platform, matching algorithm, and automation advances now allow Songfinch to fulfill orders at scale with relatively low marginal cost. The company can handle seasonal surges by virtue of its streamlined digital workflow and further personalize the customer experience by recommending particular artists or song styles. The selective adoption of AI and the rollout of Instant Song demonstrate that Songfinch is working to stay at the forefront of tech innovation in its sector.

As it looks to scale growth during the next three years, the challenges of market saturation and demand generation will loom larger. Having grown nearly 24,000% in three years, the company may have already reached many of the customers who are most excited about gifting custom songs. There is a risk that growth could plateau if Songfinch doesn't continue to improve its platform and roll out new products.

While acknowledging these challenges, Williamson envisions a bright future for Songfinch that combines the creative talents of independent musicians with a rising demand for personalized songs that deliver an emotional impact. From John Williamson's perspective, Instant Song is just the beginning of a new era in creative music-making at scale; an era that will respect musicians' rights and stoke consumer demand for new musical experiences. Williamson's vision is to use AI and other emerging technology as an "Iron Man suit" that enhances, rather than replaces, human artistic creativity.

Here's how he describes it,

> My take on the future of AI in music is to look at the creative artist community as being like Tony Stark, and innovative tech, like our Instant Song capability, as kind of an Iron Man suit for the artists. Both elements can add value separately, but something is still missing- either the scale or the soul. When you combine them to get the best of both, you are creating a totally new model for the future of the musical superhero. At Songfinch, I believe we are in the best position to achieve that.

John Williamson and Songfinch are still mapping out a profitable path to summit this particular entrepreneurial mountain. Based on his ability to pivot, innovate, and achieve extreme growth in a new market sector, Williamson seems poised to make it all the way to the top.

◆ ◆ ◆

What unites the founders featured in this chapter is an ambitious vision to create market leading brands in emerging categories and unwavering commitment to building consumer value into their product. Ben Goodwin, Shane Heath, Adam Kroener, and John Williamson believed that consumer brands could evolve into something life-changing, and they each set out to challenge traditional market leaders to prove it.

Their 100X growth was built on a foundation of personal conviction and willingness to stay the course. They tested messages, sampled product in-person, mixed batches late into the night, and pivoted as needed. Each faced moments of doubt: OLIPOP's failed first attempt with Obi, Shane Heath's near-burnout before landing his first investment, the Kroener's lean early years as they fine-turned their backyard-to-backyard strategy, and Williamson's failure to find product-market fit down before Songfinch pivoted toward emotional resonance.

What pulled them through was the conviction that building a product people loved, supported by a company that embraced the essential elements of scalable growth, was the most viable path to building an enduring consumer brand. That path takes time and extraordinary commitment, but the results are exponential.

4
Outsized Business ROI and Bottom-Line Impact

TO REACH 100X GROWTH in the business services sector, an innovative product is just the starting point. Convincing a skeptical business owner, corporate buyer, or procurement officer to try an unproven product from a startup requires more than vision and advanced technology. In the B2B world, high-value contracts and long-term relationships depend on solving real problems, delivering clear ROI, and proving bottom-line impact.

The companies featured in this chapter faced that challenge head-on, and prevailed. Odeko, Relay, Autosled, and Harness each launched into markets where customer loyalty to legacy systems and old habits ran deep. To move the needle on adoption, the founders started with a deep understanding of the pain points and business frictions their target customers experience. Then they piloted a solution, and listened carefully to early adopters. If their initial product didn't demonstrate resounding product-market fit, they iterated, improved, and adjusted until the value proposition was clear and compelling.

That interactive persistence allowed Relay to develop a banking platform tailored to the day-to-day needs of small business owners. It helped Odeko pivot from predictive inventory software to a vertically integrated fulfillment platform that reduced costs and chaos for independent cafes. It drove Autosled's design of cost-saving "self-dispatching" technology that solved an outdated, friction-heavy auto transport system. And it sharpened Jyoti Bansal's focus at Harness on creating modular tools that enterprises were willing to pay for because they demonstrably increased developer efficiency and reduced costs.

These founders embedded themselves with customers, built close relationships with early adopters, and listened intently to every complaint and compliment. At Odeko, founder Dane Atkinson pivoted the entire business model after realizing that his software didn't solve the most urgent problems of coffee shop owners. At Relay, Yoseph West gave customers his personal number, fielded their calls at all hours, and used those conversations to shape a cash management product that now serves over 100,000 small businesses.

Autosled's David and Dan Sperau literally walked car transport drivers through their first app downloads to ensure they understood the value of the self-dispatch model. Harness grew by turning each product into a mini-startup with its own revenue target and roadmap, requiring every solution to win or lose on its own merits.

These startups grew by crafting solutions that met business customers where they were and demonstrated measurable value. All four companies made early choices that defied conventional startup wisdom—pivoting away from high-margin SaaS business models (in Odeko's case), embracing modular pricing (Harness), and offering freemium features with real utility (Relay). They focused on high customer ROI and made sure that value was visible in the customers' bottom line and operational performance. In doing so, they built a base of loyal early adopters who acted as evangelists, further accelerating growth.

100X growth in B2B markets requires delivering products that make customers more successful, with solutions that dramatically increase profits, reduce costs, save time, boost operational performance– or ideally a combination of all four outcomes. Customer success is what inspires B2B entrepreneurs and powers the scalability flywheel for their own companies.

Odeko

Dane Atkinson, founder and CEO of Odeko kicks off our conversation by talking about his passion for supporting small businesses. It turns out there's a bright line between Odeko's 100X growth over the past five years and this unwavering commitment.

As for his decision to pivot Odeko from an AI-powered predictive analytics startup to a warehouse and truck-based fulfillment service? That improbable path from zero to $150 million in revenues via coffee shop inventory deliveries is the beating heart of Atkinson's story. Here's how it starts,

If you indulge me, I'll start with our WHY (my vision and mission for this company). So personally, I've been on a quest throughout my life to try to encourage entrepreneurship and support small business owners. I think the power of large corporate structures is insane, and yet it doesn't capture anywhere near the full power of the human spirit. So many people don't fit into the typical corporate world – like me with ADHD. I think that those of us who are entrepreneurs, who are lucky enough to build solutions, should be trying to make it possible for others to realize their dreams. But there are not enough entrepreneurial voices speaking on behalf of the small business community.

Atkinson points out that over 90% of all US companies are small businesses, and that these companies provide most of the country's jobs, and economic output every year. Small business owners are 30 million strong, and they are incredibly innovative. What's more these owners are driven by a passion to succeed, to build better lives and support the communities where they live. If you look around, that passion and the human force behind it are everywhere. But in Atkinson's experience, few entrepreneurs who want to build their own high-growth, scalable ventures take the time to figure out how to create products that will help small businesses succeed,

Small business owners are awesome. They understand local organizations and relationships in a way that corporations with distant headquarters never will. It's not like these owners are hard to find. Walk into any small café or bar and you will see them at work. Ask them about their goals, and what is holding them back in terms of daily business challenges, and you will learn so much. Because the lessons they can teach are that owning a business means taking responsibility, trying to make the world better, being a good employer, stepping up to all those things that create more understanding, more capable human beings. In many ways, my whole journey as an entrepreneur has been about building companies that will help small business owners be successful. That's the underlying WHY that inspired Odeko.

Atkinson knows from first-hand experience that these owners face daily frustrations and often struggle to grow their companies with limited financial resources. He has learned that small business owners are skeptical about investing their hard-earned dollars in the latest digital solutions. It can be deceptively easy for startup ventures to find early adopters for free services, but almost impossible to convert those users into paying customers,

> *The beauty of small business owners is they'll listen to your sales pitch, and even try something that's a good match. But the bane is that small business owners will almost never buy a product or service if you can't demonstrate that it will save them money, or clearly improve their bottom line. No matter how much time your service may save them, or how it may tee up future growth, you will have an uphill battle. There's minimal tolerance for abstract ROI calculations combined with a deep, deep skepticism that owners have about paying for new solutions.*

The importance of demonstrating the bottom-line benefits of a new product became painfully clear to Atkinson at previous startup, SumAll, which offered free analytics for small business data. SumAll attracted over half a million owners to try the free version. Most of them loved it. But that rapid free adoption didn't lead to a viable path to monetization. Atkinson ran into a firmly grounded reluctance to pay for a "nice to have' solution.

One lesson he carried forward is the critical importance of understanding small business cost structure and developing solutions that will move the needle on reducing costs or increasing revenue – ideally on both. The SumAll experience also underscored the need to make product/market fit a top priority,

> *I'm a huge believer in understanding a customer's actual fit for your product. Don't start by building every possible product feature. It's better to sell a pilot version, go live with a small group of customers first, listen to their feedback, and adjust. I think too many entrepreneurs get fixated on particulars of their business idea and revenue model. A new venture is much more likely to succeed if you focus on trying to create value for a customer, and find out what those customers have to say after they try your solution.*

Piloting a Predictive Inventory Management System
In designing the original Odeko product, Atkinson focused on a major cost center and massive headache for independent coffee shops and cafes – managing

their inventory. Inventory management often required placing orders with different vendors through phone calls or disparate systems, and dealing with erratically timed delivery of supplies. This wasn't just a logistics headache for business owners. They paid higher prices for supplies compared to big chains because their low volume orders didn't qualify for bulk discounts.

To level the playing field, Atkinson envisioned an advanced inventory management system tailored for small businesses, starting with coffee shops,

> *Independent coffee shops typically spend 40% of their revenue on COGS (cost of goods sold), which is almost double what Starbucks spends on it. And even with that high cost, just getting the goods delivered is incredibly unreliable. They have to juggle a dozen vendors. They get invoices from everybody, with payment terms that are all over the map. It's just very operationally complicated. And it puts the owners who are working the hardest at a competitive disadvantage.*
>
> *I wanted to level the playing field and empower every coffee shop (and all independent food retailers) to compete effectively against their conglomerate competitors. Supporting all the small retailers on Main Street would be awesome. But the entrepreneur in me knew that it would be a mistake to take on the entire small business food retail sector all at once. So Odeko focused on coffee shops, and the first version of the small business solution stack that we developed was a digital inventory management system.*

On a technical level, the Odeko inventory management solution was a clear cut success. Unfortunately, it didn't ring the bell for the owners who became early adopters. As Atkinson recalls,

> *Our first Odeko product was predictive inventory reordering software. It was amazing. We could predict within 15 minutes intervals, literally how many specific types of coffee and food items a particular shop was going to serve its customers with impressive reliability and consistency. It was achieving 95% accuracy predicting inventory/sales/demand within three days, 90% within seven days of what people would buy in a particular coffee shop.*
>
> *We were convinced that this would be a game-changer for the little guys. We could provide them with the kind of AI predictions that Starbucks*

and Dunkin were using, saving them time and money, and making the ordering process seamless with features and benefits that they didn't have before. We got funded and we launched in New York, selling our solution to about 100 of the top independent coffee shops in the city. Our solution did make a difference in order management and efficiency. And because it was a pure SaaS solution, it was a very, very attractive business model for Odeko.

But looking more closely at the market fit-- honestly, it was not so great. The Odeko system just wasn't catching fire. I wasn't seeing any excitement from the early buyers, or any signs of real hunger for this kind of system in the whole independent coffee shop market.

Early customers who tried the inventory software confirmed that it worked well. The more that Atkinson talked with coffee shop owners, however, the more he realized it wasn't solving their deeper pain points. The system accurately predicted what items to order, but the staff still had to do the work of ordering, overseeing multiple vendors, and scheduling physical deliveries. And even though data showed that chronic over-ordering resulted in throwing out hundreds of dollars in unused food every week, many owners didn't trust its predictions would always be accurate, or save enough money to justify a monthly subscription fee.

Fortunately, Atkinson's mindset is to listen carefully to customer feedback – even when it's disappointing. With every conversation he learned more about the day-to-day inventory problems that were driving owners to distraction,

From a system perspective, Odeko's technology was working really, really well, but when I started checking in with our early customers, I could tell there was something missing. I was hoping to see the value of our service reflected in an excited, enthusiastic response – kind of a sparkle in the eye confirming that we had solved a major problem with running their business better. I was constantly asking customers, is this great? And because we had good relationships and open conversations, they told me the truth.

One coffee shop owner said, "It's an awesome system, but honestly when the pastries arrive late and just get thrown on the counter and I don't have milk three days out of the week because my vendor didn't deliver it, I don't care that Odeko's prediction data is great."

Pivoting to Deliver Compelling Product Market Fit

Atkinson and his team kept talking to their early customers, trying out different ideas, and thinking about what solution would ignite real eagerness to buy,

> *I knew that Odeko had to totally change its approach and step up to solving the real pain point, which was centered on managing the fractured vendor ordering and erratic daily deliveries. One morning, I called the Birch Coffee owner, and asked him, what if Odeko could actually deliver everything, deliver all of your supplies during the night, so that everything would be ready to go when the shop opened in the morning. Right away on the phone, he was saying, "That would be fantastic, it would be awesome! When could you start?" The offer to handle all deliveries created so much excitement, I could hear it over the phone. Every owner I talked to about this option, I heard the same level of excitement.*

This was the feedback Atkinson had been waiting to hear. Implementing this end-to-end solution, however, would require a radical pivot. He needed to transform his company into a full-service logistics, delivery and supply partner for independent cafes and coffee shops. As a serial entrepreneur, Atkinson was well aware that this pivot would change Odeko's business model in a way that the startup's investors hadn't signed up for. It was on his shoulders to convince these investors to support a very different path for achieving Odeko's mission.

In late 2019 and into early 2020, Atkinson worked on transforming his AI-based solution into a full-service logistics provider. Instead of selling software as a service, they would be handling daily deliveries of whatever supplies their customers needed. This meant Odeko would operate warehouses, purchase goods (coffee beans, milk, syrups, cups, baked goods, and business supplies) in bulk from vendors, and then use its data engine to efficiently stock and deliver those goods to individual cafés. Essentially, Odeko would become both the brains and the brawn of their customer's inventory management.

Obviously, running trucks and warehouses is far more labor and capital-intensive than a pure SaaS model. Instead of an early path to profitability, Atkinson was asking his investors to embrace a longer journey with a more uncertain outcome. Not surprisingly, some Odeko investors found such a radical pivot hard to support. Atkinson recalls board members warning him about all the downsides of moving away from the original model. His conviction, enthusiasm, evidence of pent-up market demand, and his prior entrepreneurial track record won the day.

Odeko transformed itself into an all-in-one operations platform that consolidated ordering and delivery of everything a café needs. Starting in 2020, a café owner could purchase all their supplies, choosing from hundreds of national and local brands via an Odeko portal or app. Then Odeko would deliver the order in a single drop off, even delivering perishable items direct to the shop's refrigerator, up to seven days a week, positioning Odeko as a single, tech-powered supplier. It was a compelling offer, saving customers a massive amount of time on vendor management and significantly lowering their cost of goods sold because Odeko passed on a high percentage of the discounts it received through unified bulk buying.

The new value proposition resonated because it removed a massive pain point, saved time, and delivered immediate cost savings with many other tangible benefits, including the predictive features of the original product. Unlike generic promises of increased productivity that many small business solutions make, Odeko was offering measurable, bottom-line value. The immediate customer response was all Atkinson had hoped for, and the company's business model pivot would eventually generate the extreme revenue growth he had predicted to investors. By 2025, more than 14,000 independent cafés, coffee shops, and food businesses around the US were using Odeko's platform to streamline their operations.

Before reaching those heights, however, Odeko had to survive a black swan event, the widespread shutdown of New York coffee shops during 2020 at the height of the pandemic.

Surviving COVID and Leapfrogging into Recovery

Odeko rolled out its new model with a handful of New York City pilot customers in early 2020, successfully unlocking market demand and rapid customer adoption. Then, just weeks after Odeko's growth started to accelerate, business was upended by the COVID-19 pandemic. Nearly all of its client cafés were forced to close or severely curtail operations as lockdowns hit New York and other cities. Odeko's revenue plunged to zero overnight in spring 2020 and suddenly a startup that had just found its footing faced an existential crisis. Even after cutting the startup team by half, Atkinson recalls that Odeko had only 4–5 months of cash on hand with little prospect of raising new funding in the middle of a pandemic-induced sector shutdown.

At this crossroads, Atkinson's resilience came to the fore. He refused to give up on Odeko. Instead, he and the remaining Odeko team designed a project to support the city's hard-pressed health care providers by delivering free coffee and pastries to hospitals. This "Coffee for Hospitals" campaign accepted donations from the public, used these funds to purchase coffee and pastry from local cafes, and delivered them in the company's recently purchased trucks. This goodwill initiative benefited front line healthcare workers, generated much-needed income for the cafes, and kept the company's team active in the field. The campaign didn't make any money for Odeko, but it provided a much-appreciated service that demonstrated Odeko's community-centric culture and strengthened relationships with both cafes and suppliers.

In addition to keeping his company active in New York, Atkinson looked beyond the local shutdowns for potential strategic partners. These efforts yielded a partnership that turned into a financial lifeline. A young startup called Cloosiv, based in Charlotte, NC, had launched a mobile order-ahead app for independent coffee shops. When the pandemic hit, Cloosiv experienced a surge in demand for its apps with proportionate revenue growth. Atkinson connected with Cloosiv's CEO Tim Griffin to explore collaboration. They quickly recognized a potential win-win opportunity and agreed to a merger.

With their runway extended, Odeko added more warehouse capacity and expanded their supplier network to prepare for coffee shop reopening. The company's work in building high-trust relationships during the pandemic resonated with many independent café owners who felt abandoned by their former distributors and were ready for an advanced logistics service from a trusted partner.

Extreme Growth Takes Off

In 2021, as independent coffee shops reopened in New York and nationwide, Odeko experienced a groundswell of demand for its end-to-end solutions that is reflected in their revenue numbers. In 2021, Odeko's revenue grew from effectively zero to about $40 million. By 2022, revenue had rocketed to over $100 million, and by late 2023 the company surpassed a $150 million annual revenue run-rate. In the span of just a few years, Odeko went from near-death to one of the fastest-growing startups in the country.

Odeko turned customers into evangelists by doubling down on outstanding service. Dane Atkinson employed several counter-intuitive, labor-intensive strategies to reinforce early demand, build momentum, and deepen loyalty during this take-off growth phase. Doing things that don't scale was one such strategy. The Odeko team was willing to go to great lengths to make sure its early customers felt special. Odeko staff personally visited cafes, learned their routines and supply storage locations, and performed unattended overnight restocking. This white-glove treatment for early adopters helped Odeko iron out kinks as quickly as possible.

Coffee shop staff could count on all of their day's supplies being in place before opening. Odeko's delivery staff even took photos of the stocked shelves so owners could remotely verify that everything was in order. For overworked small business owners, this was truly game-changing. The trust and customer satisfaction flywheel began turning faster and faster: each successful delivery and each dollar saved reinforced the value, and café owners told their peers about the transformational value of Odeko's service.

By securing highly respected and popular independent cafes as marquee customers in each local market, Odeko created reference points that made other owners more comfortable signing up. While it was labor-intensive to earn, this customer-driven virality was far more cost-effective than a generic mass marketing campaign. Odeko's marketing during its early growth was primarily grassroots: it relied on industry events, referrals, and leveraging the strong community word of mouth among local café owners in each new region that it entered.

The company strategically opened warehouses in new regions as clusters of demand emerged, spreading first along the East Coast and then to the West Coast. By early 2025, Odeko boasted warehouses or local distribution hubs in 15 major U.S. markets, from New York and Boston to Chicago, Los Angeles, Atlanta, and beyond. In areas without a nearby warehouse, Odeko served cafes via third-party shipping or regional partners, ensuring even cafes in secondary cities could join the platform. This gave Odeko a national footprint, though its densest concentrations remain in urban areas. Alongside geographic growth, the platform's catalog of suppliers and products also scaled quickly. Odeko now carries hundreds of national and local brands, from staples like Oatly oat milk and major coffee roasting companies to niche artisanal bakers and emerging local beverage makers. By aggregating the buying power of thousands of cafes, Odeko is able to negotiate better pricing from these suppliers and pass on savings, reinforcing and expanding its value promise.

Even with the weight of a cost-intensive vertical logistics solution, and pressure to improve operating margins, Atkinson remains committed to sharing savings from bulk ordering with his customers. It's an essential element of his mission to be a value-generating partner for small business owners,

> *It's very simple. Our marketplace revenue is just transactional based on the volume., When you buy through Odeko, we take a percentage of that volume for managing the order, including delivery services that bring it to your door There's no subscription, or base level of volume, or extra SaaS fees or membership dues or any hidden fees. In fact, we pass on to our customers a lot of the savings we negotiate on high-volume ordering. That way we are creating incentives to become an Odeko customer, with no barriers to a new client getting onboard. And when you think about the way coffee shops economics work, if we reduce their 40% cost of goods down to 34% or so, there is a massive amount of capital that runs on our marketplace.*
>
> *Beyond the marketplace, we are building out some value-added services that are subscription based. Some people pay us for routing their own inventory. They may pay us for a different software stack. We are starting to offer insurance coverage and equipment financing, like for a new espresso machine. Today, those revenue streams are still very small. From a ratio standpoint, the bulk of our revenue still comes from the marketplace transactions, and our profitability is from using volume ordering to negotiate better pricing for vendors.*

Technology and Infrastructure: Scaling a Hands-On Supply Chain with AI

That commitment to sharing the savings generated in the marketplace puts pressure on Odeko to improve its unit economics by operating more efficiently than the competition, and continually improving its internal productivity. Behind Odeko's white glove service is a sophisticated technical infrastructure that blends old-school logistics with cutting-edge automation.

The warehousing, trucking, and in-store delivery components of Odeko are intrinsically labor-intensive. That means technology, with AI and data analytics must serve as the force multiplier to create efficiencies and scalability.

The company's origins as an AI platform continue to bear fruit in the form of predictive algorithms that forecast demand for each café and each product. Every day, Odeko's systems analyze factors like historical sales, seasonal trends, weather, and even local events to anticipate what items and quantities each shop will need in upcoming days. This drives an "auto-replenishment" feature: many café owners now trust Odeko's system to generate their suggested order each week, which they can tweak or approve in one click. The AI's accuracy means cafés using Odeko have significantly less food waste and fewer emergency stock-outs. In practice, Odeko's portal now provides cafes with sophisticated analytics dashboards that track ordering trends and inventory turnover, helping owners make data-informed decisions.

On the logistics side, Odeko has built internal software for route optimization and warehouse management. Each night, as orders stream in from customers, Odeko's system consolidates them by warehouse and plans efficient delivery routes for the next morning. A single truck supplies multiple cafés in the same neighborhood with diverse products, which is far more efficient and environmentally friendly than each vendor operating its own truck. The logistics technology also coordinates inventory levels across Odeko's network of warehouses. For example, if a boutique coffee roaster in Portland joins the platform, Odeko can predict how much of that coffee will be sold in New York or Dallas and pre-stock the regional warehouses accordingly, reducing the need for costly rush shipments. The platform even integrates with suppliers' systems in some cases, automating purchasing when stock at an Odeko warehouse runs low.

Expanding National Operations with a Collaborative Playbook

Odeko's collaborative approach to geographic expansion, with an emphasis on alliances with suppliers and small distributors, is a crucial component of scalable growth. The company seeks out partnerships and positions itself as a new channel for the vendors selling to local coffee shops. As it expands, Odeko is becoming an aggregator that provides services for niche supply chains: instead of 100 bakeries each sending their own truck out, those bakeries can partner with Odeko to handle last-mile delivery to all the cafes. This collaborative approach turns potential rivals into partners. It helps to create a virtuous cycle: the more cafés Odeko serves in a given region, the more attractive it becomes to suppliers (big and small) who want access to those cafes; the more suppliers and products it offers, the more value it delivers to cafés, attracting more of them as customers. In essence, the company has created a shared value ecosystem where Odeko is the central connective tissue between local businesses on both the demand and supply side of the coffee economy.

Odeko also partners with point-of-sale (POS) companies and other technology providers that serve small businesses. Square and other POS vendors like Toast list Odeko in their app marketplaces as a recommended integration solution for inventory management and ordering.

By 2025, Odeko's network spanned the country, and the company was beginning to eye adjacent food verticals. Odeko's branding has recently shifted to include "coffee shops, cafés and other food establishments." Odeko now faces what Atkinson recognizes as every high growth company's "blue ocean" problem,

> How do we extend into new sectors, when there are so many unserved small business needs in retail, or even just in the food sector? We can see how the Odeko services could help all these different communities in all these different ways. Odeko needs to be disciplined and pick the path where we can add value all the way through. Deciding where and how to expand, without over-extending is a demanding, tough stage of growth. It's fun, but it's tough.

Financial Strategies to Balance Growth, Opportunity, and Profitability

These tough decisions are complicated by Odeko's reliance on external funding for growth, and the timing of future profitability. As of March 2025, when a Series E round of $126 million was announced, Odeko had raised about $350 million in a combination of equity and debt funding. According to Atkinson, the foundation for profitability is in place, but he is still seeking to scale Odeko and increase its reach to more markets and customers,

> We've raised quite a bit of money, and we still have a lot to do. So as a business, we're not profitable. That's partly by design, partly by the

nature of only being four years old, and because we're intentionally trying to continue to grow and scale as the priority now. The way I think about profitability is that a company needs to demonstrate that it's able to turn the levers to become profitable when the time is right. For Odeko, during the last two years, it's all been about EBITDA, and, ironically, two years from now the emphasis may all be about growth again. Basically, if you neglect the fundamentals and unit economics, if you go too far one way the other, it's really hard to recover.

Odeko recently acquired Butter Insurance, a specialist provider of insurance to small businesses, to start offering tailored insurance policies to its current customers. This move into fintech/insurtech services reflects Odeko's strategy to diversify its revenue model and deepen its relationship with customers. Such diversification will be an important lever for increasing customer lifetime value and retention with products that provide new revenue streams with higher margins.

By controlling more of the value chain (from ancillary services vendors to goods-sold suppliers to café to consumer), Odeko not only increases revenue per customer but also creates a more daunting moat against competitors by offering integrated logistics, software, and ancillary business services.

Delivering a Customer-First Culture

Guided by Atkinson's vision, a customer-centric perspective is embedded in Odeko's DNA. From engineers deploying code that optimizes a route, to a loader double-checking an order, everyone knows that an inventory mistake means a small business could suffer that day. On the flip side, every smooth delivery is helping an entrepreneur succeed. This sense of responsibility is a powerful staff motivator and cultural glue.

It's clear that Dane Atkinson's priorities are still rooted in his original mission for founding Odeko; empowering these small businesses and their owners to thrive. Odeko doesn't just want to be just another vendor for small business owners, it aims to be their go-to, can-do partner in all aspects of operations. Championing local small businesses generates goodwill for Odeko's brand and helps to attract partners, customers, employees, and investors who are enthusiastic about the WHY that inspires Dane Atkinson.

Even with these advantages, Odeko's interconnection with the success of its small business customers brings its own challenges, especially in a volatile economy. If consumer coffee shop spending decreases, then cafés will order less, directly impacting Odeko's revenue. When asked about the key performance metrics he tracks, Atkinson puts the overall success of his customers at the top of his list,

I'd say that customer retention is a lagging indicator. It's important, and of course it should be tracked. But I find you can never make pivots in your company fast enough based on tracking just your NPS scores or retention scores. You have to look for subtler signs of your customer's success, and ideally, tracking how customers are achieving their goals and the trends that impact the people buying their product. If you're selling to coffee shops and they're starting to see increases in revenue, that's an important metric. If the cafes are attracting proportionately more customers than Starbucks, or seeing deeper customer loyalty, we want to track that. True, we don't own that outcome directly, but we're part of that outcome, and such trends are usually better indicators of the health of the whole system and the potential for more growth or possibly decline.

Even while acknowledging these issues, Atkinson is enthusiastically optimistic about continued growth,

Honestly, it's tough to be precise across those three years. I hope it will be something like the last three years. Obviously, we're at a different quantum so it's harder to get 1,000% growth, or 11,000% growth. Our target for next year is more in the 50, 60% growth, which is conservative, but we're building a lot of pieces, and then hopefully we'll be increasing that yearly growth rate after that. In three years, we should have almost tripled from the revenue we have today

With Atkinson at the helm, Odeko is on track to build an enduring, scalable services platform, while staying true to the founding vision of championing small business owners. Odeko's journey from near-zero to $150M in revenues may be just the prologue to a larger narrative of how technology can revitalize local businesses rather than replacing them. It's a story still being written, but one that has already proven that by solving a tough-to-scale problem, and delivering measurable value, a business can scale beyond what most people believe is possible.

Relay

The language that small business owners speak is cash. 92% of small business owners actually make financial decisions based on their bank balance. But in the traditional banking context, a business bank balance is just a static bit of information. A business owner may have a $100,000 bank balance today. That's great — but that owner also has bills due, company payroll coming out next week, maybe also some sales trips scheduled. Do they have enough money coming in to cover all that?

We realized that the killer app for financial services is actually better visibility into the company's bank account and the bank balance. Our vision for Relay started there, and expanded to become a cash management solution that is deeply interconnected with a small business's back office. Our mission is to increase financial visibility for small business owners, enable them make better decisions, and ultimately help millions of entrepreneurs build profitable businesses. **Yoseph West, Co-Founder and CEO of Relay**

Yoseph West and his Co-Founder Paul Klicnik understood the language of small business owners when they launched Relay in 2018 to "deliver cash flow clarity." From his prior fintech experience, West believed that Relay would solve a major pain point by delivering an integrated suite of account and cash management tools. He also knew that the small business sector is a tough market to penetrate. Advanced features alone would not convince budget-constrained companies to adopt a new cash management product. The Relay solution had to demonstrate clear ROI out of the gate – saving money, enhancing the customer's bottom line, and boosting their operational efficiency.

Lots of well-funded fintech startups had already tried to turn the 30 million plus small businesses in the United States into paying customers, and failed to get sustainable market traction. The few who had succeeded were formidable competitors. The Relay founders needed to hit the bullseye on product value, cost-effective customer acquisition and retention, and flawless execution to be a credible contender.

I asked Yoseph West to tell me how his startup stayed on target to attract over 100,000 small business customers and achieve almost $100 million in annual revenue by 2025 – and how he plans to grow from here. He describes building deep relationships with early customers, and using their feedback to ensure that the Relay solution really matched their needs,

> *I became really close with our early customers. I gave them my personal phone number and was always reachable. I wanted to be known as some-one customers could call when they have a problem, the founder who would answer their phone calls. I would listen to their issues no matter what. That made a big difference. I can't tell you the number of custom-ers who are still with us to this day, even though they had bumpy experi-ences at the beginning. Certainly, building those early relationships was beneficial from a customer retention and revenue perspective. But even more important than that, it really helped Relay to empathize with the customer and understand the challenges that they're facing at a deep level. The closer you are to those early customers, the more successful a startup is going to be.*

Cash Flow Clarity Goes to Market with a Personal Touch
Throughout 2019, the Relay team worked on developing what West called a "minimal loveable product" with a set of cash flow visibility features that would be especially useful to small companies. Relay's initial offering al-lowed businesses to open multiple checking accounts easily, categorize funds (for taxes, payroll, operating expenses, etc.), and monitor balances in each.

To avoid the cost and regulatory complexity of operating as a bank, Relay partnered with federally insured U.S. banks to hold deposits and issue cards. This partnership model allowed Relay to offer its customers U.S. checking ac-counts and other financial services even though it is headquartered in Toronto, Canada. After a small seed round of funding to support product development, Relay raised $4.4 million (USD) in October 2020 and prepared to launch its solution to small businesses across the United States – right in the midst of the widespread disruptions of the COVID-19 pandemic.

For a new digital banking product, launching during the pandemic was actually fortuitous. Many small business owners had long relied on the local branch of banks that were now struggling to maintain services during lockdowns. Relay's fully-online business banking appealed to owners needing to open accounts and manage cash without visiting a branch. By positioning itself as a no-fee, modern alternative for everyday business banking, Relay began to accumulate a base of users across the United States.

West was intensely hands-on in Relay's early go-to-market efforts, making time for phone calls, video meetings, and even in-person visits to potential partners and customers. He still believes in a high-touch approach to building relationships and getting close to customers, and the value of listening carefully to their issues and suggestions for product enhancements.

One lesson that Relay learned from early customer feedback was the importance of integrating into their existing workflows rather than expecting the customers to change their financial management behavior. Relay initially launched with the idea of multiple accounts linked to internal budgeting – that feature was well received, but it was not enough for many customers. The team soon realized that to truly solve the cash flow visibility problem, Relay also had to plug its solution into all the places where money moves in and out of a business. This led to a strategic adjustment: prioritizing integrations with accounting and finance software sooner than later.

Relay learned that if its solution didn't sync with QuickBooks, for example, many business owners or their accountants wouldn't fully adopt it. Thus, Relay expedited development of direct bank feeds to QuickBooks and Xero, and integration with Bill.com, Expensify, and other popular tools. Such integrations were not trivial to build but they became a crucial step for cementing a lasting relationship with early adopters and gave Relay credibility and stronger visibility among the many business owners and CFOs who were already using those tools. Relay's listing on the QuickBooks and Xero app stores meant that any small business searching for a bank feed solution or a better way to manage finances could discover Relay during their search for accounting add-ons. This tactic effectively piggybacked on the distribution of much larger companies, giving Relay market reach it could not have achieved on its own.

Importantly, such integrations also provided a major boost to small business financial efficiency. It was one of many steps that Relay would take to meet customers where they are, and to solve the problems that mattered most to their financial success. By becoming the hub that connected payroll services, payment processors, and expense tools, Relay adjusted its product roadmap to deliver measurable customer benefits and ROI in the real-world context of small business operations.

Professional Partnerships and a Freemium Customer Acquisition Strategy

Relay's freemium "Starter" plan included many high-value features, making it a powerful way to jumpstart word-of-mouth customer acquisition. By offering a robust free business banking and cash management service with no monthly fees, no minimums, and no overdraft fees, Relay drastically lowered the barrier for customers to sign up. A small business could try Relay with zero switching cost, using it alongside an existing bank account initially. This encouraged many curious owners to give it a shot – after all, if it didn't work out, it wouldn't cost them anything. Many did try, often for a specific purpose like segregating taxes or tracking a particular project's finances, and then gradually expanded their usage once they experienced the benefits, increasing the likelihood of their conversion to a paid "Grow" account.

This product-led acquisition was fueled by the inherent virality of multi-user access for a company's accountant, or fractional CFO, or other trusted advisors. If a business owner found Relay helpful, they might invite their business partner or bookkeeper or financial advisor onto the platform since setting up multi-user access was easy and free. Satisfied users would mention Relay in entrepreneur forums or local business groups, resulting in new sign-ups. Additionally, Relay's strategy of making the product sticky – via integrations and embedded functionality – meant that once a customer was on board and had connected Relay to their whole back-office, the switching costs increased. Switching was less and less likely as customers utilized more of the features in the paid account tier. This stickiness improved lifetime value and justified spending more to acquire each customer, creating a positive unit economics cycle.

Another cornerstone of Relay's customer acquisition strategy was developing relationships with accounting professionals and other business advisors who work closely with small business owners. Relay created product features and tools that made advisors' lives easier while providing better outcomes for their clients. This approach proved particularly effective because advisors often manage multiple clients with similar cash flow challenges, creating opportunities for referrals and recommendations. Relay's offering was naturally appealing to accountants because it solved many of their own workflow issues: it provided client companies with granular account separation (helpful for bookkeeping), it allowed accountant access with proper permissions (no more sharing bank passwords), and it synced with accounting software to reduce manual data entry.

By partnering with accounting firms and pitching Relay as a way for advisors to deliver more value, Relay converted a number of these professionals into evangelists and even a de facto salesforce. The company created an Advisor Partner program where accountants and bookkeepers could get certified on Relay and, in return, receive benefits like a directory listing (exposure to businesses using Relay who might need an accountant). This two-way incentive – accountants bring clients to Relay, and Relay brings clients to accountants – was a cost-effective driver for customer acquisition. The channel partnership strategy also increased customer retention, since customers who were acquired through an accountant or professional advisor were especially likely to stay because their trusted advisor was embedded in the banking process with them.

Gathering Momentum to Scale

By 2021, Relay was poised for accelerated growth, buoyed by new capital and a widening customer base. The company raised a Series A round of $18.2 million CAD (~$15 million US), led by Bain Capital Ventures, and reported it was on track to process over $1 billion USD in transactions by the end of that year, reflecting how quickly businesses were adopting the platform for everyday banking. Revenues at this stage were modest but beginning to accumulate through interchange fees and interest on deposits. Relay's freemium subscription option, with no monthly fees on the standard service, had been deliberately structured to help drive adoption by keeping direct costs low for customers. Even with mostly freemium account customers, Relay could generate some revenue from the volume of customer activity on their platform, rather than via upfront fees. This approach created alignment with customer success: fast-growing clients would naturally bring more volume (and thus more interchange revenue) as their businesses grew. Relay moved into 2022 with continued momentum in customer growth and product enrichment. The company's revenue tripled over the prior year, a testament to a fast-growing customer base and increased transaction volumes.

Several strategic moves underpinned Relay's transition to even more rapid growth during 2023. One was a headline partnership with the *Profit First* organization, and the popular *Profit First* cash management method created by Mike Michalowicz. This method is based on small business owners and their financial team setting up and managing different account "envelopes" or sub-accounts for predictable business expenses and revenue streams, including a dedicated "profits" account. Over 3,000 Profit First method followers were already using Relay by the time the partnership was announced, and Relay's team rolled out new features (like automated allocation transfers) tailored to Profit First's multiple-account approach. This move not only brought in new customers; it also cemented Relay's reputation as the go-to platform for cash flow management.

Another catalyst for growth in 2024 was the introduction of premium account tiers with increasingly advanced features and customer benefits. While the standard Relay "Starter" account remained free, the "Grow" account at $30 per month, followed by the "Scale" account at $120 per month offered power users and fast-growing companies advanced capabilities such as same-day ACH transfers, higher limits, and expanded bill pay and invoicing tools together with higher interest rates on their account balances. These premium accounts allowed Relay to start monetizing a subset of its customer base more directly. Many small businesses were opting to upgrade to the paid plans as their needs became more sophisticated. Meanwhile, even free users generated rising interchange and float revenue for Relay because the overall volume of transactions and deposits on the platform ballooned.

Product development in 2023 and 2024 also expanded Relay's value proposition for existing and new customers. Responding to user feedback that access to credit was a top priority, Relay launched its first lending product: a business credit card. The card offered 1.5% cashback and integrated controls for spending by category or project, effectively extending a short-term credit line to help companies manage cash flow crunches. This was the first step in Relay's broader plan to offer credit solutions. West also had a longer-term goal of providing a revolving line of credit to customers. Instead of just helping businesses manage the cash they had, Relay would be providing small companies with additional liquidity when needed. Doing so required careful financial management on Relay's part, since underwriting loans and bearing credit risk is a different business than transaction-based banking. However, with fresh funding in hand and a wealth of customer financial data to inform underwriting, Relay decided to expand in this direction.

These initiatives aligned with Relay's vision of delivering AI-powered predictive cash flow analytics and becoming the all-in-one financial command center for small business – essentially, using data to proactively advise customers, for example, alerting users about potential cash shortfalls or optimal times to make purchases.

With revenue growth and customer acquisition continuing to accelerate, Relay plans to expand its scope to become a comprehensive platform offering integrated banking and fintech services to small businesses. This next stage of growth reflects West's understanding that small business financial needs evolve over time, and that growing companies want platforms that can scale with their needs rather than forcing customers to switch providers as they mature. Rather than pursuing rapid scaling at any cost, his company has grown by focusing on deep customer and partner relationship, sustainable growth and operational efficiency – and delivering on its initial promise of delivering cash flow clarity. The company is on a path to achieving profitability in the year ahead, thanks to its own disciplined financial management.

Relay's evolution from a multi-faceted cash flow management tool toward becoming a comprehensive financial command center illustrates how extreme growth can be achieved while maintaining focus on core customer problems.

Autosled

David Sperau starts our conversation about Autosled by talking about how his auto industry career became a startup catalyst. David and his brother Dan grew up knowing their way around dealer showrooms and service bays. Their grandfather and father were industry veterans, and the brothers both gravitated to automotive careers right out of college. David recalls his early years of "working my way up through a couple of dealer groups in the Atlanta area, and getting lucky enough to buy a car dealership myself," and his satisfaction in mastering the complexities of new and used car retailing.

The catalyst was repeatedly encountering an industry-wide pain point – vehicle transport. David recalls spending countless hours on the phone tracking delayed transport trucks, hunting down paperwork, and appeasing impatient customers. On one particularly exasperating afternoon, after chasing the location of a late-arriving vehicle and scrambling to overnight a title, David vented to his brother Dan, "There just has to be a better way to do this." At that moment, he decided to take on the challenge of deploying digital technology to reinvent automotive transport logistics.

Dan was the ideal partner to help him turn frustration into a smarter, tech-driven alternative to manual tracking and mountains of paper. Dan's expertise was in managing finance and operations, and he had logged over a decade of consulting for dealership groups. Like David, he was well aware that the industry's transport logistics were mired in outdated manual processes. Both brothers saw that the simple act of moving a car – whether a dealer trade or a customer delivery, was costing dealerships a disproportionate amount of time, money, and operational performance. Even small dealers felt the pain, while larger auto groups, faced with coordinating hundreds of shipments and unpredictable delivery dates, were desperate for a different way to manage vehicle transport.

David and Dan quickly realized that everyone in the vehicle logistics chain was frustrated, not just the dealerships. Their mission expanded to transforming all aspects of vehicle transport by inventing and deploying a 360-degree digital platform to address multiple industry pain points. In practice, that meant building an online system where car dealers, fleet managers, auction houses, and even individuals could instantly find trusted transporters to ship vehicles. To replace the old patchwork of phone calls and faxes, the Autosled digital platform would be designed to connect large and small dealerships with the transport providers who actually moved the cars, ranging from independent drivers to companies. The platform would feature a secure, reliable, web and mobile interface. As a foundation for future scalability, the system would be easy enough for both dealers and transport drivers to use in self-service mode.

From Idea to Startup: Building a 360° Logistics Platform

Fired up with the vision of streamlining vehicle transport for the 21st century, David and Dan built the foundation for Autosled during an intensive year of business planning and coding. As their vision took shape in design prototypes, the cofounders filed a patent application, "Method and System of Automated

Vehicle Transportation," in October 2018 to establish Autosled's proprietary rights to a system that "empowers users such as car dealers and transporters to ship cars more efficiently, ...and more directly, continuously, and automatically" than currently available systems.

In plain language, future dealership customers could use the platform to arrange the transport of a vehicle to any desired US destination, just by posting the job on Autosled's platform, then confirming an agreement with a vetted auto carrier who claimed the load and committed to the desired pickup and delivery schedule. Auto transport providers, for their part, could see available trips (loads) on their phone, sign up for a load that fit their route and available capacity, and get the vehicle moved with minimal back-and-forth. "Self-dispatching" was the term Autosled used – carriers essentially dispatching themselves by accepting jobs via the app interface to the Autosled platform instead of being matched up with jobs by a third-party middleman or broker.

Autosled's platform was designed to address all the frustrations David had experienced firsthand in his dealership career. In addition to matching dealers with carriers through self-dispatching, it offered real-time GPS tracking on every shipment and digital bills of lading, so dealers no longer had to manually follow up to determine the location of vehicle shipments, or worry about lost paperwork. Payment was handled electronically. Instead of waiting for paper invoices and mailing thousands of checks every year to various transport vendors, a dealer could pay through Autosled's secure and rapid driver payment system.

Fast-tracking driver payments also gave Autosled a very attractive benefit to offer independent drivers. It helped to ensure that the transport providers prioritized jobs from the Autosled platform, and stayed loyal, and ended another hassle for dealers whose inefficient manual payment systems had previously triggered awkward phone calls from drivers looking for their money. In short, Autosled's technology aimed to deliver transparency and efficiency for all sides: dealers could track the status of each shipment on the platform in real time, and transporters could manage jobs, fill unused slots on their trucks, and get paid all in one place. What had been a disjointed, analog process was poised to become a one-stop, integrated digital workflow.

Crucially, the platform was designed to enable automated matching of dealership transport requests and the responses by vetted, insured drivers – the feature that Autosled's founders called "self-dispatching." This built-in

scalability feature eliminated the need for manual oversight and removed potential bottlenecks as the demand for and use of the platform accelerated in
future years.

With the development of their proprietary solution underway, the cofounders were poised to launch in 2019 from their home base in Rockville,
Maryland. To support their market entry, they needed to secure financial
backing and recruit a small group of pilot customers to put their system to the
test. As David recalls the company's launch sequence, Autosled incorporated
in the middle of 2019, and the cofounders pitched their solution to a local
business group of angel investors a few months later.

> We already had a good relationship with this angel group, so we explained
> how our platform would massively improve auto transport logistics, and
> how we needed seed money to pilot it and launch the company. Some
> investors in the group liked the idea, and next thing we knew, we had a
> million-dollar angel investment to build out and pilot test the platform.
> By the middle of 2020 we had completed the software and it was ready for
> pilot customers. We signed up a small group of local dealers and trans-
> port drivers to put it to the test.

To ensure that their platform could scale, the Sperau brothers decided to pilot
all of its features with a group of local dealerships and transport drivers, testing both the dealer and transporter features of their two-sided network. They
learned that persuading old-school car haulers to trust a new app took patience and a hands-on approach. David and Dan often walked drivers through
downloading the Autosled app and taught them how to upload photos and
status updates for each vehicle move.

To win over dealership managers, Autosled offered a compelling adoption
model. Instead of charging fixed subscription fees or requiring long-term contracts, dealers could work with Autosled on a simple pay-per-shipment basis.
That made trying out the service easy and low-risk for dealers. The company
also carried a $5 million insurance umbrella to give the dealers and car own-
ers peace of mind, knowing that their vehicles were fully protected in transit.
These strategic choices – removing friction for early adopters and building
trust through insurance coverage – helped Autosled gain traction in its local market. Soon, the company's platform had facilitated hundreds of vehicle

moves, proving that it was viable for multiple users. That was an important milestone, but a more ambitious test of the system and its ability to scale was still ahead.

In fact, for much of 2020, Autosled still operated in a semi-manual mode. The platform was performing well, but the operations team often found themselves intervening behind the scenes, matching a tricky shipment to a reliable driver or nudging a carrier to update their app and check it for new listings.

The Aha Moment That Propelled Growth

Job one for Autosled was demonstrating that its platform and its innovative self-dispatching technology could truly scale and operate in fully automated mode to match up dealers and carriers. That proof point finally arrived at the end of 2020, in what the Sperau brothers still call their "aha moment."

In December 2020, a vehicle shipment request was posted by a dealer in Pennsylvania and accepted by a transporter entirely through the Autosled app, without anyone at Autosled being involved. The driver delivered the car, the digital paperwork flowed, and payment was deposited, all automatically. Dan Sperau recalls turning to David and saying, "Did that just happen?" It had. The brothers finally got to celebrate seeing a load self-dispatch through their system, moving from request through delivery and payment without the need for any human intervention.

That first truly autonomous transaction proved that Autosled's marketplace model could function as a "force multiplier" that would let a small team handle transport requests at scale. From then on, the company's confidence, customer acquisition, and revenues all started to snowball. As David summarizes this memorable turning point,

> It worked! The self-dispatch feature worked perfectly. And, you know, we've just been growing ever since.

Autosled soon found that pandemic-driven trends actually played to its strengths. Dealerships in 2020 had faced acute inventory shortages and were increasingly swapping vehicles with one another or sourcing cars from farther away to satisfy customers. Traditional vehicle transport was too sluggish for this new urgency. Autosled's promise of enabling contactless delivery, real-time GPS tracking, and direct contact with transporters gave it a timely edge.

The company leveraged the demand for increased logistics efficiency to land a partnership with 20 Group Dealer Trades, a network of franchise and independent dealerships that trade used cars among themselves nationwide. As the exclusive transportation provider for 20 Group's dealer-to-dealer exchange platform, Autosled acquired a built-in customer base eager to move transactions onto their system. The 20 Group deal was an early milestone that signaled Autosled's arrival on the national stage.

Throughout 2021, Autosled built out its two-sided network by signing up more dealerships and adding more transporters. The cofounders' long-standing familiarity with auto transport pain points and focus on listening to its customers shaped their roadmap for enhancing the platform. For example, many transporters told Autosled they struggled with slow payments in the industry, which reinforced the company's commitment to its Quick Pay feature. This feature became a competitive differentiator that attracted more and more independent drivers to the platform, encouraged their active engagement, and built loyalty. Dealers, for their part, requested features like instant online quotes and bulk upload of multiple vehicle orders, which Autosled's developers implemented in a cycle of continuous improvement. The result was a dynamic flywheel of improved product-market fit, leading to high user satisfaction and increased adoption during the critical early growth period.

By the end of 2021, Autosled's bet on solving an entrenched problem with technology was paying off in both usage metrics and revenue growth. The company moved thousands of vehicles that year and generated an estimated $4.4 million in revenue. Achieving these milestones attracted an additional round of seed funding from angel and early-stage investors. This funding provided a runway to expand the customer base and beef up the operations and development team. It also paved the way for an even bigger capital raise, bringing marquee investors into Autosled and setting the stage for hypergrowth.

Scaling Up with Marquee Venture Investors

Autosled entered 2022 riding its early momentum and attracting notice far beyond the local dealer community. In March 2022, the company announced a $5 million Series A funding round from investors whose industry ties and strategic expertise validated Autosled's platform and the technology that powered it. Lyndon Rive, a familiar name in Silicon Valley circles as the co-founder of SolarCity, led the round. After personally experiencing the headaches of

automotive logistics during Tesla's rollout of the Model 3, Rive was impressed
with Autosled's advanced features and proven performance. He and other investors were ready to bet on widespread adoption of a solution designed to
eliminate bottlenecks in a sector that had been lagging in innovation. The
Series A round brought Autosled's total capital raised to over $7 million. This
was a small amount compared to the funding digital platform innovators in
other industries, but it was enough to power the company to a new level of
customer acquisition and operational scale.

During 2022, Autosled invested this new capital in growth initiatives as
well as bolstering its internal capabilities. The company expanded its carrier
network westward, onboarding many independent truckers in the Midwest
and West Coast to become a coast-to-coast solution. It also started forging
relationships with large dealer groups, winning business from franchise dealerships that recognized the efficiencies Autosled could bring. By late 2022,
Autosled's user base had swelled and its platform was handling far more volume without requiring proportional staff increases. In fact, more than 85% of
all vehicle shipments were now being self-dispatched by carriers through the
app with no manual involvement, a powerful proof point for Autosled's scalable model.

Extreme Growth Breakout

By 2023, Autosled was a markedly different company than the operation that
David and Dan Sperau founded in 2019. It had venture investors, an enlarged
leadership team, and a growing reputation as an innovator in auto transport.
The solution that two brothers launched with a handful of mid-Atlantic dealerships had, in a few short years, become one of the largest digital auto carrier
networks in the country and was experiencing the kind of rapid growth that
most startup founders can only dream of.

The company had increased its vehicle moves by 10X in just over two
years, and was partnering with over 1,000 retail automotive dealerships nationwide. This growth in dealer demand was matched on the driver supply
side: Autosled's network of transporters exploded to over 11,000 active carriers across the United States. The implications for capacity were significant –
with thousands of actively engaged truckers on their platform, Autosled could
offer dealers near-instant coverage for shipments almost anywhere in the
U.S., a key competitive advantage over regional brokers. It also meant that

on any given day, thousands of cars were moving via Autosled's system. The
company's revenues climbed accordingly.

One striking example of Autosled's operational adaptability was how it
handled the surge in dealer-to-dealer trades caused by regional inventory im-
balances and shifts in market demand. Autosled saw this trend and responded
by developing a new Dealer Exchange Network feature to let dealers coordinate two-way swaps more efficiently. The tool allowed a dealer to request an
outbound vehicle shipment to another dealer and an inbound one back in the
same order, ideally to be handled by the same transporter as a round trip. This
new feature cut down on wasted trips and gave haulers transparency that a delivery was part of an exchange, so they could plan for a return load. By adding
such features, Autosled demonstrated its ability to stay ahead of industry demand, helping to increase retention and build business among its dealer users.

Another growth vector for Autosled in 2023 was its expansion into serving
OEMs (automakers) and large fleet owners. Having largely built its reputation
in used-car and dealer trade shipping, Autosled began forming partnerships
to handle new vehicle logistics from manufacturing plants and ports. One opportunity was coordinating last-mile delivery of new cars from rail yards to
dealerships, applying its marketplace approach to a domain long dominated
by less efficient legacy transport firms. The company also began contracting
for public sector vehicle moves, for example, reallocation of state-owned vehicles or moving police cruisers from upfitter to precinct. While these segments
were nascent for Autosled, the strategic intent was clear: the platform that had
proven itself in dealer logistics could be extended to larger enterprise uses.

Meanwhile, Autosled doubled down on marketing to maintain its growth.
In keeping with the company's lean operations and agile management style, instead of allocating budget to traditional, high-cost advertising, Autosled favored
promotional incentives and strategic marketing campaigns that could be linked
directly to new customer acquisition. One national promotion, for example,
effectively subsidized the first shipments for new dealer clients. This grabbed
attention within the industry and also gave dealers who signed on for the promotion immediate tangible value, increasing the likelihood of converting them
to repeat customers. Autosled's leadership was willing to incur short-term costs
like these promotions for long-term gain in their key growth metrics.

Decisions about marketing and customer spend were made with a keen
eye on improving overall unit economics. By handling payments and charging

service fees on their platform, Autosled ensured that each completed shipment contributed to overhead. The more the platform automated dispatch and reduced manual work, the more profitable each transaction became. Dan Sperau highlighted the self-dispatching rate of over 85% as a critical factor in keeping operational costs in check even as volume soared. Essentially, Autosled's software was doing the work that an army of brokers would otherwise have to be paid to do.

In 2023, Autosled applied for the annual *Inc. 5000* list (which ranks America's fastest-growing private companies) as well as *Deloitte's Technology Fast 500*. Autosled earned the #12 spot on the 2024 Inc. 5000 list of fastest-growing companies in the nation, making it the single fastest-growing automotive or logistics-focused company on the entire list. Similarly, Deloitte's Fast 500, which spans North America, ranked Autosled as the #9 fastest-growing tech company in 2024 – again the highest-ranked automotive logistics platform on that prestigious list. Deloitte reported Autosled's revenue growth at an eye-popping 14,001% over the measured period. For the Sperau brothers, seeing Autosled listed among the nation's top startups was a proud moment – and a far cry from the early years of working to convince skeptical dealers and carriers that their platform was reliable.

Financial Discipline and Profitability on the Road to Market Transformation

Unlike some tech startups that burn cash in pursuit of top line growth, Autosled's leadership kept a disciplined eye on their financial management and cash flow. The company's business model and scalable digital platform have powered both rapid growth and sustainable profitability. Autosled earns revenue on each vehicle shipment (usually as a percentage service fee or margin on the transport cost) and operates a capital-light model without owning any trucks or heavy assets. This marketplace model has allowed the company to scale revenue faster than expenses, and to achieve a fundamental financial milestone by becoming consistently profitable in 2023.

As David Sperau sums it up,

> *In the company's first few years we were focused on improving the platform and expanding market reach. Revenue-wise, our take was just really small. Then the number of users and revenue growth both really kicked in,*

and we started seeing the benefits of our digital platform technology. We turned the corner from burning cash to breaking even in June 2023, and our cash flow has been positive ever since. Our first profitable full quarter of operations was the third quarter of 2023 and we haven't had a down month or quarter since then.

And in 2023 we reached $37 million in revenues. For 2024, we are looking at about $42 million in revenue, and for 2025 or maybe 2026, we are aiming to reach $60 million. Our goal by 2029 or 2030 is to grow to annual revenues of $100 million, which would be incredible.

Autosled is a rising star in an evolving industry. The vehicle transport and logistics sector in the U.S. is enormous and historically fragmented. Even the largest car-hauling companies only account for a small slice of the market, with thousands of independent carriers hauling cars on routes nationwide. This fragmentation is precisely what Autosled's marketplace thrives on, knitting together many small players through a unifying tech platform. The company's current strengths position it well to capture an increasing share of this market. It has a significant first-mover advantage in offering a truly digital, end-to-end solution that many competitors are only now attempting to emulate. Its network effects are growing: more dealers and shippers on the platform attract more transporters, and vice versa, creating a self-reinforcing ecosystem.

The company has built considerable brand goodwill, especially among car dealers who appreciate that it was "built by car people, for car people." In a business as trust-based as auto transport, those relationships, combined with the advanced features of the Autosled platform, are a significant competitive moat. As the automotive retail sector continues its trend toward online sales and remote customers, Autosled's value proposition will become even stronger. More consumers are willing to buy vehicles from out-of-state sellers, whether through online retailers, auctions, or distant dealerships, which adds to the demand for shipping cars reliably across long distances.

The U.S. auto transport market offers ample room for continued growth. Total expenditures across this sector are expected to exceed $50 billion in 2025. There are roughly 18,000 new-car franchise dealers in America and tens of thousands of independent used dealers, many of whom still rely on old-style methods for transport. Even with the inevitable competitive challenges from new entrants and larger industry players, Autosled has reason to be optimistic about the long haul, and proud of achieving such impressive milestones in its first five years.

The remarkable journey from David Sperau's frustration with legacy logistics to a multi-million-dollar enterprise demonstrates the power of addressing an old problem with fresh perspective and innovative technology. As of 2025, Autosled's strengths – an intuitive platform, a massive transporter network, strong customer relationships, and a dedicated team – give it a solid springboard for sustainable future growth. With continued innovation and gold-standard customer service, Autosled is well positioned to truly revolutionize vehicle transport.

Harness

Does scoring a first multibillion dollar exit make it easier for founders to go on building more unicorn companies? That seems like a good question to ask Jyoti Bansal who sold AppDynamics, his first company, to Cisco for $3.7 billion in 2017. That same year, Bansal launched Harness, an end-to-end software delivery platform, followed in 2020 by Traceable, an API security startup. By 2022, Harness was already valued at $3.7 billion. In early 2025, Harness and Traceable merged, achieving a multi-billion-dollar valuation backed up by an estimated $250 million in combined annual revenues.

When Jyoti Bansal slows down briefly to talk about what it takes to become a 100X entrepreneur, it's no surprise that he's often asked whether it gets easier to achieve extreme growth with your second and third startups.

Bansal's answers are refreshingly unassuming for a serial entrepreneur who already has two unicorns to his credit. As it turns out, his insights and advice are relevant to founders at every stage of growth. For example, Bansal believes that founders should be involved in their company's early sales efforts, even when they know that building an efficient and predictable sales machine is essential to scaling over time,

What you need to do in the very early stage of your company, to get from the founding idea, to your first product release, to the first million dollars of revenue — those things are hard. I think it really doesn't matter how much prior experience you have. These early steps will remain hard and

you just have to do them. At AppDynamics, in the initial years there was much more hustle and less science than you would imagine to meet our sales goals. I initially thought at Harness, we wouldn't need to hustle as much, but actually it was just like the early days at AppDynamics. Every deal mattered, and as the founder, you need to do whatever it takes to close those early deals.

So, I knew that I had to be involved on the front line trying to close the deals. But the second time around, you also understand that building a sales machine is essential to systematic company growth, because the hustle doesn't scale. So you start building toward that sales machine as soon as possible. At Harness we built up very predictable sales machine a bit earlier than most startups would do.

In our conversation, Bansal emphasizes that all startups have to grow "one step at a time" regardless of how ambitious the vision is, or how enormous the total market opportunity may be. He outlines the flexible five-point process that he has used to scale three successful companies so far,

First you need to identify a major problem, a big, expensive problem that customers will pay you to solve. At Harness, we identified a trillion-dollar market opportunity to reduce all the time that engineers waste in the software development and delivery process.

Second, build the best possible product to solve this problem. Be innovative. In the software market, if you can't be a technology leader, that's a challenge.

Third is go-to-market execution, from product-market-fit to sales and distribution. That's where a lot of startups fail. Even with the best technology, without great distribution you can't scale the business. And that includes setting milestones and measuring success at every step.

Fourth is taking care of all your customers, listening to what they really need, and continually delivering value – value for customers is core.

Fifth, what's most important in the end is your people and your culture. Create the right culture for long term success; for me that means hiring smart people, and creating a high degree of transparency, accountability, and collaboration.

I believe in setting a 'mountaintop goal'—early at Harness, it was reaching $100 million in revenue. Now, it's a billion. You can't just have the goal; you need to map out strategic steps; you need a clear path that people will believe in. The path might change, but the direction stays the same.

Strategic Steps for Scaling a DevOps Powerhouse

So how did Bansal employ this advice in starting and scaling Harness? When he launched Harness in 2017, the big problem he had identified was a trillion-dollar inefficiency at the heart of software engineering. From his experience at AppDynamics, Bansal knew that tech giants like Google and Netflix had built sophisticated internal tools for continuous software integration and delivery, but most companies—even large enterprises – didn't have such advanced capabilities. As a result, their overall software delivery processes were typically slow, expensive, and error prone. That gap was at the heart of a trillion-dollar market opportunity. As Bansal told us,

There are about 40 million software developers in the world. The cost of their software engineering time is about $4 trillion—and 25% to 30% of that time is just wasted effort. Enterprise engineering time can be optimized with the right toolchain for DevOps, for quality, application security, cost management and financial operations – all the work that's not really the creative work of software engineering, but the plumbing and the mechanics that takes so much time.

Bansal's founding goal was both straightforward and massively ambitious: to build a platform that could make software engineering faster, more efficient, and less error-prone for enterprises. The Harness solution would ultimately expand to automate all those non-creative, repetitive tasks that slowed down developers and hampered software deployment across the enterprise. But true to his own framework for scaling, Bansal approached this goal with a methodical, customer-centric mindset. He didn't try to address all the inefficiencies in one step; he started by picking one focus for the Harness launch.

The first problem Harness tackled was Continuous Delivery (CD) as a service – automating the process of deploying code from development to production. By launching with a managed CD platform, Harness aimed to eliminate much of the manual toil and scripting that bog down enterprise software releases, from testing and deployment to security checks and cost optimizations.

True to what he had learned at AppDynamics about the importance of founders taking the lead in early sales, Bansal talked with dozens of potential customers, including their software teams, to validate the product-market fit. He deliberately sought out candid feedback by making cold calls and having hard-hitting conversations to ensure he heard the unvarnished truth about software delivery pain points.

This hands-on customer discovery process helped confirm that many companies were indeed struggling to reliably deploy code and saw high value in a solution like Harness. Importantly, it also revealed that some of the Harness assumptions about the market sweet spot were incorrect. The founding team had expected that Continuous Delivery as a service would resonate first with mid-size tech companies. However, Bansal discovered by reaching out to prospects that large enterprises – banks, retailers, and healthcare firms with thousands of developers – had the more urgent pain point, because their legacy development processes were so slow and expensive.

Based on this insight, Harness focused on targeting large enterprises, investing in features that would meet their needs. This paid off in landing Fortune 100 customers sooner than anticipated. Another lesson came from pricing trials: Harness initially wasn't sure if a consumption-based model or per-seat model would be best for their customers -and for generating scalable revenue. Through pilot programs, they learned that enterprises preferred predictable annual budgets for such a platform, leading Harness to stick with annual seat licenses rather than less predictable usage-based pricing—a win-win for Harness and its customers. Bansal describes this iterative process of testing product-market fit to fine tune the product, packaging, and sales approach as a "product-market-sales fit" model. It allows Harness to prioritize the most in-demand solution with the clearest ROI for users and to distribute it effectively to the right enterprise buyers.

Scaling Startups Within a Startup
From the start, Bansal envisioned Harness as a multi-product platform that would scale by building modular solutions and selling each module independently. He calls this strategy the "startup within a startup" model.

Our first product was continuous delivery, and then we started working on how companies and developers could simplify their testing, how they could simplify cost management, and compliance. We started by taking one development problem at a time and building solutions into our platform. As of now, we have 15 modular products. It's almost like a chest of tools where each tool is designed to address one particular part of software development and deployment in a much more effective way.

Each of our 15 products operates like a startup inside Harness, with its own CEO equivalent (the general manager), roadmap, and goals. We don't bundle them together; every product must win on its own merit. That's how we ensure excellence across the board.

In practice, that means each Harness product module—whether for CD, feature flags, cloud cost management, security, reliability and more—is sold independently. No bundling. No cross-subsidization. From Bansal's perspective, this model encourages best-in-class innovation across the entire platform. There are no tag-along solutions being bundled with product leaders just to drive adoption. As Bansal put it, "We're not going to bundle things together. We have to win the business on the merits of each one of those [products]. Otherwise, they will never become the best products in the market." Since a customer can buy just the Harness testing module without buying its Continuous Delivery or cloud-cost modules, the customer will renew that testing module only if it clearly delivers value. While this raised the bar for Harness in its early years, it also created internal team accountability and clearer product-market fit signals. At renewal time customers vote with their wallets on each module, keeping the entire Harness team laser focused on customer success.

What's more, each product is run like its own venture, complete with its own general manager, roadmap, sales, revenue, and growth targets. Bansal's leadership style empowers these teams with autonomy while holding them to high standards of customer satisfaction and revenue contribution. The expectation is clear: if a product module isn't delivering value and revenues on its own, it won't be propped up by the other Harness products.

Bansal's "startups within a startup" model creates a very powerful scalability engine for Harness, especially when it's linked to his "mountaintop goal" of reaching $100 million in recurring revenue. In fact, Harness reached the $100 million milestone in 2023 – and Bansal promptly defined the next mountaintop goal as achieving $1 billion. At the same time, each of the company's internal startups has internalized their own goal of achieving a $100 million in revenue for their product module. Their efforts become the scalable foundation for Harness to reach its company-wide billion-dollar milestone. At Harness, there will always be a higher mountaintop to climb. Bansal notes that he is planning to continue adding more product modules to the Harness platform; in the next three years, he aims to double the number from 15 to 30.

Growth Through Strategic Acquisitions

Strategic acquisitions have also supported a rapid growth trajectory, in part by bringing on board already successful companies to accelerate the release of one or more new product modules. Harness acquired Drone.io, which was focused on Continuous Integration (CI), ChaosNative (resilience testing), Split.io (feature flags), and several other companies to broaden its platform. Each acquisition was carefully integrated into the company's modular product model. These acquisitions, especially Drone.io and ChaosNative have also enabled Harness to work more actively with the open-source developer community. The open-source modules act as top-of-funnel lead generators to showcase Harness's technical capabilities, increasing credibility and lowering the cost to acquire developers' attention.

For example, Drone started as an open-source solution, and had attracted a sizable community of CI users. Harness not only pledged to keep Drone open-source, but also began open-sourcing additional parts of its own platform over time. It released, for example, an open-source feature called Lightweight Execution Engine (LEE) and later a project called Gitness, a GitHub alternative. These moves signaled to the developer community that Harness wasn't a closed black box; developers could adapt and even contribute to its tools. This strategy drives awareness and adoption at the practitioner level without adding to Harness marketing spend. A software engineer might encounter Drone or LitmusChaos (from the ChaosNative acquisition), start using it for free, and later discover a paid Harness module with deeper enterprise features. Harness thus employs product-led growth in parallel with enterprise sales – a powerful combination. When the sales team engages with a new prospect, they often find pockets of Harness or Drone open-source users already existing internally, smoothing the conversation.

In 2025, Harness announced its most significant acquisition yet: a merger with Traceable, the API security startup co-founded by Bansal in 2020. The merger unified software delivery and security into a single DevSecOps platform and brought Harness's projected ARR above $250 million.

The merger decision reflects Bansal's insight that enterprise buyers' needs are evolving: many development and security teams are now jointly responsible for software delivery pipelines. The expanded Harness offers best-of-breed solutions in enterprise software deployment and application security protection, using shared data and AI to integrate DevOps and AppSec workflows.

AI as an Advanced Product Feature and Internal Efficiency Engine

Harness was an early adopter of artificial intelligence and data analytics, both in its products and internal operations. In fact, when we ask him about using AI today, Bansal replies that Harness has leveraged machine learning since its launch in 2017. The platform uses machine learning to optimize testing, detect anomalies during deployment, and recommend fixes. One of Harness's differentiating features from the start was Continuous Verification, an AI-powered engine that monitors the health of new software deployments. When a company deploys a new version of an application via Harness, the platform automatically checks metrics and logs (application performance, error rates, etc.) and uses machine learning to determine if the release is behaving normally. If an anomaly is detected – say, a spike in error rates – Harness can automatically trigger a rollback to the previous version without waiting for human intervention. This capability is essentially an AI safety net for deployments, and it sets Harness apart from manual CI/CD pipelines.

Looking ahead, Bansal believes that generative AI will flood organizations with new code and microservices—making AI-powered software delivery and management platforms all the more valuable and indispensable. Harness aims to become the must-have platform for using AI agents for DevOps, FinOps, QA, compliance, and security.

This AI integration is more than a product strategy—it's also an internal engine for operational efficiency. Harness uses analytics to track customer usage, prioritize product development, and flag accounts for upselling. Internally, it uses AI for code generation and test optimization, enabling fast innovation with a lean team.

Metrics That Matter at Harness

Jyoti Bansal is a self-professed metrics-driven leader, but typical financial metrics and a drive to profitability have not been at the top of his list. At Harness, the key performance indicators (KPIs) that Bansal prioritizes are a blend of business, product-centric and customer-centric metrics. Since founding, Bansal has focused on the following four areas as the barometers of success:

- **Revenue Growth:** Annual Recurring Revenue is Bansal's "ultimate measure" of business expansion. Harness tracks revenue growth both at the company level and at the level of each product module. Each product / startup within Harness is expected to meet its revenue targets to demonstrate both market traction and customer value. If a particular module isn't growing, that flags a problem to address (be it product-market fit, sales execution, or competition). It's notable that growth is measured as evidence of value delivered and market capture, not just for its own sake.

- **Customer Happiness:** Harness uses customer satisfaction metrics – from Net Promoter Score surveys to renewal rates and qualitative feedback – to ensure it is truly solving problems for users. This metric is deeply tied to retention and lifetime value. One concrete metric Harness tracks is the renewal rate per product since high renewal rates indicate happy customers. Additionally, usage metrics serve as a proxy for happiness – if customers are executing millions of deployments and expanding usage, they're clearly finding value. Bansal has made customer happiness such a core value that it factors into performance reviews and bonus calculations for teams, aligning incentives toward user success rather than just new sales.

- **Innovation Rate (Product Excellence and Competitive Win Rate):** Bansal tracks how fast each team is innovating and whether they're winning against the competition in their respective domains. Internally, teams keep an eye on metrics like the number of new features delivered, the speed of release cycles, and adoption of those features. But even more telling is the external lens: are we beating the competition? If a Harness module is repeatedly losing deals, that's a sign the product needs improvement. Conversely, consistently winning and perhaps even commanding a price premium is a sign of product leadership. Another facet of innovation is how much value new product modules add. Whenever Harness launches a new product, Bansal is watching how quickly it gains market traction. Essentially, he is measuring Harness's ability to continuously find product-market fit for new offerings – a true test of long-term innovation capacity.

- **Efficiency and Unit Economics:** Bansal is very conscious of cost and efficiency metrics as a measure of efficient growth at Harness. He gives weight to metrics like gross margin (being a software SaaS, Harness's gross margins are high, but the cost of supporting on-premise installations and the cost of cloud infrastructure for its SaaS are monitored), customer acquisition cost (CAC), the ratio of customer lifetime value to CAC, and operating burn.

Each internal startup is expected to move toward profitability as it matures. Bansal believes, however, that a relatively new product module with $1 million revenue shouldn't be held to the same profit standard as a well-established $50 million product; there are stage-appropriate cost targets. For example, a newer product might be allowed to be in investment mode (not profitable) while growing to $10M ARR, but a mature product should have healthy margins. By measuring unit economics per module, Harness can allocate resources efficiently. This also ties into a blended metric of "efficient growth" – growth rate relative to burn rate. Bansal notes that in 2023, Harness tripled its revenue without proportionately increasing headcount or costs.

Together, these four pillars – growth, customer satisfaction, innovation, and efficiency – form a balanced scorecard for Harness. When capital markets tightened a few years ago, the company quickly doubled down on efficiency —cutting spending, optimizing team productivity, and tripling revenue with only a 20% headcount increase between 2021 and 2023.

Leadership and Culture

At the core of Harness's execution is Bansal's inclusive, learning-oriented leadership. He believes there's no one-size-fits-all formula for entrepreneurship—success requires passion, curiosity, and adaptability alongside a viable scalability strategy. That philosophy informs the culture at Harness, where teams are empowered to run like mini-startups, and are also supported with centralized resources and mentorship.

Bansal is highly engaged with customers, products, and people. He encourages transparency, avoids micromanagement, and prizes continuous learning. That means hiring the right people, listening to users, and adapting quickly when markets change. The startup-within-a-startup model allows for risk-taking without top-down control. It also creates opportunities for internal talent to rise—many early engineers now lead product teams.

Looking Ahead: Goals for the Next Three Years

True to his vision of building a high-value solution for a massive enterprise pain point at Harness, Jyoti Bansal has articulated ambitious goals for the company's next chapter. He wants to establish Harness as the best-in-breed enterprise platform for both software delivery and security. The company has set its sights on becoming a $1 billion ARR company by the end of the decade, if not before. Only time will tell how the next chapter unfolds, but if the past is any indication, Bansal and his Harness team will continue accelerating toward a sustainable, high growth future

◆ ◆ ◆

The founders featured in this chapter didn't just bring new products to market—they reshaped how their industries solve fundamental problems. By focusing on clear financial outcomes, demonstrating value from day one, and listening intently to their earliest users, these entrepreneurs earned the trust of some of the most skeptical buyers in business.

They learned, sometimes the hard way, that enterprise and small business customers won't adopt a new solution unless it moves the bottom line. That meant pivoting when needed—as Dane Atkinson did at Odeko—and stepping directly into the shoes of early users, like Yoseph West did at Relay. It meant embracing high-touch onboarding and strategic relationship building, like Autosled's founders did with every dealer and driver. And it meant building products that could stand alone, deliver ROI, and scale independently—as Jyoti Bansal insisted at Harness.

What unites all these companies is a shared commitment to creating compounding customer value, not just software features. Their stories are grounded in discipline, humility, and a deep respect for the customers they serve. That's what turned their solutions into platforms, their users into evangelists, and their revenue lines into hockey sticks.

In the B2B world, trust is earned slowly— based on consistent value and ROI. These 100X entrepreneurs earned enterprise trust by proving they could make a difference not just in theory, but in the financial and operational value their solutions deliver to every customer.

5
Leveraging Data and AI to Outperform the Competition

IN TODAY'S HYPER-COMPETITIVE business landscape, mastering data and deploying AI tools are no longer optional—they are table stakes for scaling successfully. Every company featured in this book uses data and AI in some form to power their growth. The three enterprises featured in this chapter—Rarebreed Veterinary Partners, Crisp, and ProxyPics—stand out for how deeply data and AI are embedded into their strategy for 100X growth. In these companies, advanced data infrastructure and AI-driven operations are an engine to outperform the competition and transform entire industry sectors.

Dan Espinal, Are Traasdahl, and Luke Tomaszewski each set out to solve entrenched inefficiencies in traditional industries. Each founder faced intense challenges: Espinal needed to standardize chaotic veterinary data across 130+ clinics, Traasdahl had to convince retail giants to share proprietary data with a tiny startup, and Tomaszewski watched his crowdsourced photography marketplace burn cash for three years before the market caught up to his AI-powered vision. Their ambitious visions led them to invent entirely new methods for extracting value from data; methods so innovative that they have been patented and are now difficult for competitors to replicate.

At Crisp, Traasdahl's refusal to prioritize short-term revenue or marketing spend in favor of focusing on "data under management" helped the company build a data network powerful enough to serve giants like Walmart and Target. The early years devoted to product-market iteration, done side-by-side with marquee customers, yielded a robust retail analytics platform that has scaled to manage over 600 million PODs by 2024. Crisp now underpins operations for over 80 of the top 100 CPG brands in the U.S., using AI to turn raw data into real-time retail insights.

Rarebreed, under Espinal's leadership, created a proprietary operating system that not only tracks every transaction and staffing event across its national network of veterinary clinics, but also applies AI to optimize clinic-level operations. From predictive staffing models to an interface that allows managers to ask plain-language questions and get data-driven recommendations, Rarebreed's analytics flywheel is transforming the operations and customer service aspects of veterinary medicine and freeing up care provider time to focus on keeping pets healthy.

ProxyPics, meanwhile, reinvented manual property inspection and appraisal with a combination of advanced technology, crowdsourcing, and old-fashioned grit. Its founder, Tomaszewski, pioneered the use of AI to auto-generate detailed property reports from photos. While his innovations were initially "too far ahead of the market," they now position ProxyPics as a go-to partner for major lenders, insurance companies, and facility managers. Real-time computer vision, fraud detection, and floor plan creation have vaulted the company to a spot on the Inc. 5000 and an expanding national footprint.

Together, these companies illustrate the compounding value of data and AI when it's integrated into operations, refined into insights, and used to power feedback loops that drive staff efficiency, customer value, and high-quality, scalable growth.

Crisp

My opening question for Are Traasdahl, CEO and cofounder of Crisp, is what inspired him to start Crisp after an entrepreneurial career in wireless. His response is far-ranging and visionary,

> In 2016, I sold my former company [Tapad] and took my family on a long trip around the world. We saw so much hunger in some countries, and wasted food in other places. I realized the world is spending so much energy making food, and transporting food, and keeping it cold, for so much of it to just go to waste. Food is one of the largest industries in the world; billions of people need food products three times a day. Finding some way to reduce food waste in the global supply chain – that was my inspiration for Crisp.

*My prior companies utilized a tremendous amount of data to solve busi-
ness problems in the mobile sector, meaning that I come from a data background. So, when I started looking at the problem of food supply chains
more closely, my natural focus was on data flows in the food industry. It
became clear that the existing data infrastructure mostly depended on
outdated, legacy systems—some of these systems were still based on an
EDI standard that was created around 1973. That's the year I was born!
Software had been stitched and glued together to connect these hundreds
of millions of companies handling food in some way around the world. I
had an inspiration then to create a modern data infrastructure, create
this advanced connective tissue, a platform to allow companies in a really
complex supply chain to collaborate better by leveraging data to improve
their own operation and also reduce food waste. My vision for Crisp became building a smart tech platform using advanced analytics that drive
action as a way to reduce waste in all stages of the supply chain, and
especially in retail sales.*

I'm eager to hear how Crisp managed to scale up from this vision to the extreme growth company it is today. But when I ask Are to describe his growth
priorities and metrics, he answers with a critique of conventional startup
metrics.

*I think in the first three or four years of a company's life, many of the
typical metrics that founders and investors apply to measuring startup
traction are very overrated. For example, I see a lot of founder pitch decks
where establishing product market fit includes a price point, and a timeline for proving that you can actually sell your product for that particular
price. But introducing this type of product market fit metric too early in
a company's lifecycle leads a lot of companies to go wrong at the start.
Founders feel pressured to claim product market fit just as soon as some
businesses buy their product. At that point, they don't know if those buyers are happy with it. They don't have any churn numbers. And they don't
know if their product actually solves the buyer's problem.*

Traasdahl clarifies that he's a firm believer in measuring what really matters.
It's just that from long experience as a serial entrepreneur, he knows that

what matters in years one through three of a startup's growth is usually very different from what becomes critically important in later phases,

> *The problem with starting out with a long list of standard SaaS metrics is that founder priorities inevitably change over time. My priority for Crisp today is so different from what it was a year ago, or four years ago. All these metrics have importance at some point, but what is the most important is very dependent on the stage of the company, the customers you need to reach, and the product you plan to offer.*

Instead of trying to hit all the standard metrics, Traasdahl prioritized building the core technology for his data-driven platform into a robust, scalable technology infrastructure, knowing that without the right foundation, the company could not deliver the advanced supply chain insights he envisioned. From the start, he identified data as Crisp's "hero metric,"

> *We decided to prioritize how much data we have on the platform, and work on constantly expanding the amount of data we have under management. That is our **hero metric** — how much data do we have on the platform. We needed supply chain data. That's our oxygen. We needed data to build the technology, to enable the technology to build the products that we can then take to the market through business development and sales and marketing. By focusing on the metric of data under management, we were also measuring network effects. We're measuring our growth through the network and its data, versus growth through traditional SaaS metrics. That hero metric underpins our growth and our customer-related metrics; How much usage does our platform have? How many transactions are happening on the platform? It's also a way for us to measure velocity.*

If you step back and think about all the challenges Crisp had to overcome to achieve its current market success, Traasdahl's decision to start by building out and testing the platform in stealth mode, and focusing on data under management, makes perfect sense.

In 2018, Crisp was a small startup aiming to become a key player in a crowded, multi-trillion-dollar industry. Between 2016 and 2019, Traasdahl and cofounder Dag Liodden operated in stealth mode, self-funding development,

prototyping, alpha testing, and enhancing the Crisp platform in close collaboration with a small group of brands and retailers who provided feedback as
well as access to their data. It wasn't until 2019 that Crisp publicly launched
its first product, and announced a $14.2 million Series A investment.

The Crisp team developed the next generation of their product by iterating features to tackle real-world issues in inventory tracking, demand forecasting, and shelf availability. In Traasdahl's words, *"if they pay us $1 it needs
to drive $10 of value,"* an ROI that he believed would justify the product's fu-
ture price point when Crisp reached the stage of prioritizing revenue growth.

From Customer Buy-In to Surging Growth

By focusing on data and customer fit instead of revenue until it could demonstrate ROI, Crisp secured enthusiastic buy-in from its pilot customers, including some of the world's largest global retailers. Instead of maximizing
revenue, Crisp prioritized gaining indispensable feedback from these key customers. That was enough to attract an additional $12 million in pre-revenue
investment, followed by a $35 million Series B investment early in 2022.

When it was ready, Crisp moved decisively from piloting and product iteration to growth, dramatically expanding its customer base, product feature
set, and the pace of acquisition, accompanied by significant revenue increases.
After years of planning, product enhancements, and marquee customer collaboration, it's not really accurate to call the growth inflection point that Crisp
reached in 2023 -2024 as "sudden" but the leap was certainly explosive. By the
end of 2023, Crisp had earned a spot on Deloitte's Fast 500 company list, with
3-year revenue burst of 11,380%.

The company has continued growing, from roughly 600 customers in early
2023 to over 7,000 by mid-2025. What's more, these customers were all now
paying at appropriate levels based on the volume and value of their use of
Crisp's platform. The strategy of building a robust product, validating its market fit through deep iteration with early customers and feeding it a constant
stream of high-value data paid off in scalable, 100X growth.

Under the Hood of the Crisp Platform

How does all that data under management add value to the Crisp platform, and
most importantly, to its customers? At its core, Crisp is a cloud-based data integration and analytics platform built specifically for the retail and consumer

goods industry. The technology automatically ingests data from dozens of disparate systems – including retailer POS databases, inventory management systems, distributor ERP feeds, and even external data like weather or demographics – and harmonizes it into a coherent, query-able format. One of Crisp's distinguishing features is its ability to standardize and clean data across sources in real time. In the legacy world, a CPG team might log into 10 different retailer portals, each with its own data schema and update cadence, then manually copy that data into spreadsheets for analysis. Crisp eliminates that manual toil by acting as an authorized data agent for the brand: with the brand's permission, Crisp pulls their data from each retailer (using APIs or automated retrieval from retailer portals), decrypts and stores it securely, and updates it daily (or more frequently if the source allows). All data is normalized – e.g. consistent product codes, store identifiers, and time periods – so that users can see a unified view of sales, inventory, orders, and other metrics in one dashboard or data feed.

The outputs of Crisp's platform are flexible to suit different user needs, from technical leads to managers across the organization. Many clients use Crisp's web-based dashboards and analytics platform, which provides intuitive visualizations and reports for roles from sales to supply chain. For instance, a sales manager can log in to see up-to-date sell-through by region, identify any distribution voids or track the lift from a promotion last week. A supply chain planner might use Crisp to monitor inventory across all distribution centers and stores, spotting which locations are at risk of stockouts and which have excess, enabling proactive rebalancing or production adjustments.

These real-time insights represent a leap from traditional weekly or monthly reports found in syndicated data sets. Crisp can feed data into more than a dozen different internal data destination systems, from data warehouses to leading vendor products, to plain Excel. Crisp is designed to act as a platform that pipes clean retail data into whatever workflow the customer prefers. This reflects a key evolution: Crisp pivoted around 2021–2022 from being a "forecasting application" to being primarily a platform company, after its early pilot testing made it clear that many large clients were not seeking to adopt yet another standalone dashboard. Instead, Crisp built robust APIs and connectors so that its clean data and analytics could plug into existing enterprise workflows and systems, making Crisp more extensible and valuable, as its data becomes embedded in daily operations of the client.

Crisp's platform offers a way to enhance supplier performance and drive operational excellence at scale. The Crisp presence in both Bentonville, AR (home to Walmart) and Minneapolis, MN (home to Target) facilitates close collaboration with enterprise brands working with the world's largest retailers. For large CPG manufacturers, Crisp provides a unified lens to manage complex, sprawling businesses. Take Nestlé USA as an example: Nestlé deals with an enormous portfolio (1,500+ SKUs) across multiple divisions and distributors. Historically, Nestlé's teams struggled with fragmented data – for instance, trying to consolidate sales reports from UNFI (a major distributor) with their internal systems. Now that the UNFI Insights portal is powered by Crisp, Nestlé staff can access accurate, easy-to-understand reports on each SKU's weekly sales and inventory by store, complete with real-time heat maps and store-level stock tracking. For Nestlé and other global manufacturers like Kraft Heinz, and Mars, Crisp's value lies in turning a deluge of retailer and distributor data into a stream of real-time intelligence that informs production, logistics, and sales strategies across their largest accounts.

Consumption-Based Pricing with PODs

Crisp operates a data platform business model with a consumption-based pricing structure tailored to the scale of each customer's data. The primary pricing unit is "Points of Distribution" (PODs), which Crisp defines as the total monthly count of unique store-SKU combinations for a brand. In simpler terms, one POD is one product in one store; a brand selling 10 products across 100 stores would generate 1,000 PODs (plus any e-commerce transactions, which are counted separately). This metric serves as a proxy for the volume of data Crisp must ingest, process, and host on behalf of the customer. The more stores and SKUs a brand adds to the Crisp platform, workload – and thus the higher the subscription tier.

This usage-based pricing model aligns with Crisp's value proposition: customers are essentially paying for the breadth of data coverage and integrations they utilize. A small regional brand in 1,000 stores with a limited product line will be onboarded at a relatively low cost, while a Fortune 500 CPG selling tens of thousands of SKU-store combos pays more commensurately. In effect, Crisp's revenue scales with the success of its clients: more products on more shelves or websites translates into more data to manage and higher fees, a model that investors favor for its built-in growth and net retention potential.

Unsurprisingly for a company that has challenged the rules for SaaS start-ups, this consumption-based approach via PODs is unconventional compared to typical enterprise SaaS pricing (which might charge per user license or a flat annual fee). However, it closely mirrors Crisp's data-first philosophy. Since Crisp's costs (cloud infrastructure, data engineering) and the value delivered are both tied to data volume, POD-based pricing creates a fair usage-based system. Brands essentially pay for what they consume – i.e. the complexity of their retail distribution data – rather than for an arbitrary number of seat licenses.

By the end of 2024, Crisp was connected into more than 50 major data sources, including retail chains, grocery distributors, online channels, and more. These connections grew an impressive 3588% from 2023 to 2024. Each integration (for example, adding a connection to a regional supermarket chain's data) can bring in thousands more PODs under management. Because Crisp's pricing monetizes this volume, the company's incentive is to cover as much of the retail universe as possible onto its platform, solidifying its position as a one-stop data hub. This strategy has paid off: by late 2024 Crisp had over 80 of the top 100 CPG brands as customers and dramatically increased its "share of shelf" data in the market. The POD pricing model thus not only generates revenue in proportion to customer scale; it reinforces Crisp's network effects – the more data sources and brands join Crisp, the more valuable it becomes for everyone, and the more PODs there are to monetize. Traasdahl's "data under management" metric is proving itself to be a true growth hero. His data-first mindset underpins Crisp's competitive advantage today, as the company shifts into a phase of accelerating sales and monetization.

Heroic Data in Action: Real-Time Analytics and AI at Scale

Crisp's technology stack heavily leverages AI and advanced analytics to deliver prescriptive insights, not just raw data. For demand forecasting (Crisp's original use-case), the platform's algorithms combine historical sales with a wide range of external signals – seasonality, holidays, pricing changes, even weather – to generate more accurate predictions of future demand. Traasdahl noted that Crisp's models benefited from cross-brand data: while a single yogurt brand can forecast its supply needs, dozens of yogurt brands from the same parent brand in Crisp's system allow even more granular, comparative forecasting, improving accuracy via broader context. In 2024, Crisp won industry recognition as "Overall Data Solution of the Year" for retail, in part due to its integration of real-time data with AI to automate decision-making. And in 2025, Crisp was recognized with SupplyTech Breakthrough "Artificial Intelligence Innovation Award" for developing technology that transforms fragmented retail data into unified, AI-ready insights.

Another aspect of Crisp's AI-integrated platform is its emphasis on store-level and item-level detail, going beyond what legacy systems like EDI or traditional ERP provide. Crisp pulls item-level POS and inventory by store per day, something many suppliers historically lacked access to in a digestible form. With store-level data, brands can do things like heat-map their product's performance to see which stores or regions are trending up or down, correlate sales with local events or demographics, and execute truly localized supply chain management. Crisp also incorporates on-shelf availability metrics – for instance, identifying phantom inventory (when a store's system shows stock but shelves are empty) or tracking how quickly a product sells after restock, which can indicate if shelf placements or planograms are effective. By having this fine-grained view across all retail partners, Crisp's clients can tackle problems that older tools would miss.

But the true value of data is about more than reporting. Crisp plans to launch an agentic AI platform that enables users to design and deploy systems of agents that can operate in modes ranging from "chat mode" all the way through fully autonomous mode where the agents are running in the background, surfacing issues in real-time and opportunities as they arise. Building on top of a strong data foundation, Crisp AI Agents will help CPGs turn their data into insights, and insights into action.

Positive Impact: Reducing Waste

Crisp has kept Traasdahl's original vision of reducing food waste at the heart of its strategy. This vision permeates the company's culture and value proposition. By enabling better demand forecasting, inventory management, and fewer stockouts or overstocks, Crisp's platform directly contributes to waste reduction. For instance, if a supplier can see that a product is overstocked in one region and understocked in another, they can redirect shipments or adjust production, preventing spoilage. A retail chain on Crisp can quickly spot when an item isn't selling in certain stores and take action (markdowns, transfers) before it expires, also cutting down on waste. In 2025, Crisp acquired Shelf

Engine, the AI pioneer in demand forecasting and automated ordering. The Shelf Engine platform is now in use across more than 7000 stores, helping to reduce millions of pounds of food waste.

Traasdahl summarizes Crisp's impact as creating a "positive triple bottom line – good for our customers, good for the business and good for the environment". By aligning profitability with sustainability, Crisp taps into a powerful incentive loop: companies have economic reasons to prevent waste (it's literally throwing away money), and Crisp gives them the tools to do so efficiently and systematically.

Transforming Supply Chains with Collaborative Data

Crisp closed a $72M Series B equity round in October 2025, bringing the total equity raised to $97M since inception. Its strategic acquisition targets had expanded beyond the U.S. to encompass UK companies, Atheon and ClearBox, establishing a footprint in Europe. With the UK acquisitions, Crisp is executing on Traasdahl's stated goal to "take Crisp international;" Crisp can now boast a global data network and product capabilities that cover grocery, big-box retail, and even foodservice – positioning it as a far more comprehensive solution.

"Data under management" also reflects Crisp's strategy of positioning itself as core infrastructure rather than just a tool. Traasdahl believes that the industry needs to standardize around an agreed-upon data model – akin to how financial services adopted common networks. Crisp and its many partners will be a key facilitator of that standardization. From this long-term perspective, maximizing data under management isn't just about current insight delivery and revenue growth; it's about achieving a central market position. The metric encapsulates both the scale of Crisp's proprietary data asset and the strength of its network effects – two factors highly correlated with the company's valuation and competitive edge.

The dramatic growth in customers, transactions on the platform, and PODs demonstrate that Crisp is capturing a unique dataset and achieving network-based growth. Data has become a direct barometer of the company's progress toward its vision of a globally connected, data-driven retail supply chain. This hero metric bodes well for achieving Traasdahl's founding vision of reducing waste in the global supply chain with a scalable, AI supported model for growth.

Rarebreed Veterinary Partners

Dan Espinal, CEO and Co-Founder of Rarebreed Veterinary Partners doesn't fit the typical profile of a first-time founder. For one thing, novice entrepreneurs don't usually manage to raise $900 million for their startup idea. Regardless of how much funding they raise, most startups don't grow their revenues over 10,000% in three years, or make it into the Inc 5000 top ranks of America's fastest growing companies. How do all these pieces fit together at Rarebreed?

In our conversation, Dan talks about his path to entrepreneurship as the culmination of a career in venture investing, M&A consulting, strategy, and corporate development. His role at IDEXX Laboratories, a global pet health-care firm that develops advanced animal diagnostic tests and veterinary practice management software, crystalized his long-standing passion for animal welfare and the human-animal bond into a founding vision for Rarebreed Veterinary Partners,

> *Before I got directly involved with animal health at IDEXX, I worked in venture investing in a firm in Boston where I got to see companies get started. I always found myself kind of in awe of the entrepreneurs who put it all on the line to create companies. They seemed so determined to bend reality to their will. But I realized that I'm almost too optimistic to be a good investor. I think you need a healthy dose of skepticism.*
>
> *When I got into one of our operating companies on the biotech side, working with different teams, from accounting and HR to product engineers, and scientists, my job was getting everyone to row in the same direction, towards a common objective. I found that incredibly gratifying and realized that my calling was in operations, not being an investor. From there, I was recruited to run corporate development and strategy at IDEXX in Portland, Maine. I fell in love with the animal health business, and the veterinary industry and I co-founded Rarebreed in 2018 with Sean Miller. Like every entrepreneur, I wanted to change the world for the better. Starting a company isn't easy. It has tested every element of me. But it's the best decision I've ever made.*

The veterinary industry called out to Espinal for change when he realized that problems like high veterinarian burnout rates, professional isolation, and the mounting administrative burdens of small practice groups could be

solved with a different vision for animal care. Veterinary professionals typically work solo or in small independent practice groups. They lack shared resources, business support, and the economies of scale that could allow them
to focus on their passion—caring for animals. Many work longer hours for less
pay than their human medicine counterparts, despite having invested in long
and expensive animal care education, and incurring student debt loads comparable to physicians.

Dan Espinal's founding vision centered on elevating the veterinary workplace and bridging a critical gap he had observed: veterinarians lacked the
support and resources common in human medicine. The problem extended
beyond the professionals to the pets and families they served. Without systematic approaches to care delivery, quality could vary dramatically from
practice to practice. Data collection was inconsistent, making it difficult to
identify trends, gaps in care, or opportunities for improved outcomes. Espinal
believed that pet owners often faced difficult choices about their animals' care
not because of medical necessity, but because of system limitations.

Reimagining Veterinary Care

With these issues in sharp focus, Rarebreed set out to "reimagine the veterinary experience and make work actually work for people." The startup's mission from the outset was to deliver exceptional care to pets, delight clients,
and provide what Espinal calls "a kick-ass work experience" for veterinary
practice owners and employees. In practical terms, this meant building a company that cares for its people and clients equally – proving that a veterinary
business can put employees first and run efficiently while delivering superior
levels of animal care. To achieve this, Rarebreed worked to create a network of
veterinary clinics, provide centralized resources and support, and free up the
care team and front-line providers to do the work they loved.

Rarebreed's pragmatic and investor-friendly business model is to acquire
standalone veterinary practice groups and roll them up into the Rarebreed
Partners organization. Once it buys a   veterinary practice—typically taking
a majority ownership stake—Rarebreed works to boost both performance and
revenues. Upon acquisition, Rarebreed clinics gain access to a full suite of
shared resources that independent veterinarians often lack: strategic guidance, marketing, staffing and HR support, accounting, IT systems, and more.

That eye-popping $900 million investment provided the funds to power

Rarebreed's acquisition of about 130 veterinary care groups between 2019 and 2025. By way of context for this investment, between 2017 and 2024 U.S. private equity groups have invested over $60 billion acquiring veterinary clinics and animal health specialty practices. It turns out that Espinal's experience in venture investment, M&A, corporate development and operations is a perfect match for steering this model to financial success.

As I learned during our conversation, acquisitions and operating expertise are not what differentiates Espinal's leadership of Rarebreed. Dan's passion for animal welfare, his deep belief in the value of human-animal bonding, and commitment to improving the lives of veterinary care providers are what make Rarebreed stand out among the dozens of veterinary roll-up firms operating in the U.S. today.

As Espinal describes it, his company's strategy is to provide newly acquired practice groups with the resources needed to empower the staff to focus on delivering the best possible care for their animal patients and the highest quality of service for their human pet families. Importantly, Rarebreed's model is deliberately flexible for each partnership. The company "rejects[s] the one-size-fits-all partnership model" and works with practice owners to structure ownership and roles in ways that suit each clinic's needs. In many cases, the clinic owners retain a minority stake or receive performance-based payouts, aligning incentives post-acquisition. This tailored approach, combined with heavy investments in culture and technology, has enabled Rarebreed to execute a rapid roll-up strategy while maintaining clinical quality and staff engagement across its growing footprint. The emphasis is on bringing operational, financial, technical, quality enhancement, and administrative expertise into each practice group it acquires.

Creating Value for All Stakeholders

Rarebreed's differentiated strategy creates value for all its key stakeholders: veterinary employees, clinic owners, and pet-owning clients. For veterinary professionals, Rarebreed positions itself as an "employer of choice" that fundamentally improves their quality of work life. In an industry notorious for burnout and turnover, Rarebreed offers veterinarians and support staff higher pay and better benefits than industry norms, along with creative incentives and a positive culture. Espinal notes that Rarebreed has "great pay and benefits" and also provides "incentive-based compensation, as well as plenty of advancement opportunities, continuing education and a mentorship program" to its team members. Espinal firmly believes that team members who feel valued "provide better care for pets and owners," creating a virtuous cycle of employee satisfaction and client service. By making veterinary medicine a more sustainable, rewarding career, Rarebreed is also helping address the industry-wide talent shortage – an important selling point as many stand-alone practices struggle to recruit enough veterinarians.

Rarebreed offers clinic owners a chance to join a larger platform while retaining what makes their practice special. The front-line veterinarians who join the Rarebreed network report being able to focus on clinical care in ways they never could in stand-alone practice settings. Espinal ensures that his company "takes care of the people who take care of pets," prioritizing staff well-being and development. The company's network model also creates a community of peers – instead of operating in isolation, veterinarians become part of a collegial network of Rarebreed professionals who can share knowledge and cover each other's needs (for instance, referring patients to PetMedic urgent care or consulting on complex cases). All of these benefits make Rarebreed an attractive exit or partnership option for clinic owners looking for both financial and operational support.

The company's approach to compensation reflects this philosophy in ways that set it apart from traditional veterinary practices and most other businesses. Every single employee at Rarebreed—"from a client service representative, a kennel cleaner to a practice manager to a field director to a head of operations"—participates in some form of incentive-based compensation. This isn't just token profit-sharing; it's a comprehensive system designed to ensure that when the business succeeds, everyone who contributes to that success benefits proportionally.

At the practice level, every partner has the ability to earn quarterly profit sharing based on clinic profitability. In 80% of Rarebreed practices, key personnel have actual ownership stakes through joint ventures or profits interest plans tied to practice growth. At the corporate level, every employee participates in the management equity incentive plan, creating alignment between individual efforts and company-wide success.

For clients and pet owners, Rarebreed's growing network aims to deliver a superior veterinary care experience. By standardizing best practices and investing in training, Rarebreed clinics strive for consistently high medical quality. Clients also benefit from the expanded services and access that a network can provide. Through initiatives like urgent care centers and telehealth triage, pet owners can get timely care advice and off-hours options that individual clinics typically cannot offer. As Espinal explains, the goal is for pet parents to feel they are "part of this medical system for pets" where they "get the best care possible" across all needs. Higher employee engagement further improves customer service: a veterinary team that feels appreciated is more likely to go the extra mile for patients.

Finally, Rarebreed's stakeholder-centric approach creates long-term value for its investors and shareholders. Rarebreed focuses on building a trusted brand in veterinary care, not just a collection of clinics. This brand equity and the company's sustainable practices (like profit-sharing and community-building) contribute to durable growth. As Espinal frequently emphasizes, doing right by employees and customers isn't at odds with profitability – it is the strategy to achieve it. Rarebreed's rapid growth and industry accolades to date suggest that this stakeholder-forward model is yielding competitive advantage. The company is effectively proving that entrepreneurship can be a force for good in veterinary medicine when the interests of doctors, pet owners and investors are genuinely aligned.

Relationship-Centered Customer Acquisition with Operational Efficiency

Rarebreed's approach to acquiring new partner clinics is strategic and relationship-driven. Rather than mass marketing or bidding for every available hospital, the company targets practices that fit its culture and geographic strategy. Espinal notes that Rarebreed expands by "building density and building clusters" in its regions – acquiring multiple clinics within a market to create local synergies. Standard operating procedures are implemented to integrate new clinics swiftly without disrupting their local character. When courting an owner, Rarebreed emphasizes its flexible partnership model and mission of care. Many sellers are drawn by Rarebreed's reputation for not simply absorbing clinics, but helping them thrive. As noted, Rarebreed eschews a uniform acquisition template; it works "with hospital owners to create a relationship that works for them," whether that means the owner stays on as managing doctor, retains equity, or takes on a new leadership role in the broader company. This tailored, trust-based acquisition strategy has helped Rarebreed win deals even in a highly competitive consolidation market.

Once a clinic joins Rarebreed, a well-defined integration process kicks in to realize value for staff and clients. On the technology front, Rarebreed deploys its centralized systems to connect the new practice. The company's proprietary data platform can integrate with various clinic management software, aggregating and normalizing the incoming clinic's data and plugging it into Rarebreed's analytics dashboards. This allows the Rarebreed support team to immediately start monitoring key metrics and identifying improvement opportunities at the clinic. In many cases, Rarebreed introduces new services or operational tweaks to enhance the clinic's performance. For example, Rarebreed has encouraged clinics to adopt wellness plans (subscription preventive care packages) to smooth revenue and improve pet health over the long term. It also tackles inefficiencies like in-clinic retail: a typical vet hospital stocks thousands of SKUs (foods, medications, supplies) which consume space and staff time. Rarebreed's integration playbook includes offloading such inventory to an online delivery system – so pet owners still get their pet food or meds, but "from the warehouse to the consumer direct" – freeing individual clinics from storing and managing retail products. Changes like these lighten the workload for clinic staff and let them focus on care delivery, which boosts productivity and morale.

Critical to Rarebreed's integration strategy is aligning incentives and preserving the clinic's human capital. Espinal highlights that "every hospital... has to be self-operating" with "one or two people...thinking like owners in a practice" to truly succeed. Rarebreed therefore strives to retain key veterinarians and managers at each acquired location. Joint ownership and meaningful profit-sharing mean that when Rarebreed improves a clinic's financial performance, the staff tangibly share in the upside. Such incentives help ensure that new team members buy into Rarebreed's system rather than feeling like cogs in a big corporate machine.

From the client perspective, Rarebreed aims to make the integration of a new clinic as seamless as possible – ideally invisible except for positive changes. Clinics generally keep their local name and staff members, including the veterinarians, so pet owners continue to interact with the care providers they already know and trust. Over time, clients may notice improvements such as upgraded facilities or equipment, additional services such as urgent-care hours or telehealth consults, and perhaps enhanced customer service protocols. This careful integration strategy – blending centralized efficiencies with local autonomy – is a cornerstone of Rarebreed's ability to grow rapidly via acquisitions without diluting the quality of care or alienating staff and customers. Each new practice is woven into the Rarebreed fabric at a manageable pace, so that the result is a stronger combined enterprise that still feels personal and community-based.

Building a Scalable Growth Platform with Integrated Data

Early in Rarebreed's development, Espinal made a data management decision that would prove fundamental to the company's long-term success. While other veterinary consolidators focused primarily on acquisition speed and cost synergies, Rarebreed invested heavily in building what Espinal calls "an integrated and deep back end that provided analytical insight into what was happening operationally every single day with every single client transaction or personnel scheduling issue and workflow."

Integrating data across all its partner clinics was challenging and expensive. Veterinary data is notoriously messy. Unlike human medicine, where regulatory requirements and insurance reimbursement demands have driven standardization, veterinary practices have evolved with tremendous variation in their data collection and management approaches. As Espinal notes, "from practice to practice, the way a veterinarian may put in his or her information into their electronic medical record system could be very different."

When a board member questioned whether Rarebreed was spending too much "building a Maserati where a Ford would do fine," Espinal held firm. The data standardization investment wasn't about having the most sophisticated system; it was about creating a foundation that could support the kind of multi-site healthcare business he envisioned. "When every acquisition had incompatible data, we would have a big problem getting to the next growth milestone if we didn't invest early to build an integrated data back end," he explains.

The Rarebreed Operating System is a proprietary infrastructure that emerged from this investment. It comprises four critical components working in harmony: delivering veterinary services, generating data from those services, constantly analyzing that data, and creating internal incentives to drive better care delivered to more patients. This Operating System model is a flywheel that generates momentum as it grows, with each component reinforcing the others.

The practical impact has been transformative. Practice managers who once struggled to make sense of complex operational data can now ask simple questions in natural language and receive actionable insights. A manager might ask, "Why is revenue down last month?" and receive a detailed analysis: "Volume is down because pets ages two to four have not adopted wellness services." The system can then recommend specific interventions: "We recommend you send out a notification with a discount for wellness visits to this demographic."

Funding, Financial Management, and Profitability Milestones

Rarebreed's aggressive roll-up acquisition strategy has been powered by significant outside investment. From its founding, the company recognized that scaling a multi-site veterinary operation would require substantial capital. Early on, Rarebreed raised $40 million across two rounds of financing. As the company expanded, it attracted larger backers: by mid-2022 Rarebreed partnered with Revelstoke Capital Partners, a private equity firm that took a majority stake and provided a major infusion of growth capital. This enabled Rarebreed's landmark acquisition of Vet's Best Friend, a 47-clinic group, making Rarebreed one of the country's largest veterinary practice consolidators. As noted, by late 2024 Rarebreed had raised close to $900 million to fuel its expansion –reflecting investors' confidence in the firm and in Dan Espinal's leadership.

Alongside these large capital injections, Espinal has kept a careful eye on operational and financial efficiency. Thanks to his management and the strong organic performance at acquired clinics, Rarebreed achieved profitability in 2021 and has been profitable ever since. Espinal affirms that "profitability definitely matters to us," even as the company continues to invest in growth. Veterinary care offers attractive economics – unlike human hospitals encumbered by insurance bureaucracy, a multi-site vet business can target operating margins around 25%. There are fewer regulatory and insurance billing frictions, and clients pay directly for about 98% of the services delivered. Rarebreed's strategy is to realize those efficiencies and share the upside with clinic staff through profit-sharing, while reinvesting in expansion.

Rarebreed's growth strategy has balanced "inorganic" acquisition-driven growth with improving the underlying operations to generate cash flow. Espinal describes Rarebreed as a "balance sheet intensive business" – buying and building clinics ties up capital and takes time to yield returns. His dream, he says, is to have the company's own cash flows eventually fund further acquisitions, eliminating dependence on outside capital. In the meantime, Rarebreed uses external funding to accelerate expansion, while simultaneously strengthening its operational processes so that each acquired clinic contributes positively to the bottom line as it matures. This balanced approach became even more crucial as market conditions have changed. "A few years ago, everybody valued growth, and today people value cash flow," Espinal notes, acknowledging that Rarebreed must "do both" – continue growing while generating healthy cash yields.

By instituting disciplined operational processes and systems early, Rarebreed avoided the trap of many roll-ups that "grow really fast and then struggle to build processes later." As a result, it has been able to maintain profitability even during hyper-growth. Going forward, with higher interest rates and more cautious investors, Rarebreed has become even more selective about acquisitions, focusing on the best opportunities and tightening internal operations to maximize returns on invested capital. This capital-efficient strategy – scaling rapidly, but not recklessly – is positioning Rarebreed to sustain its expansion without sacrificing financial stability.

Leveraging AI and Data Analytics for Competitive Advantage

Espinal has instilled a data-driven mindset in the company. Rarebreed's integrated data platform not only connects clinics but also powers advanced analytics and AI applications that set Rarebreed apart in the industry. One such initiative is the use of large language models (LLMs) to democratize data insights. Espinal explains that Rarebreed is piloting an "Alexa"-like interface for clinics – essentially an AI assistant that lets local managers or veterinarians query their data in plain language and get immediate answers. This kind of AI-driven decision support is uncommon in independent vet practices, giving Rarebreed a unique operational intelligence across all of its clinics and practice groups.

Another area where Rarebreed employs AI is in back-office process automation. Running over 130 locations means handling a high volume of routine tasks, including in HR and administration. Espinal notes that "every time you hire an employee, let go of an employee, promote an employee, change a position, that creates all kinds of work streams" in a multi-site business. Rarebreed uses AI and software automation to handle many of these tasks, from onboarding paperwork to scheduling workflows, which reduces administrative overhead and errors. The company is constantly reviewing repetitive manual processes and figuring out how to automate them. This not only cuts costs – it frees up managers to focus on higher-value activities like patient care and team development. Rarebreed's early investment in an integrated HRIS (Human Resources Information System) and other enterprise tools, bolstered by AI automation, has allowed it to scale efficiently without a proportional explosion in corporate headcount.

Rarebreed also leverages data analytics for strategic planning, particularly through predictive modeling for a seasonally variable business. To optimize staffing and resource allocation, Rarebreed uses techniques like Monte Carlo simulations to forecast demand and the appropriate staffing level for each clinic. By inputting historical data and variables, like time of year, day of week, local events, Rarebreed's analytics can predict, for example, how busy a certain emergency hospital will be the day after Thanksgiving and schedule staff accordingly. These data-informed adjustments help manage the cost of service – ensuring clinics are not overstaffed during slow periods or caught short-handed during rushes. It's a level of rigor more akin to advanced retail or airline operations than a traditional vet practice, and it translates into both better customer service and healthier margins.

Additionally, Rarebreed's integrated data approach enables it to innovate rapidly. The company has patented elements of its "Rarebreed Operating System," which continuously collects and analyzes data across all clinics and feeds key performance indicators back to managers in real time. Rarebreed sets targets for metrics like preventive care uptake or client satisfaction and tracks them closely, using dashboards to nudge clinics toward best practices. Espinal describes it as aligning the "biology of business" (human behaviors and incentives) with the "chemistry of business" (the financial model) through leveraging digital infrastructure.

These efforts give Rarebreed a technological sophistication that is rare in veterinary care. In an era where many vet clinics still run on paper records or siloed software, Rarebreed's AI and data mastery not only boost internal productivity but also serve as a competitive advantage – enabling superior service offerings like 24/7 telehealth advice informed by patient data. These make the company an attractive partner for tech-savvy pet care innovators. By treating data as a strategic asset, Rarebreed is effectively building a modern, smart veterinary network that rivals the analytical prowess of much larger healthcare systems.

Performance Metrics Paired with Behavioral Metrics
In steering Rarebreed, Dan Espinal keeps a close watch on a mix of people-focused and performance-focused metrics. He divides these into what he calls "key behavioral indicators" or KBI (for internal culture and staff health) and traditional business KPIs (for operational and financial outcomes). On the people side, Espinal and his team regularly measure employee turnover rates and even conduct periodic "relative value" surveys asking staff which benefits they value most, so they can adjust offerings to maximize perceived value. These efforts feed into metrics like annual attrition: the company sets target ranges for staff retention and aims to beat industry benchmarks, using this as a barometer of organizational health. High engagement and low unwanted turnover are top priorities, given that talent is a limiting factor in veterinary care. Espinal considers his company's people metrics as leading indicators; if engagement dips or turnover rises, it signals issues that need addressing quickly.

On the practice performance side, Espinal monitors what he calls the "standard" metrics for a multi-site healthcare business. One fundamental metric is volume – how many patient visits or procedures each clinic is doing. Volume ties directly to revenue, but Rarebreed looks deeper at what composes that volume as well. Related to volume is quality of care: Rarebreed examines the mix of services in each visit, for example, are pets getting comprehensive preventive care or just basic shots, as a measure of clinical quality and client value. Another critical metric is cost of service, essentially a productivity and efficiency gauge. Espinal breaks this down into how many patients a doctor sees per hour and how much support staff is required per doctor – capturing how efficiently each hour of veterinary time is utilized. If a clinic can increase throughput without sacrificing care through better scheduling, increasing technician support, etc., the cost per service goes down, improving margins. Similarly, Rarebreed tracks the cost of goods sold – ensuring that clinics manage their inventory of medications, pet food, and supplies efficiently with minimal waste. This is especially relevant given Rarebreed's moves to central-ize some inventory management to reduce costs.

Customer satisfaction is another key performance metric. Espinal wants to know, "Are our clients feeling they're getting the value that they expect?" A high NPS (Net Promoter Score) indicates strong loyalty and word-of-mouth, which bodes well for long-term growth. Finally, Rarebreed measures clini-cal outcomes through preventative care uptake. One KPI that Espinal tracks closely is the rate at which pet owners adopt preventive health services like wellness exams, diagnostic blood work, and dental cleanings at Rarebreed clinics. This metric reflects both quality of care and client education, as higher adoption means pets are getting more proactive health screening. Espinal's conviction in this area comes from data: he cites a study of 220,000 pets which found that in about 25% of middle-aged cats and dogs, lab tests revealed hid-den issues that would have been missed without preventive diagnostics. By tracking and pushing to increase preventive care utilization, Rarebreed aims to improve patient outcomes by catching illnesses early.

By keeping a finger on the pulse of these KPIs and KBIs, Espinal and his management team can make data-informed decisions and quickly address any area that is lagging – whether it's an uptick in staff burnout or a decline in client satisfaction at a particular hospital. Metrics are not just numbers to Espinal; they are tools to align everyone in the company around delivering great care, great service, and great workplace experiences, which are the pil-lars of Rarebreed's mission.

A People-First Company Culture

From the beginning, Dan Espinal has cultivated a company culture at Rarebreed that sets it apart in the veterinary field. He believes that culture is a crucial strategic asset and an essential element of achieving all the com-pany's goals. The company invests heavily in team development: offering mentorship programs, continuing education funds, clear career pathways, and internal promotions. Achievements are celebrated and feedback is solicited regularly, reinforcing a positive loop. This attention to culture has paid off in high retention and an employer reputation that helps Rarebreed attract top talent. It also shapes how Rarebreed integrates new acquisitions –through the lens of culture, not just financial metrics. Espinal firmly believes that keep-ing the veterinarians and staff happy is foundational for Rarebreed's success:

"We're able to keep our veterinarians and we're able to keep them happy," he explains, because Rarebreed has worked tirelessly to support its employees and to achieve "best-in-class retention".

Dan Espinal's personal leadership style is a major driver of Rarebreed's culture. Espinal inspires his team with a sense of higher purpose. He views both veterinary medicine and entrepreneurship as callings, not just jobs. The Rarebreed mission – to improve the lives of pet caregivers and pet owners – imbues employees' day-to-day work with meaning. Espinal often speaks about the "human–animal bond" and the societal value of caring for companion animals, reinforcing that Rarebreed's work has real impact beyond profits. By being transparent, principle-driven, and passionate, Espinal has built a loyal and high-performing team. Early employees and investors have been drawn in by his conviction. "It's amazing what a few people who are inspired by a mission can do. They're ten times as valuable as people who just want a job," Espinal notes. That belief captures his leadership philosophy: find great people, give them a mission and support, align their incentives with that mission, and then trust them to "get done what needs to get done." The result is a company culture that not only achieves business objectives but also uplifts the individuals within it. That's an accomplishment in any industry setting, and especially in the typically performance-first, bottom line driven world of acquisition-based business models.

Rarebreed and the Future of Veterinary Practice

Looking ahead, Dan Espinal has set ambitious goals to lead Rarebreed to the next level of growth and impact. Quantitatively, his "moonshot" objective is to quadruple Rarebreed's delivery of animal care. "I have a goal to treat 4 million patients per year. We treat a million today," he says. In fact, Espinal envisions Rarebreed becoming a truly national veterinary network operating as many as 500 locations across North America.

As Espinal leads the company toward achieving these ambitious growth targets, he is positioning Rarebreed to become a model for the future of animal healthcare in America. The trends driving demand for veterinary services—increasing pet ownership, humanization of pet care, longer pet lifespans, and growing awareness of the human-animal bond—suggest sustained opportunities for growth and continued transformation of the industry in the years ahead.

In Espinal's own words,

We want to show the world that we can pay our people the best, drive the most profitable business, and take the greatest care of clients and patients. That's what we mean by industry-defining.

This encapsulates his aspiration for Rarebreed's impact: to set a new benchmark in veterinary medicine on all fronts – employee well-being, financial performance,

ProxyPics

Luke Tomaszewski, founder and CEO of ProxyPics, has a gift for viewing roadblocks and industry pain points as entrepreneurial opportunities. That deep-seated instinct served him well as the founder of two Chicago-based appraisal companies, before it inspired him to start yet another business. As Tomaszewski recalls, it was a particularly acute appraisal pain point back in 2008 that eventually led him to found ProxyPics almost a decade later,

In 2008-09, during the mortgage default crisis there were so many foreclosures that I was constantly driving around taking photos of properties before we could do an appraisal. It was a lot of wasted time day after day. Back then, crowdsourcing was becoming more popular; smartphones were getting smarter. While I was driving for hours to take some simple pictures, I kept thinking, 'it would be so much easier if I could just pay somebody in the neighborhood to take these photos.' For years, that was just a general idea, but every now and then it would pop back into my head. Eventually, a plan for ProxyPics started to take shape.

By 2016, Luke's pain point solution had crystallized into envisioning ProxyPics as a marketplace where appraisers and other real estate professionals could connect with local photographers to source the photos they needed. He saw ProxyPics as a win-win value proposition. Busy professionals could efficiently outsource simple fieldwork and local photographers (dubbed "Proxies") could earn extra cash for quick gigs. ProxyPics would play the role of an Uber – build the platform, create a mobile app to match up demand and supply, and earn money by charging the professionals who ordered photos.

Tomaszewski was in a position to self-finance the company's startup costs, so he didn't need to run the gauntlet of pitching to outside investors. Unfortunately, he had underestimated both the complexity of establishing a two-sided marketplace in a traditional industry sector, and the time and money needed to achieve profitability.

I knew that ProxyPics had managed to overcome early setbacks to score a spot on the 2024 Inc 5000 list with a very impressive 3-year revenue growth rate of 4,754%. There was clearly a lot to learn from this turnaround story, so I asked Luke to talk with me about the problems he had encountered and what strategies he used to pivot from a near-disaster to profitability.

Growing Pains in Building a Two-Sided Marketplace

The first challenge Luke Tomaszewski encountered was the classic chicken-and-egg problem of building any two-sided marketplace —ProxyPics needed a critical mass of clients willing to pay for photos and it had to recruit Proxies in enough locations to deliver those photos in a timely way. Luke originally planned to roll out ProxyPics services incrementally, one geographic region at a time. A region by region launch strategy would have allowed Tomaszewski to leverage his long-standing experience and extensive network of connections in the real estate and appraisal industry to set up local ProxyPics pilots in selected cities. Setback number one was finding that his potential clients wanted a service that could offer nationwide coverage from the start. Even more daunting was realizing how many of the industry's legacy regulations and rules blocked widespread adoption of digital solutions. Before 2020, for example, mortgage guidelines often required a licensed appraiser to personally inspect a property, limiting the extent to which lenders could use crowd-sourced photos in lieu of an official visit.

Populating the platform with Proxy photographers seemed easier at first; Luke just advertised on social media to attract them. Client demand was slow to materialize, however, making gig assignments scarce. Many Proxy photographers who had joined the platform lost interest. To rekindle Proxy engagement, Luke devised some clever but expensive solutions, like creating "fake jobs" just to keep a core group of Proxies on the platform. As he recalls,

In the early days, we'd have to pay to acquire a new Proxy, or data collec-
tor, by posting a lot of Google, Craigslist, and Facebook ads, to get people
to download our app and hopefully take photos for us when we had a job
in their area. The problem that we ran into quickly is somebody would
download our app in say, Los Angeles. But if we didn't have any active
jobs for them within about a week, that person would delete the app. We
started burning even more money creating fake assignments to take pho-
tos we didn't need, just to keep them on board.

Behind the scenes was the challenge of developing a ProxyPics platform and mobile app that was secure and user friendly. Luke didn't have the technical expertise for this, so he outsourced all the software development. However, what seemed like a practical strategy turned into a costly misstep. The outsourced software didn't meet requirements and had to be scrapped. That experience prompted Luke to hire a ProxyPics CTO and eventually a small in-house team for other key roles. His decision paid off in the long term, but meeting payroll added to ProxyPics' mounting expenses at a time when revenues were painfully slow to ramp up. With no investor funding, Luke had to dig deeper and deeper into his own pocket to keep operating. It was a very painful few years, but he just wasn't willing to give up,

For almost three years, we had heavy financial losses. Luckily my ap-
praisal companies were doing well, so all of the profits from those com-
panies started flowing into ProxyPics. And I sold almost all of the real
estate I owned to help fund it. That's how we were able to survive. We got
really close to saying it's time to throw in the towel; we just didn't have
any more money to keep going. Then finally, we stopped the bleeding and
had our first break-even year.

In retrospect, the turnaround from burning cash, to achieving a modest profit, to rapid acceleration and increasingly profitable growth stemmed from several strategic steps that Luke implemented during these early years, including advances made possible by the company's embrace of algorithmic models, machine learning, and AI, plus an industry-wide shift to adopt digital documentation. The essential foundation was Luke's entrepreneurial innovation, indomitable resilience, and confidence in the value that ProxyPics could deliver.

An Algorithmic Solution for Crowdsourcing Quality

As part of its turnaround, ProxyPics had to address early issues in the quality of photos taken by tens of thousands of independent Proxies. Inevitably, a subset of the Proxies didn't take their assignments seriously and delivered substandard photos, or even claimed a gig and didn't follow up on it. These instances of uneven quality and delivery delays compromised the service promise ProxyPics made to its clients, so finding a solution became a top priority.

Step one was to back up the quality guidelines in the Proxy app with a system enforcing quality with internal review and feedback. Proxies now receive ratings on all of their work, which encourages professionalism. Low ratings can lead to a Proxy being removed from the platform to protect quality standards. Step two was to establish a cohort of Proxies to undertake more complex or high-stakes jobs, for example photography inside a home or building condition assessments. To qualify, these Proxies had special training and passed background checks.

One of the most innovative aspects of ProxyPics' strategy for improving quality and consistency was implementing an algorithmic approach to managing a very large crowdsourced workforce. The company developed a sophisticated system for evaluating all of its Proxies and assigning them to tiers based on the quality of their work. This algorithm was also used to reward top quality performance by automatically offering new gigs to the highest rated photographers first. As Luke describes it,

> *Tiers are maintained by an automated system, with five levels that are based on a matrix of things like quality of your photos, the speed of your delivery, level of training, your availability to accept gigs, and so on. As Proxies improve on these metrics, they can automatically move up towards the top tier.*

This system ensures that the best performing Proxies get priority for new jobs, and helps to keep all of the Proxies accountable and motivated to deliver their best work. One measurable outcome is improved speed of delivery for client orders. A more qualitative benefit for the company is that establishing vetted Proxy tiers proved to its clients that ProxyPics was serious about holding its gig workforce to professional standards. Instead of an undifferentiated crowdsourced approach, ProxyPics implemented an efficient and cost-effective system to balance openness with necessary filters.

Importantly, the tier system has created a positive flywheel for revenue growth at the same time as reducing the costs of recruiting and managing what is now a Proxy workforce of well over 150,000 gig workers nationwide. Clients are happier with the deliverables, and more likely to increase their order flow. This in turn creates more opportunities for top tier Proxies to earn fees. ProxyPics no longer needs any paid advertising to attract new Proxy photographers. In fact, hundreds of potential Proxies download the mobile app daily and register for assignments based on positive word of mouth.

Leveraging Technology to Deliver More Data and Value

Initially, ProxyPics delivered just the requested photos to its clients, perhaps with a brief explanatory note. But as clients started asking for more detailed information about properties, the company integrated new technologies to transform a simple photo-taking app into a more comprehensive – and higher value—property data collection solution.

Underpinning ProxyPics' ability to deliver this higher value is the company's embrace of data analytics, machine learning, and most recently advanced AI tools to augment human capabilities. Tomaszewski, a tech enthusiast at heart (if not a hands-on practitioner), has made technology innovation a core part of ProxyPics' operations. As the pace of technology adoption accelerated, the ProxyPics mantra essentially became: real-time photos, transformed into meaningful data. To achieve this goal, ProxyPics is leveraging AI tools to automate the once tedious tasks of image annotation and reporting.

Rather than taking on the steep cost of developing AI tools from scratch, the company has partnered with leading AI companies to integrate high-value features into the ProxyPics platform. In collaboration with CubiCasa, ProxyPics added the ability for Proxies to perform quick floor plan scans using a smartphone, generating accurate layouts to accompany photos in a report. In partnership with FoxyAI, the company integrated computer vision and machine learning models for property inspection automation. This technology reduced ProxyPics data collection time by up to 50% through automated property condition assessment, quality scoring, real-time fraud detection, and predictive analytics for pattern recognition. In the past, after a Proxy took photos of a property's interior, they had to manually fill out a lengthy questionnaire, detailing everything from the flooring type in each room to the model of kitchen appliances – so that the client had in-depth info about the property's features. This manual step had "long been considered an annoying but necessary part of the job," Tomaszewski notes.

Today, much of that annotation and ever deeper property condition insights are provided by AI tools. ProxyPics integrated OpenAI's multimodal GPT-4 model into its workflow in 2023–24, enabling the system to analyze photos and automatically populate standard property questionnaires with the details detected through its analysis. If a Proxy uploads a picture of a basement, for example, the AI can identify that it's a finished basement with vinyl plank flooring and even note the presence of, say, a sump pump, all without the Proxy's manual notes. The result is a faster, more consistent data collection process: Proxies can focus on taking excellent photos, while the AI handles the tedious documentation task in seconds – eliminating human error and variance in descriptions.

ProxyPics continues to add new capabilities to its platform and mobile apps, including LiDAR 3D scanning capability, 360-degree photo capture, offline mode functionality, AR-based floor plan scanning, and background upload features. The platform maintains multi-layer quality control through AI-powered review, manual oversight, geolocation verification, time-stamp validation, and sophisticated fraud detection algorithms. These advanced technology features differentiate ProxyPics from its competitors. Equally important, they make ProxyPics' deliverables richer in detail, more accurate, more instantly useful – and more valuable to their clients.

Profitability and Growth Through Industry Transformation

Instead of giving up when he encountered skepticism and regulatory barriers in the real estate, lending, and appraisal sector in the early years of ProxyPics, Luke focused on improving the quality of his company's products and demonstrating the reliability of its data, while also advocating for industry change. When the pandemic lockdowns forced the issue in 2020 and accelerated the adoption of remote solutions in real estate and mortgage lending, his perseverance paid off. ProxyPics' model gained wide acceptance as not just a convenience but a necessity—and the future-facing digital development of the industry.

The year 2020 marked a turning point for product innovation as well as revenue growth at ProxyPics. One new product released during the pandemic was ProxyPics Direct, a "self-inspection" service launched to enable remote data collection when physical visits by appraisers were impractical. By 2021, ProxyPics Direct had effectively expanded the company's toolkit from pure crowdsourcing to a hybrid model, positioning ProxyPics as a versatile inspection platform under any conditions.

ProxyPics achieved a landmark breakthrough by becoming the first approved Property Data Report provider for Freddie Mac's ACE+PDR program and the first software vendor verified to submit PDRs (Property Data Reports) using the Uniform Property Dataset.

These advances coalesced in the Property Data Report product that ProxyPics rolled out in 2022 as part of its Freddie Mac partnership. Instead of just an exterior photo, the PDR delivers a lender a full packet of data in 72 hours on average, including exterior and interior photos, answers to standardized condition questions, and an automatically-generated floor plan, all formatted to Freddie Mac's dataset requirements. For lenders, this dramatically simplified the process of approving certain refinance loans; for ProxyPics, it marked a significant and profitable shift up the value chain from a crowdsourced photo vendor to a provider of end-to-end property inspection reports.

A Stronger Foundation for 100X Growth

In retrospect, even the missteps of the early years at ProxyPics contributed to a stronger foundation for future growth. When outsourcing key elements of its initial platform development resulted in errors, Luke decided to hire a dedicated ProxyPics CTO and bring other key roles in house. By 2025, ProxyPics was still a lean operation, with under 50 employees, but it now has specialists in operations, customer success, and technology to handle the complexities of managing a fast-growing national platform. Delegating and trusting new leadership was a learning curve for Luke as a founder-CEO used to doing things himself. Embracing delegation was an important step that demonstrated ProxyPics' ability to adapt its organizational structure and management processes.

After seeing that early Proxy photographers delivered inconsistent quality of work, ProxyPics developed an advanced, automated model to create a five-tier system that now cost-effectively manages quality metrics for about 180,000 of Proxies nationwide. The company's training and vetting program is well-regarded by its clients and has created a moat that competitors will find hard to replicate.

Finally, by using the painful wait for industry acceptance to enhance its products and systems, ProxyPics positioned itself at the perfect intersection of customer demand and its own ability to deliver advanced, AI-based solutions when digital transformation in property assessment accelerated.

Each challenge met and each mistake corrected has refined ProxyPics' model – making the company's service more resilient, more reliable, and better prepared for the next stage of growth.

These turning points have put ProxyPics on the path to consistent profitability and rapid revenue growth over the past several years. Today the company is well positioned to expand into more industries, effectively increasing its product's value and revenue potential in the years ahead. Facility management is emerging as a significant area for growth. ProxyPics now helps corporations ensure their distributed locations are well-maintained with photographic documentation of parking lot conditions or nighttime lighting audits across hundreds of sites. Fraud prevention is another area ProxyPics services are addressing; for instance, verifying that a remote asset actually exists or checking that a borrower's claimed home improvements were indeed made (with photographic evidence) to deter fraudulent loan applications.

In another expansion breakthrough, ProxyPics onboarded its first client in the insurance sector in 2025, penetrating an industry that has at least as many regulatory barriers as real estate and mortgage lending and achieving one of Luke's key goals for the year.

In addition to ranking #59 on the 2024 Inc. 5000 list of the fastest growing companies in the U.S., ProxyPics was recognized for its leadership and innovation in the mortgage tech sector as the 2025 *HousingWire* Tech100 Mortgage Winner. But Luke Tomaszewski is by no means ready to rest on these laurels. Looking ahead, he has ambitious plans for continued product enhancement and expansion into new markets. ProxyPics revenue was approaching eight figures in 2024. Luke believes that at a minimum ProxyPics can double its revenues every year for the next five years. That's a truly remarkable turnaround story.

From a personal and entrepreneurial perspective, Luke is eager to keep innovating, expanding the verticals that ProxyPics serves, and staying profitable while having fun. As he thinks about the future of ProxyPics, he is not interested in moving towards an exit anytime soon,

At this point, the number of customers is growing and so is our revenue. I don't think about the future of ProxyPics with an eye on potential exits, or imposing revenue targets the way an outside investor might do. We are growing the company, and we're having fun innovating, building new products that solve problems. I'm really happy with that. In fact, I feel that what we have achieved so far is only the beginning.

◆ ◆ ◆

Crisp, Rarebreed, and ProxyPics serve vastly different sectors—retail analytics, veterinary medicine, and real estate data collection—but their rise to market leadership is grounded in a data-centric vision, AI-based innovation, and the perseverance to build trust in skeptical markets. Each founder recognized early on that unlocking real value for customers required more than collecting information—it demanded transforming that data into actionable intelligence through purpose-built platforms, advanced analytics, and strategic applications of AI.

These entrepreneurs all faced significant headwinds before achieving 100X growth. Traasdahl at Crisp spent years piloting and refining his platform with feedback from global retail giants, foregoing early revenue to ensure measurable value and ROI. Dan Espinal at Rarebreed invested in building a proprietary operating system, pushing through doubts to standardize messy veterinary data and empower local clinics with predictive tools. Luke Tomaszewski at ProxyPics bet everything—his savings, his properties, and years of effort—on the conviction that AI and crowdsourced data could modernize a rigid, regulation-heavy industry.

Their persistence turned lagging industries into high-growth markets. Their platforms are now indispensable to the businesses they serve, and their success highlights a critical truth for all founders: The future belongs to those who can harness data not just to inform—but to lead. When AI and analytics are woven into the fabric of operations, new entrants can outperform their competition.

6

Hyper-Efficient Operations for Quality That Scales

OPERATIONAL EFFICIENCY IS the unglamorous but essential engine behind every true scale-up story. In the companies featured throughout this book, we've seen how product-market fit, converting early adopters into evangelists, and demonstrated ROI drive early growth. But when the goal is to achieve long-term 100X growth, efficiency becomes the difference between sustainable success and self-sabotage. Companies that can scale operations without compromising quality, culture, or profitability are the ones that truly break out from the pack. In this chapter, we profile three founders—Michael London of Uwill, Aaron Smith and Callie Turk of FlexCare Infusion Centers, and James Dean of Oxygen8—who built hyper-efficient operational frameworks from the ground up. These frameworks enabled them to deliver exceptional quality and unlock long-term profitability together with extreme growth.

Uwill's promise to universities—to connect students with a licensed therapist in ten minutes or less—would be impossible without a back-end infrastructure fine-tuned for speed, quality, and compliance. Their routing algorithms, therapist network management, and intake processes have been engineered to operate with hyper efficiency. When Uwill acquired other companies to expand its reach, these operations became the basis for seamless integration—allowing the firm to expand its services to reach thousands of new users without disrupting quality of care.

FlexCare Infusion Centers relied on operational efficiencies as their 100X growth foundation. Co-founders Aaron Smith and Callie Turk spent their first year refining every aspect of the clinical and administrative experience at their Oklahoma City clinic. Their investment in standard operating procedures, clinic-in-a-box expansion models, centralized intake and inventory systems, and consistent payer contracting enabled rapid expansion. FlexCare scaled from Oklahoma to over 30 clinic locations across multiple states in less than five years—all while maintaining top-tier patient and referring physician recommendations, strict insurance reimbursement compliance, and a highly productive and motivated team. Their ability to maintain high-touch patient care while rapidly scaling clinical capacity made them a prime acquisition target for Optum, one of the largest healthcare services companies in the U.S.

Oxygen8 took a different but equally effective route to achieve hyper-efficient operations. Rather than developing and building proprietary clean air technology from scratch, James Dean partnered with top-tier European HVAC firms, adapting and certifying their proven systems for North American markets. Oxygen8 generated early revenues with cutting-edge solutions and streamlined operations that bypassed the time and expense of in-house R&D. At every stage of growth, Dean emphasized nimble execution, lean operations, and modular scalability—winning market share with proven product quality, cost-effective sales and marketing, and profitable expansion strategies.

These three founders—each a serial entrepreneur with hard-won insights from earlier ventures—understood a fundamental truth: if your operations can't handle 100X expansion, neither can your business. Quality, brand reputation, and customer trust are fragile assets during periods of rapid growth. To capitalize on explosive market demand, a company's operations must be engineered for hyper-efficiency and excellence from day one.

Uwill

Michael London's founding vision for Uwill fuses social mission and entrepreneurial rigor. A serial entrepreneur with four prior startup exits, London's career has focused on education technology ventures that deliver positive social impact. "I wouldn't be starting a new company only for the money at this point," he says at the start of our conversation, noting that his founding vision for Uwill was to use his experience to radically improve access to mental health for college students.

In 2019, London was hearing a frequent concern from higher education leaders: student mental health was in crisis. Traditional campus counseling centers were stretched thin and oriented around in-person services for on-campus students. Large segments of the student population were underserved. London realized that this crisis was an opportunity to "create a solution based on technology that would truly be complementary to what was offered on college campuses," bridging gaps for students unwilling or unable to attend in-person counseling.

Michael London's prior ventures had built credibility, expertise, and deep relationships in higher education. He leveraged these strengths to partner to pilot Uwill's platform with a small number of early adopters. London positioned Uwill not as another teletherapy startup, but as an extension of campus mental health services designed to relieve counseling center overload while significantly expanding student access.

The timing was prescient: when the pandemic struck and campus life went virtual, the demand for remote counseling solutions exploded. Uwill was ready to meet the moment, accelerating its rollout as colleges urgently sought ways to support students' well-being with online therapy options. This convergence of London's social-impact vision and acute market need laid the foundation for rapid growth.

Scalable Access to Student Mental Health Services

At the heart of Uwill's success is an innovative business model that delivers mental health support as a scalable subscription service for institutions. Unlike traditional counseling or telehealth services that charge per session or per hour, the company offers what London calls an "environment" – a comprehensive mental wellness platform tailored to each client campus. Schools partner with Uwill on a subscription basis, typically through multi-year contracts, to provide their students with a suite of services including on-demand therapy appointments, a crisis line available 24/7/365, and virtual wellness programs. Importantly, Uwill's contracts are not metered by individual counseling sessions. "We're not counting sessions. We're giving you what you feel you need, pricing it accordingly and exceeding expectations," London explains of the approach. In practice, this means a university might pay a flat annual or multi-year fee for Uwill's platform to ensure access for its entire student body, rather than purchasing a specific number of counseling hours. Uwill's pricing scales primarily with the size and needs of the institution – but always within a flexible framework, and with a model of value delivered rather than a simple markup on therapist time.

This model has SaaS characteristics with an essential twist. On one hand, Uwill's offering behaves like a cloud service: an upfront subscription provides client institutions with broad access for its users, and usage can fluctuate without incurring per-use fees. On the other hand, Uwill's mental health support is grounded on real human-to-human services, not some AI-based system. Uwill maintains a network of licensed counselors, vetted to ensure consistently high quality in each live online session they conduct. And while the educational client pays on an annual or multi-year subscription basis, Uwill pays its counselors for each session delivered.

Balancing these factors, London designed service level agreements based on the type of school and projected client "utilization bands." This approach helped to ensure that even if student demand and usage occasionally spikes, the service remains financially viable for the client and profitable for Uwill over the life of the contract. For example, a large residential university will predictably see higher utilization than a small online college, so pricing and capacity planning account for those differences. In all cases, the focus is on long-term partnership: over 80% of client institutions sign auto-renewing or 3-5 year agreements, in effect making Uwill a permanent part of their campus wellness infrastructure. Uwill becomes the behind-the-scenes extension of the college's counseling center – whether that means providing unlimited teletherapy to students who need it or, conversely, handling only overflow and after-hours crises while campus staff manage routine counseling. "We can be who you want us to be, and it should complement what you offer," London says, highlighting the flexible customization options that make Uwill's services a fit for many different institutions' needs.

The revenue mechanics of this model are a foundation for expansion in tandem with cash-conscious financial management. Uwill invoices colleges (its B2B clients) for services upfront on a term basis (annual or multi-year), and only compensates its counselors (who are 1099 contractors) after sessions take place. This means positive cash flow – the company gets paid in advance and can manage payouts in arrears, which significantly eases working capital demands. It's a deliberate contrast to many venture-funded startups that burn cash to subsidize growth. London, influenced by his prior ventures, designed Uwill around unit economics that made sense from the start. "If you have something of value, you should be able to sell it profitably and operate it profitably," he argues, noting that Uwill didn't fall into the trap of chasing unicorn-style growth at the expense of massive losses. This disciplined approach set Uwill on a path to early profitability while building a sustainable and highly efficient operational foundation for scale.

Measurable Value, Operational Efficiency, and Financial Discipline

Uwill's growth strategy is characterized by a blend of efficient operations and ambitious goal-setting. In the early years, London focused on sales and customer acquisition as the primary engine for growth, personally leveraging his network to sign up the first cohort of colleges. Uwill leveraged its initial $5.2 million in angel startup funding to achieve profitability by its third year of operations, an impressive milestone for a young edtech company. As the product proved its value and word spread in higher-education circles, Uwill's client list expanded rapidly. By May 2023 the company had over 150 colleges on board, including prominent names like Dartmouth College, University of Michigan, and Florida Gulf Coast University.

This traction teed up a $30 million Series A funding round led by Education Growth Partners, a private equity firm focused on education technology. The capital infusion was earmarked to scale the business – enhancing the platform's technology, recruiting more therapists, and ramping up sales to reach even more campuses. It provided Uwill with a war chest to support its expansion, but the company's financial trajectory was already distinguishing it from typical startups. London recalls that by year three his company was "very profitable," all while never "burning a lot of money" even in the ramp-up phase. This prudent growth – scaling revenues nearly in step with expenses – made Uwill attractive to investors precisely because it wasn't a cash-burning risk.

From day one, Uwill has focused on delivering clear, measurable value for both the institutional clients and their students. That strategy paid off by creating a virtuous cycle of adoption: satisfied institutions renewed and expanded their commitments, providing capital to invest in further growth without deep losses. By late 2024, Michael London anticipated reaching $25– 30 million in revenue for the year, capping off a trajectory of doubling revenues annually while maintaining profitability. This rapid growth rate earned Uwill the #27 spot on the *Inc. 5000* list of fastest growing companies in 2024. It was #1 for growth among Massachusetts-based companies, as well as raking

#18 on the Deloitte Technology Fast 500, cementing its reputation as a rising star in education technology and mental health.

London emphasizes that marketing and lead generation has become increasingly important for Uwill. The company invests in branding itself as a thought leader in student wellness and its national brand recognition is growing. Uwill's sales team targets colleges and universities across all 50 states, and the company has also succeeded with innovative channels such as statewide partnerships. A notable example was Uwill's agreement with the New Jersey Office of the Secretary of Higher Education in 2023 to provide 24/7 teletherapy access to students across 45 colleges in the state. This first-in-the-nation statewide initiative effectively turned a government entity into a channel partner, subsidizing Uwill's service for numerous institutions in one sweep. It demonstrated Uwill's creative approach to scaling distribution, and the partnership's success led New Jersey to renew it through 2026.

Customer Acquisition and Long-Term Retention

Uwill's client growth is impressive; even more striking is its ability to retain and expand existing relationships. More than 90% of colleges that contract with Uwill continue their partnership in subsequent years. That's an extraordinary retention rate in B2B services, and achieving it is not by chance. London views client retention as one of the clearest measures of Uwill's value: "we retain clients at a very high rate – in the 90-something percent overall," he notes with pride. "When someone's willing to pay for your services again and again...that says something,"

From the beginning, Uwill structured its offerings and contracts to foster long-term integration into a campus' support system. Multi-year agreements with auto-renewal clauses are common, which reduces churn. But beyond contract structures, Uwill earns loyalty by delivering consistent results and making itself indispensable to campus mental health and well-being efforts. University leaders see Uwill not as a short-term stopgap but as an ongoing extension of their counseling resources. As more and more of the student body benefits from the teletherapy provided by Uwill, replacing this flexible, extensible counseling platform becomes a daunting task. In essence, Uwill creates a value proposition that makes renewal the obvious choice: students are getting help, the institution's own counseling staff workload is more manageable, and the administration has a scalable solution for a persistent problem.

To achieve such stickiness, Uwill pays close attention to customer success and usage data. The company shares detailed usage reports and outcomes with client institutions (within the bounds of privacy laws) to demonstrate impact and transparency. One of the most impressive commitments that the company makes is a radical reduction in the time it takes to match students seeking help with qualified therapists, compared to the norm for on-campus appointment availability. Uwill will typically schedule a student with a chosen counselor in under five minutes, no matter where the student is located. If a student is in crisis, Uwill's platform connects them to a counselor within 30 seconds.

London notes that being "transparent with all data" – for example, providing dashboards of how many students utilized therapy and the average wait time for appointments – builds trust with schools. It helps shift the conversation away from a simplistic cost-per-session mindset to a broader understanding of value. If an administrator ever questions, "We only had X counseling calls this month, is it worth it?" Uwill can highlight that many of those calls addressed serious issues and point out that quickly connecting a student to a therapist may well have averted a severe mental crisis. Given staffing and budget limitations, providing a counseling service available around the clock, seven days a week, is beyond the reach of most colleges and universities. But administrators understand that providing such access is a critical issue in the minds of many students today – and even more so in the minds of their parents. A partnership with Uwill can become a vital and cost-effective service extension, while proving the institution's commitment to student wellbeing.

In practice, usage rates tend to fall within predictable ranges, which Uwill and its clients mutually understand. As of 2023, Uwill's platform was available to over 1.5 million students and roughly 5–10% of those students actively used the service for counseling, according to London. That level of utilization – tens of thousands of counseling sessions – is significant, yet it remains manageable and sustainable given Uwill's therapist community size. Knowing these patterns, Uwill can reassure new clients that its service can handle peak demand (such as during exams or after holidays when mental health needs spike) without breaking the model. And for clients, a 5-10% usage rate often means hundreds of students are getting support that the campus might otherwise struggle to provide, a clear win for student outcomes.

Leveraging AI and Data Analytics for Human-Centered Service

While Uwill thrives on delivering human-to-human teletherapy services, technology plays a critical role in its operations and the robustness of its platform. London's philosophy is to use technology pragmatically to enhance service delivery, not as a replacement for human care. For example, Uwill has developed a proprietary matching algorithm that pairs students with the most suitable therapist based on the student's preferences and needs. London describes this as an "AI light" solution – essentially a smart routing system that takes into account factors like a counselor's specialty, availability, and the student's presenting issues to achieve a compatible match quickly.

Using the Uwill platform, students can request an appointment, choose a therapist, and arrange an appointment time within a few minutes. If a student is in crisis, Uwill's platform connects them to a counselor within 30 seconds – an almost instantaneous response made possible by an always-on triage system and available on-call clinicians. These speed metrics (which Uwill tracks diligently) are far beyond what most campus counseling centers could achieve on their own, underscoring how technology enables better access. "We really get people an appointment within five minutes, regardless of where they are in the world...same thing within 30 seconds if someone's in crisis, and we track it," London confirms, highlighting those as key operational metrics for service quality.

To further refine its ability to track the pulse of student mental health, and the potential demand for specialized services, Uwill has been developing a system for measuring counseling outcomes in a more nuanced way. London envisions a "general resiliency scale" that could be paired with progress measures that align with each student's specific issue. Instead of relying on generic one-size-fits-all surveys (like asking every student "How are you feeling on a scale of 1–10?"), Uwill's approach could, for example, track improvements in resiliency for one student or reductions in anxiety symptoms for another. This forward-thinking use of data aims to provide more meaningful insights into the impact of counseling – data that could be valuable not only to colleges but to the broader field of student mental health. It reflects Uwill's balance of technology and compassion: using analytics to ensure that the human-delivered care is effective.

While he is impressed at the capabilities of today's AI tools, London draws a sharp line at AI-based therapy replacing human interventions. In his view, the stakes in mental health are too high to hand off counseling to a chatbot or AI agent, at least with current technology. "Allowing the AI to be the support" for a student in need is risky and not something Uwill will do, he insists. London predicts some companies in the industry might try fully automated therapy, but he's not willing to take that gamble with student well-being. Uwill's adoption of AI is incremental and ethically grounded – it enhances matching, scales triage, and monitors safety, but stops short of replacing the human connection in counseling.

Metrics that Matter at Uwill

In steering Uwill's growth and operations, Michael London is highly metrics-driven. He believes in quantifying success, both to manage the business and to demonstrate value to clients. Some of the key performance indicators (KPIs) that London monitors include:

- **Student Utilization Metrics:** how many students register for the platform at each campus and how many ultimately engage with each of the services (therapy, crisis line, wellness events) over time, including the peaks and valleys of usage. Utilization data guides internal resource allocation, ensuring enough counselors are available at high-demand times; they also help clients understand student needs and the value that Uwill provides.
- **Service Delivery Speed:** the time to first appointment and crisis response time as critical quality metrics. Consistently achieving an appointment within 5 minutes or a sub-minute crisis response is a point of pride. Any slowdown triggers operational adjustments, such as onboarding more counselors or load-balancing across time zones. These speed metrics set Uwill apart and are often highlighted to schools as evidence of superior service.
- **Student Outcomes & Satisfaction:** feedback from student users is collected to help monitor outcomes. These data points provide validation that Uwill is making a difference in students' lives. High satisfaction ratings or positive outcome trends also support Uwill's customer retention, demonstrating that the value of Uwill services can't be summed up by counting the number of sessions.

- **Client Retention & Expansion:** the renewal rate of institutional clients is a crucial metric for Uwill, and includes analysis of how many clients renew contracts, upgrade to larger service packages, or expand the service scope. Internally, Uwill also measures its success in integrating the clients who come on board as a result of the companies it has acquired. Successfully onboarding 100% of acquired customers, and keeping satisfaction rates high, is a key goal for the team and a metric of acquisition effectiveness.

- **Sales Pipeline Metrics:** sales funnel metrics include number of leads, conversion rates, sales cycle length, and new client signings per quarter. By late 2024, acquiring roughly one new institutional client per week became a yardstick, reflecting the pace of growth.

- **Financial Performance:** key financial metrics include revenue (tracked against projections), profitability, and cash flow. Even as the company invests in growth, London watches gross margins and operating expenses, observing that while many founders ignore "the basics" of financial performance, for him those fundamentals are non-negotiable.

- **Employee and Team Metrics:** Finally, London tracks internal team metrics such as employee retention and productivity. One remarkable statistic: Uwill had lost only four full-time employees in its first five years (through resignations or terminations). London believes that low turnover is a key indicator of a healthy workplace and effective team building. High employee retention translates to accumulated expertise and faster execution – new hires become productive by month two on average, he notes, thanks to hiring carefully and often recruiting known talent from his past companies. London views the strength of his core team as a metric that underlies all others: if the team is engaged and experienced, they will drive the sales, service, and innovation metrics in the right direction. It's why he rates "staffing, productivity and culture" as a top priority area in scaling the business.

Together, these metrics form the dashboard for London's management of Uwill. They balance mission (how many students helped, how well) and margin (revenue, renewals, profitability), reflecting his philosophy that a well-run business achieves both impact and income. This analytical rigor, combined with Uwill's social mission, creates a powerful feedback loop for continuous improvement.

Accelerating Growth with Strategic Acquisitions

Acquisitions have become an important component of accelerating Uwill's growth over the past few years. In the highly fragmented market of student mental health services, London identified several smaller competitors and niche providers that were serving a significant number of college clients but that lacked Uwill's financial stability, scale, and advanced technology. By selectively acquiring such companies, Uwill is increasing its market reach and adding large client cohorts to its platform – a classic industry roll-up strategy.

Uwill's first acquisition came in late 2023 when it purchased Christie Campus Health (CCH), a provider of mental health and wellness support that was serving about 100 colleges. For London, acquiring CCH made strategic sense on multiple fronts. First, it added a significant block of new clients and users, expanding Uwill's coverage to over 2 million students across more than 300 colleges nationwide. Second, CCH brought valuable relationships and an experienced campus counseling team.

In 2024, Uwill acquired The Virtual Care Group (VCG), a student telehealth provider. VCG brought with it another group of about 100 colleges. These two acquisitions – CCH and VCG – are illustrative of London's broader growth-through-acquisition strategy. Strategically, the VCG acquisition wasn't just about numbers; it further demonstrated Uwill's intention to be the consolidator in the industry, uniting a scattered field of campus mental health providers under the strongest available platform.

Company Culture and Leadership with Impact

Michael London's leadership of Uwill exemplifies his deep belief that entrepreneurship can be a powerful force for good. He has built a high-growth venture that directly addresses a pressing social problem – the student mental health crisis – with a sustainable, profitable business model. This alignment of mission and margin is core to London's belief that truly helping the students and institutions it serves is the most effective strategy for building the trust and market demand that in turn fuel his company's financial success. He is described by colleagues as a "social impact leader with a passion for supporting students" and simultaneously lauded as "one of the great company builders in EdTech."

Employees understand that Uwill's goal is to create social impact *and* to be a successful enterprise. Uwill's team members embrace innovation – for example, pioneering new teletherapy techniques and outcome measures – at the same time as they carefully monitor key metrics such as customer retention and sales pipelines. Another cultural cornerstone is collaboration: because London intentionally complements campus services rather than competes with them, Uwill's employees often interface with university counseling staff in a cooperative and collaborative way.

The importance of culture is also evident in Uwill's navigation of growth challenges. Rapid expansion and acquisitions can often dilute a culture or unsettle a team, but Uwill has managed these transitions smoothly by keeping communication clear and reinforcing the mission at every step. Recognitions like London being named one of the *Boston Business Journal*'s "2025 Innovators in Healthcare" also reflect well on the team and boost morale. It signals that their work is noticed and valued in the wider community. The team's dedication and stability enable Uwill to deliver consistently high-quality service, which in turn reinforces the strong client retention and growth that the company enjoys. As London says, it's all connected.

Planning the Next Phase of Growth

Uwill has already grown to serve students at more than 400 colleges worldwide, and London believes that a realistic growth target is expanding his company's customer base to roughly 1,000 partner schools within three years. In terms of future revenue growth, he projects that Uwill can roughly triple its revenue during this period, approaching "close to $100 million" in annual revenue, with a more conservative goal to hit at least $75 million. This would mark a dramatic rise from the company's $25–30 million range in 2024.

The path to extreme growth will include deeper penetration into the higher education market through a blend of direct sales, continued strategic acquisitions, and expansion into related wellness areas. While Uwill's core offering will remain teletherapy for educational institutions, London is well aware that adding new services would increase revenue per client. One example is the company's introduction of an array of student wellness programming, such as yoga, meditation and mindfulness. Another area of growth could be providing mental health and general wellness services for the faculty and staff of client institutions.

Uwill is already establishing itself in selected K-12 schools, and London is thinking about expanding more aggressively into this market. He points out the strong parallels between higher ed and secondary education in terms of student mental health needs. "They remind me a lot of higher ed, they're just about 2–5 years behind," he says of K-12 schools, observing that school district demand for student mental health support is rising sharply. If Uwill can replicate even a fraction of its higher ed success in the K-12 arena, the total addressable market multiplies greatly – there are about 13,000 school districts and many thousands of private schools in the U.S. While Uwill won't serve all of those, even capturing key districts or networks could drive significant revenue.

Another pillar of Uwill's three-year growth strategy will be expanding its footprint outside the United States. London describes Uwill in 2025 as "international light" – they have some counselors outside the U.S. and are already serving students in 40 countries via existing client institutions. The expansion goal is to convert that international reach into formal client relationships with institutions based abroad. Going forward, Uwill will prioritize growing its presence in Canada and the United Kingdom, followed by other English-speaking parts of Europe. These markets share similar higher education systems and challenges with student mental health, making Uwill's value proposition relevant.

London's vision for the future of Uwill is to become the undisputed leader in education-focused mental health technology, in the U.S. and in select global markets. He frames this vision not just in terms of market success and revenues, but in the context of the company's human and social impact. As Michael London leads Uwill in its next phase of growth, that blend of competitive drive and social mission will remain his north star.

FlexCare Infusion Centers

For Aaron Smith, the cofounder and CEO of FlexCare Infusion Centers, the path to founding one of the fastest-growing specialty infusion companies in the United States did not begin in a boardroom or with a business plan — it began with a family crisis. Smith opens our conversation by recalling how his mother-in-law's struggle to receive timely treatment for a chronic disease sparked his determination to create the solution that would become FlexCare.

As Smith tells the story,

My mother-in-law, after living with Crohn's disease for 15 years, went into a phase where her disease became very aggressive. To treat it, her doctor referred her to receive a biologic therapy. And just by pure co-incidence or however the world works, I was working for an infusion services company at the time and had become familiar with biologic treatments. The drug she was prescribed was an effective treatment for aggressive Crohn's disease, and I was happy to hear she would be getting it. But somehow, things went off the rails after her doctor's referral. The approval to actually get her on the therapy was delayed for five months.

We worked together as a family to untangle all the paperwork problems that held up approval, so she could finally start the treatment. But that five months of waiting became pretty dicey for her health, because with Crohn's Disease, time delay means tissue loss. Biologics will stop the progression of the disease, but patients can't get that tissue back. The most frustrating thing for me was knowing that this problem should never have happened. It was a failure in the system that was wholly and completely preventable.

My takeaway out of the experience was two things: First, such a long delay should never happen—to my mother-in-law or to any other patient. Second, solving this problem will help patients and their doctors -and there's a business opportunity in doing it right.

Aaron Smith had identified a critical problem at the heart of a fast-growing, multi-billion-dollar sector of the healthcare industry: the systemic failure to efficiently coordinate care, referrals, and drug approvals for high-cost, high-impact infusion therapies. His family's experience inspired a clear and urgent mission for FlexCare: eliminate the friction in getting patients timely access to biologics, especially for those with chronic conditions. Drawing on his recent work in infusion services at another company, and decades as an entrepreneur building software and systems for healthcare innovation, Smith quickly focused on the top priorities for launching his new venture:

I knew how to build tech solutions from my prior companies, but I also knew that wouldn't be enough. I needed a founding partner with deep expertise in managing infusion center operations and protocols. Then we would require outside investors to grow the business in its early years. Given the cost of biologics, we would need to purchase tens of millions of dollars-worth of drugs every month. Even buying those drugs on credit would take significant capital resources. And I knew that actually reducing approval times for treatment and delivering high-quality care required a high-functioning software system and a skilled team that would embrace the mission of putting the patient first.

That added up to three clear priorities for launching FlexCare: Finding the right partner, then raising the capital needed to scale, and thirdly investing in the technology and the people who would support our vision for radically reducing treatment delays.

Proof Point One: Oklahoma City, 2019

Callie Turk, a registered nurse with a background in specialty pharmacy and home infusions, checked all the boxes as FlexCare's cofounder. A dedicated clinician, Turk brought deep operational and compliance expertise to the startup. She understood the shortcomings of hospital-based and pharmacy-based infusion models and was passionate about creating a more convenient, comfortable option for patients and referring physicians. Most importantly, she shared Smith's mission and determination to build infusion clinics that were "more effective, less expensive, easier for physicians and overall better for patients." Alignment around FlexCare's founding mission – "to fight for our patients as if they are our own family" – set the tone for working together with Smith on the challenge of transforming their industry sector.

FlexCare opened its first clinic in Oklahoma City in June 2019, operating as a standalone, multi-specialty infusion center offering intravenous therapies for complex chronic conditions. Unlike hospital infusion suites that often require long waits and inconvenient scheduling, FlexCare's model focused on accessibility and patient comfort. The inaugural clinic featured private infusion suites, flexible appointment times, and amenities like free snacks and entertainment to put patients at ease. This patient-centric design was very intentional – as Turk noted, they "wanted to make it not seem like you're going to a hospital or a physician's office."

From the beginning, FlexCare also worked to streamline the behind-the-scenes process for patients and referring doctors. The team handled insurance pre-authorizations, benefits verification, and appeals for denied claims, aiming to reduce delays in treatment. By seeing "the infusion journey through the eyes of patients and referring providers," FlexCare's founders hoped to eliminate the friction and frustration that so often characterized standard infusion therapy access. An important path to reducing friction was to merge clinical excellence with convenience, by delivering high-quality infusion treatments in a local, outpatient setting. That shift saved patients time and also saved the healthcare system money by avoiding costly hospital visits. This vision resonated strongly with referring physicians in the community, who appreciated having an alternative infusion site that reduced the burden on doctors by streamlining paperwork and handling patient follow-up. It also tapped into a growing need among busy patients (including working professionals and small business owners managing chronic illnesses) for infusion services that could accommodate their schedules. By late 2019, FlexCare's Oklahoma City clinic was serving a steady stream of patients and validating the market demand for more convenient infusion care.

Financially, the company's early months were modest but promising. Having opened mid-year, FlexCare generated revenue in the low six figures that first year –enough to demonstrate proof of concept. Aaron Smith had raised a small pool of capital to get the first center up and running. The founders kept the operation lean, often taking on multiple roles themselves to control costs. This scrappiness reflected their commitment to disciplined management of unit economics and cash flow from the outset, even as they pursued growth.

In practice, this meant FlexCare founders were careful not to overextend the company's financial resources early on: they negotiated favorable terms with drug suppliers, staged hiring and onboarding staff as patient volume grew, and meticulously planned the sequence of obtaining clinic licenses, payer contracts, and drug purchasing agreements to avoid cash flow gaps as they opened new locations in the coming years. These prudent practices during the founding phase laid a solid financial foundation that would support FlexCare's rapid expansion in the years to come.

Fine-Tuning the FlexCare Value Proposition and Scaling Its Operations

During 2020, FlexCare focused on proving its model in Oklahoma and building the operational backbone for future growth. The Oklahoma City flagship clinic gained traction as more physicians learned of the patient-first platform and began referring their infusion patients. Word spread that FlexCare could start new patients on therapy faster than hospitals – thanks to its "rapid referral management and time-to-treatment" processes – and could do so in a lower-cost setting, which appealed to patients, providers, and insurance payers alike. In defining FlexCare's value proposition, Smith emphasized messaging around convenience, quality, and cost: patients could receive biologic infusions locally with extended hours (including evenings and weekends) for those who "can't afford a day off work," and payers would save significantly compared to hospital infusion charges. This value proposition – better experience at lower cost – became the cornerstone of FlexCare's marketing and was communicated through the company's website, informational brochures, and meetings with insurance networks.

During this period, Smith, as CEO, concentrated on sales and marketing efforts to create local brand awareness, while Turk, as COO, refined internal operations. A key early hire was an intake coordinator who liaised with referring doctors and handled insurance authorizations. By taking on the administrative burden, FlexCare made it simple for busy specialty practices – such as rheumatologists and gastroenterologists in private practice – to send patients to their center.   In parallel, the company worked on building relationships with referring clinics through lunch-and-learn meetings, physician network events, and one-on-one outreach by Smith and his small sales team. This was essentially a B2B marketing strategy; although time-intensive, it was much more targeted and cost-effective than advertising to the general public at this stage.

Operationally, 2020 was about establishing scalable processes. Callie Turk leveraged her compliance background to implement rigorous protocols for safety, drug storage, and clinical documentation early on, which ensured the young company met all regulatory requirements for an ambulatory infusion center. She also instituted detailed nursing checklists and emergency procedures, creating what she described as an extensive library of infusion protocols. These standard operating protocols (SOPs) helped to thoroughly systematize the clinical operations. The early investment in SOPs paid dividends as the company later duplicated its model in new locations.

Another challenge in 2020 was securing contracts with major insurance payers in Oklahoma. As a new standalone provider, FlexCare had to negotiate reimbursement terms from scratch. Navigating this sequence required patience, a realistic timeline, and careful cash management, since revenue could only flow after all the pieces fell into place. COVID-19 temporarily slowed some referral streams as the pandemic curtailed elective office visits. Soon, however, FlexCare's stand-alone clinic model and extended hours became an advantage. Many immunocompromised patients felt safer receiving infusions in a private clinic with prompt appointments instead of being treated in a crowded hospital. FlexCare adapted by implementing strict infection control measures and even treating some patients in isolated suites or in their cars during the worst of COVID, ensuring continuity of care. By late 2020, the clinic's patient volume had rebounded and grown beyond pre-pandemic levels, validating that demand for accessible infusion therapy was durable.

By the end of 2020, FlexCare Infusion Centers was still a single-city operation but with strong fundamentals. The Oklahoma City clinic had treated a few hundred patients that year and built a reputation for high patient satisfaction – evidenced by glowing testimonials and a Net Promoter Score (NPS) consistently above 90, a truly impressive figure for its first full year, amidst the disruption of the pandemic. In October 2020, the company secured a private equity investment led by River Cities Capital (RC Capital), providing growth capital at a pivotal stage and officially turning the startup into a growth-stage company. With funding in hand and a proven model, FlexCare prepared to accelerate its expansion in 2021 while still maintaining a lean operating strategy and disciplined financial management.

Expanding to Provide Regional Services

Armed with new capital and momentum, FlexCare embarked on an ambitious regional expansion strategy during 2021 and 2022. By November 2021, just two and a half years after founding, FlexCare was operating five infusion centers across Oklahoma and Alabama. To achieve this milestone, FlexCare had scaled its internal operations and logistics rapidly while maintaining the high-quality, patient-centered experience of its founding mission. The still small corporate team centralized key functions to drive efficiency. For instance, referral intake and insurance verification for all the clinics were managed through a central hub, ensuring consistency and fast onboarding of patients across the network. Drug inventory management was also centralized: medications (expensive biologics like infliximab and immunoglobulin) were purchased via a group purchasing organization and distributed to clinics as needed, a cost-effective move that avoided duplication and waste.

Callie Turk oversaw the hiring and training of new nursing staff, instilling FlexCare's culture and protocols at each site. Maintaining quality during rapid expansion was a top concern – Turk's background in compliance helped here, as she ensured each new clinic met the same rigorous standards as the flagship. A lesson from early growth was to never cut corners on training: each nurse and staff member spent time at the Oklahoma City location learning "the FlexCare way" of doing things before their clinic opened. This growth marked a pivot point in FlexCare's trajectory: from a single-state operator to a regional player with multistate presence. It demonstrated the company's ability to replicate its model and proved that the concept was not location-bound.

Importantly, FlexCare remained focused on unit economics – ensuring each clinic would be poised for long-term profitability. The infusion centers were launched in areas with strong referral pipelines, and FlexCare was careful not to overspend on lavish facilities or unnecessary overhead. This discipline meant that, by late 2021, the overall company was on track with its financial resources, with the revenues from established clinics subsidizing newer ones, and moving steadily toward profitability as a whole.

By 2022, FlexCare was prepared to embark on an accelerated growth strategy. It acquired Arizona-based InfuseAble Care, instantly creating a significant footprint in the Western U.S. and nearly doubling its clinical locations from 5 clinics to 11. Within a few months, the integration was largely complete, and FlexCare could boast a seamless platform of 11 clinics operating under a consistent model across three states. The InfuseAble Care acquisition also proved FlexCare's ability to execute a roll-up strategy, signaling a maturation in the company's growth approach. By the end of 2022, the company had grown to 16 clinics across Oklahoma, Alabama, and Arizona. Revenues surged accordingly – jumping into the tens of millions as the patient count swelled. The company was now servicing thousands of infusion patients annually, many of whom were relieved to have a local option for therapies like IV immunoglobulin, monoclonal antibodies for autoimmune diseases, and other biologics.

In August 2023, Inc. magazine ranked FlexCare Infusion Centers No. 6 on the Inc. 5000 list of America's fastest-growing private companies, with an extraordinary three-year revenue growth of 35,012% (growth measured from 2019 through 2022). This placed FlexCare as the #2 fastest-growing company in Health Services nationwide, and #1 in its home state of Oklahoma. The *Inc. 5000* recognition underscored that FlexCare's founding vision had evolved into a scalable, multi-million-dollar enterprise poised for scalable growth.

Even more impressive, FlexCare's extreme growth came at the same time that the company achieved firm-wide profitability and continued to expand its clinical operations. Its long-standing financial discipline and focus on unit economics had paid off.

As Aaron Smith recalls,

Looking back to 2019, in that first half-year of operations our revenue was about $200,000. Going forward, we managed our operations to be as lean as possible in tandem with high-quality, patient-first services, to ensure that we were on a path to profitability. In our first few years, profitability was deferred by our heavy upfront investment in continued growth. We deliberately used a lot of the capital we raised to expand to new locations and grow our top line. But we kept a close eye on managing our cash and margins, so year by year, many of our clinics became profitable and FlexCare as a whole became profitable four and a half years in.

Reaching our clinic expansion and profitability milestones also bumped up our revenue goals. By the end of 2024, we had reached $300 million in revenues, and we planned to set revenue goals to be even higher for our next three years.

Marketing, Sales and Customer Acquisition: Balancing Cost-Effectiveness with Scale

FlexCare's ascent from a local startup to a multi-state brand was underpinned by multi-level marketing around its strong value proposition. From the beginning, the company crafted its brand around patient-centric, accessible care – a message that differentiated it from hospital infusion centers. The brand message had to resonate with reaching physicians (who are the referral source) and patients (who must feel comfortable choosing an independent infusion center).

The nature of infusion services meant that physician referrals were the lifeblood of the business, especially in its early years. Therefore, FlexCare's sales strategy heavily emphasized B2B relationship-building with referring providers. Aaron Smith and his team approached this much like a pharmaceutical sales operation or clinic outreach program. They hired account managers assigned to key specialties and geographies. These account managers functioned as liaisons, ensuring referring doctors had a direct point of contact at FlexCare for any needed follow up. By providing impeccable service to the first cohort of referring doctors and then sharing those success stories, FlexCare grew its referrals exponentially through word-of-mouth. In interviews, Smith emphasized how critical these physician relationships were: "If we remain dedicated to our mission, growth will remain strong," he noted, crediting provider collaboration as key to FlexCare's rapid growth. Indeed, the company's provider-focused marketing paid off when several physicians who were initially skeptical of an outside infusion center became some of FlexCare's strongest evangelists when their patients reported excellent experiences.

FlexCare gradually layered in traditional marketing and advertising strategies, especially as it expanded to new regions. The company's branding highlighted its core value proposition for patients. Marketing collateral and the website described FlexCare as *"re-imagining the infusion experience"* by offering *comfortable clinics, convenient scheduling, and faster access to treatment*. A consistent tagline communicated the patient-first ethos: FlexCare's mission statement on marketing materials read, *"we advocate for our patients like we would for members of our own families"*. This familial, caring tone helped humanize the brand in what can be a high-stress healthcare context. FlexCare also differentiated itself by explicitly advertising its time-saving and convenience advantages, knowing that many infusion patients are busy individuals juggling work and family. The clinics offered evening and weekend appointments – a rarity in the infusion space – and marketing messages underscored that *infusions don't have to disrupt your life*. By emphasizing flexible scheduling and local access, FlexCare effectively generated demand among those who previously might have delayed or avoided infusion therapy due to time constraints.

Another pillar of FlexCare's marketing was education and thought leadership. Understanding that specialty infusions are a niche service unfamiliar to many patients, the company invested in content marketing. Its website and social media shared patient success stories, FAQs about biologic medications, and explanations of how ambulatory infusion centers operate. This educational content not only served SEO purposes (many found FlexCare by searching for treatment options for conditions like Crohn's Disease or multiple sclerosis in their area) but also built trust. Prospective patients, upon reading about how an infusion center could be "more affordable and comfortable than a hospital" with the same clinical quality, were more inclined to ask their doctor about FlexCare. In one notable piece of content, FlexCare produced a short video tour of a clinic, showcasing the private suites, the reclining chairs, and the smiling nurses. This video was shared on Facebook and via targeted email campaigns to local patient advocacy groups, effectively creating brand awareness in communities of patients with chronic illnesses. FlexCare's social media presence – while not massive – was used strategically to celebrate milestones (like new clinic openings or the Inc. 5000 award) and to humanize the brand by highlighting team members and patient testimonials. These efforts cultivated an image of FlexCare as both professional and compassionate.

To scale this strategy while controlling marketing costs, FlexCare was judicious in targeting. They focused on high-yield specialties and areas: for example, rheumatologists, gastroenterologists, neurologists, and immunologists who regularly prescribe infusions for conditions like rheumatoid arthritis, Crohn's disease, MS, or immunodeficiencies. Within each specialty, they identified key opinion leaders and early adopters – doctors who were more likely to try referring outside the traditional hospital system. By providing exceptional service to those first few, FlexCare gained testimonials that helped convince more conservative physicians. This network effect meant that in each new city, they didn't have to make sales calls to every provider; rather, they leveraged influential supporters. An illustrative milestone was in Birmingham: after one prominent rheumatology group started sending patients and reported shorter infusion wait times and happier patients, several other practices in the city followed suit. By 2023, the company had built a roster of referring providers who were essentially repeat customers. Many clinics incorporated FlexCare into their standard treatment workflow (for instance, handing patients a FlexCare brochure or electronic referral during an office visit), which meant steady inbound referrals without constant reselling.

On the patient acquisition front, FlexCare had to ensure that once a patient was referred, they chose to come and then remained with FlexCare for ongoing therapy. Excellent customer experience and convenience became their de facto sales tool. The company's internal mantra was that every touchpoint – from the first phone call to schedule an appointment, to the check-in process, to the infusion itself – should exceed expectations. By doing so, FlexCare turned patients into loyal customers who would return for their maintenance infusions (often these treatments recur monthly or quarterly) and advocate for FlexCare if given a choice in the future. Patient retention and lifetime value were thus very high; an infusion patient might receive treatments for years, representing tens of thousands of dollars in revenue. FlexCare understood this and invested accordingly: they maintained a high nurse-to-patient ratio to give personal attention, used follow-up calls and texts to check on patients' well-being, and created a physical atmosphere (plush chairs, TVs, blankets) that left a positive impression. These efforts translated into stellar patient satisfaction scores., In essence, the company's customer acquisition flywheel was fueled by operational excellence. By balancing the cost of great service with the revenue of long-term treatment regimens, FlexCare achieved a sustainable model where marketing spend could remain moderate.

Scalability in sales was achieved by gradually formalizing processes. Initially, Smith himself was the salesperson, and Turk occasionally joined to provide clinical assurance to doctors. As they grew, they developed playbooks – for example, how to approach a new physician group, what educational slides to present, and how to follow up. New market launches came to follow a formula: months before opening a clinic, FlexCare's outreach team would begin visiting local doctors to introduce themselves, often even securing referral commitments contingent on the clinic opening. By the time a new site launched, it often already had a backlog of patients waiting for their first infusion, minimizing the ramp-up period. This disciplined and innovative approach to growth allowed FlexCare to scale its customer base dramatically while keeping acquisition costs reasonable – a strategy that clearly paid off given the company's explosive growth and eventual appeal to a national acquirer.

Operational Efficiency, Logistics, and Culture as Growth Accelerators

The operational backbone of FlexCare Infusion Centers was critical in supporting its fast growth. From supply chain logistics to clinical protocols,

FlexCare built its operations with scalability and sustainability in mind. One of the early operational decisions was to adopt specialized infusion center management software to handle scheduling, inventory, billing, and patient records in an integrated way. This technology allowed a lean central team to monitor all clinic operations in real time – for example, tracking medication stock levels at each site or flagging any delays in insurance authorizations. With biologic drugs being extremely costly, inventory management was a key logistical challenge. FlexCare's solution was to maintain just-in-time inventory: they worked closely with specialty distributors and leveraged group purchasing to get drugs delivered as needed, reducing on-site stock and avoiding expired product losses.

By 2022, FlexCare had created a well-oiled operations machine that could take a referral and convert it to a treated patient in minimal time. This efficiency not only improved patient outcomes by treating diseases faster, it shortened their revenue cycles. Achieving such efficiency required internal coordination across scheduling staff, benefits coordinators, pharmacy technicians, and nurses. FlexCare's operations playbook specified each step in detail, enabling the company to maintain performance consistency and deliver high patient satisfaction across 30 clinics by 2023.

Logistically, opening new centers was based on the standardized processes that Callie Turk had focused on developing and fine-tuning. The company developed a "clinic-in-a-box" model: a template for launching a new infusion center that covered site selection criteria, floorplan design, equipment procurement, staffing, and regulatory compliance. For example, they knew the ideal clinic layout – typically around 4–6 private infusion bays plus a nurses' station and a compounding room for mixing medications. They also negotiated master purchase agreements with furniture and medical equipment suppliers so that each new clinic could be outfitted quickly and uniformly. This approach cut down launch time and cost. An anecdote from internal operations was that FlexCare could get a new clinic from lease signing to seeing patients in as little as 8–12 weeks. Part of this speed came from Turk's meticulous project management and the team's experience overcoming initial hurdles. They learned to anticipate regulatory and payer hurdles: for instance, applying for state pharmacy licenses or Medicare approvals well in advance of opening.

A notable element of FlexCare's operations was the company culture of excellence that management cultivated, which in turn boosted performance. By

2024, FlexCare was recognized as a "National Top Workplace" by an employer survey, reflecting exceptionally high employee satisfaction and engagement. In a LinkedIn announcement of the award, the company thanked its team "for helping to build an industry-leading culture of excellence" and stressed that employees' "unrelenting dedication to our patients" had been noticed. This strong culture translated into superior service: engaged employees were more likely to deliver compassionate care and go the extra mile for patients. It also meant lower turnover in an industry often plagued by burnout – FlexCare's nurses and staff tended to stay, providing consistency for patients and saving on retraining costs. The emphasis on purpose-driven leadership was evident in how Smith and Turk led by example. Smith was known to drop into clinics regularly and even sit with patients to hear their stories, reinforcing the ethos that every individual mattered. Turk, for her part, closely mentored clinic managers and nurses, balancing high standards with support.

FlexCare's operational execution was marked by a combination of process discipline and adaptive learning. The team took early operational challenges – such as complicated payer contracting and the intricacies of opening new infusion sites – and turned those lessons into playbooks that smoothed the path for subsequent growth. They scaled their logistics in a cost-effective way, avoided bureaucratic bloat by centralizing where it made sense (intake, purchasing, billing) while decentralizing patient care to retain a local clinic feel, and nurtured a company culture that made all employees stakeholders in FlexCare's mission. These internal strengths were foundational to FlexCare's success.

From Growth to Acquisition: Strengths and Synergies with Optum

By 2024, FlexCare was in a dominant position in its chosen markets of Oklahoma, Alabama, and Arizona, and was exploring expansion into adjacent states. At this stage, FlexCare Infusion Centers growth into one of the country's premier ambulatory infusion networks naturally attracted interest from larger healthcare players. All of FlexCare's strengths – a strong founding vision executed flawlessly, rapid yet sustainable growth, high patient and provider satisfaction, disciplined financial management, and a track record of innovation – positioned it as an extremely attractive acquisition target.

It was no surprise, then, when Optum – one of the largest healthcare services companies in the U.S. – moved to acquire FlexCare Infusion Centers early in 2025. UnitedHealth Group's Optum, known for its aggressive but highly selective expansion into provider services, found FlexCare to be an ideal acquisition target. Their focus on FlexCare indicates that the company had established itself as a best-in-class platform in the infusion domain.

Optum's agreement to acquire FlexCare, announced in January 2025, can be seen as the culmination of FlexCare's rapid journey from startup to a multi-million-dollar leader in its field. The acquisition validated FlexCare's model and rewarded the founders and investors for their years of hard work and strategic decision-making. For Optum, acquiring FlexCare was a strategic win, granting them a dominant presence in ambulatory infusion and a talented team to drive it.

Ultimately, the story of FlexCare Infusion Centers from 2019 to 2025 is a narrative of how a clear vision, executed with focus and adaptability, created a company whose strengths not only led to impressive standalone success but also made it the perfect addition to a larger enterprise. Aaron Smith and Callie Turk's success stands as a model for building a healthcare startup with a visionary determination to solve a major problem in advanced care delivery with disciplined operations and an expansion strategy that achieved both purpose and profit.

Oxygen8

James Dean, the CEO and cofounder of Oxygen8, starts our conversation by explaining why he took a different approach to growing this company compared to his previous ventures,

> One of the things that's very different about this startup versus my first two is that both of the others were heavy in doing R&D, and creating IP, but slow to commercialize, because that work takes a long time. This time, I decided to take a completely different approach, which was to forget about R&D, forget about IP. Instead, the strategy was to look at Europe who were already making the high efficiency products over the previous few years, develop similar products for the North American market and partner with a leading Heat-Pump company to integrate with and the leading HVAC Rep Firms to get our products specified and sold.

We focused on a very quick speed to market, getting a line of products launched and generating revenue as soon as possible. And after achieving that quick start strategy, go out and raise some money to fund expansion and continue the fast growth. Fortunately, we were able to do just that based on previous strategic relationships that we had.

Like the seasoned serial entrepreneur he is, Dean manages to make the rare startup experience of everything going according to plan seem downright matter of fact. It sounds so straightforward that I can't resist asking whether he and his cofounder had it all mapped out before launching the company. Dean laughs and admits, "Well, I recently looked at our original business plan for the first time since we wrote it five years ago. It was interesting to see how close we've actually come to doing what we said we were going to do in that plan."

I learned that James Dean's Oxygen8 story encompasses much more than the successful rollout of a smart business plan. His company's growth is grounded in Dean's commitment to delivering clean air solutions that are essential to human health, and fueled by a deep belief that businesses can succeed at the highest level by doing the right thing for their employees, end customers, partners, and investors.

Starting Fast by Integrating Partners' Advanced Products

Dean and co-founder Matthew Doherty incorporated Oxygen8 in early 2020, and within six months they had secured their first customer order and shipped the product. "Matt and I started the company in January 2020 and we got our first customer order from the University of British Columbia... and developed our first product and shipped it in six months. That brought in revenue pretty quickly," Dean recalls. This first sale was a Nova ventilation system, which integrated a heat pump from partner Daikin, the world's leading air conditioning company. By incorporating Daikin's state-of-the-art variable refrigerant volume (VRV) heat pump technology instead of developing its own, Oxygen8 could offer a fully electric, high-efficiency ventilation solution with temperature control from the outset.

The foundation of Dean's quick start strategy was forming partnerships with global leaders in HVAC, controls and air filtration technologies and products. These products were already proven in regions like Europe that had strict energy and air quality standards, but were not widely accessible or well supported in Canada and the U.S. James Dean had accurately anticipated that the timing was right to capitalize on a strong and growing North American market demand for advanced air quality systems

By adapting proven technologies that met high-performance building codes and healthy Indoor Air Quality standards, Oxygen8 was able to launch products quickly, generate sales from the start, and scale up fast. Over its first few years, the company expanded its product line with extensions and larger models rather than developing proprietary solutions. Dean confirms this, noting,

> *I would call them product extensions, as opposed to brand new products. The whole idea was just to capture more of the market by expanding the product line, setting the stage for selling into more vertical markets and accelerating the customer acquisition and retention flywheel.*

Cost-Effective Collaboration for Attracting and Retaining Customers

Oxygen8's customer base has expanded rapidly since 2020, thanks to strategic early wins, a broad market approach, and the company's focus on delivering excellent customer service. That first sale to the University of British Columbia in mid-2020 gave the company credibility, validated the new company's expertise as well as generating early revenues. Local market adoption helped to give Oxygen8 early traction in British Columbia. James Dean and his team leveraged their network of relationships in Western Canada to land more projects. Dean notes that "our No. 1 market is British Columbia...which is where our factory is, so we've built relationships with the local engineers, architects, mechanical contractors, energy modelers and real estate developers" the people who specify and buy HVAC equipment. Landing over 20 more projects by early 2021 gave Oxygen8 important reference accounts across multiple verticals including education, sports venues, office buildings, senior care facilities, retail stores, residential, and commercial sites, demonstrating the broad applicability of its solutions.

To achieve national sales momentum, the company implemented a version of its product partnership strategy. Instead of building an in-house sales team from scratch, Oxygen8 partnered with 52 of the leading regional HVAC sales reps and national distributors, as well as with Daikin's extensive North

American network, to promote and sell Oxygen8 systems. Thanks to this independent sales rep network the company quickly extended their market reach across Canada and into the United States. Despite being a young Canadian startup, Oxygen8 overcame the challenge of building brand trust in the U.S. through strong distributor and partner relationships, coupled with the heightened post-pandemic awareness of indoor air quality issues. At the same time that Oxygen8 was gearing up to expand its geographic reach, well-ventilated buildings and healthy indoor air quality were becoming a compelling priority for high-use, densely occupied built environments.

Customer retention and loyalty have been priorities from the start. Thanks to the advanced tech from its partners, Oxygen8's product line featured space-saving designs that were suitable for HVAC retrofits as well as new building installations. These features boosted opportunities for customer retention and repeat business. Oxygen8 adopted a very customer-focused approach to deployments, recognizing that HVAC retrofits can disrupt business operations if they are not meticulously planned. Project case studies on the company's web site include client quotes about "the easy installation process and the ability for the Oxygen8 team to step in and install...without extreme disruption to their business". By prioritizing the quality of the client experience and minimizing downtime and complexity, Oxygen8 was well positioned to leverage client referrals to win new business. Oxygen8 has become known throughout the industry as "Fresh Air that Fits."

Oxygen8 also invests in educating and supporting its customer base as an intrinsic component of its acquisition and retention process. Recognizing that consulting engineers and architects are both key influencers in HVAC system selection, Oxygen8 produces thought leadership content for them. The company regularly creates and shares YouTube videos, white papers, and project profiles that design engineers and architects can use to demonstrate their role in innovative solutions. By co-authoring case studies and providing continuing education to these buyers and influencers, the company positions itself as a trusted advisor. This content marketing not only attracts new leads but also deepens relationships with existing clients and industry professionals. The company has also developed a web-based product selection and configuration tool "Configur8" that enables their customers to easily select, customize and price their Oxygen8 systems on their own and instantly provide the technical documentation for their design engineers.

These integrated strategies have helped to accelerate sales growth and expand market reach since the company's launch. Oxygen8 shares and celebrates its momentum on social media, noting that the 200th order shipped in March 2022, and marking the impressive milestone of shipping their 2,000th order three years later in spring 2025. Ultimately, Oxygen8's trajectory in customer acquisition and retention reflects a blend of strategic market focus, channel partnerships, superior customer experience, and a bit of fortuitous timing – the company was in the right place with the right solution as healthy indoor air and energy efficiency became a top priority worldwide.

Disciplined Financial Management with a Focus on Profitability

From the outset, Oxygen8's leadership has managed finances with an emphasis on sustainable, profitable growth rather than growth at all costs. James Dean avoided common startup pitfalls by ensuring the company was well-capitalized yet disciplined in spending. Initial funding came from equity investments by people who knew and trusted Dean, as well as Canadian government support programs for cleantech startups. He highlights that, "We have been very fortunate to receive support from the Canadian Federal Government and BC Provincial government for non-dilutive grants and interest free loans that have helped fund manufacturing equipment to insource some of our key components, as well as fund R&D to develop new products."

Oxygen8 raised a seed round of about $4 million USD in 2021 from strategic and angel investors to jump-start production and sales, and in total has raised about $9.6 million to date – a relatively modest sum given its rapid revenue growth. In 2024, the company reached annual revenues of $33 million and turned a profit, allowing it to reinvest earnings into operations and continued expansion. In 2025 is on track to achieve close to $50M in revenue and recently expanded into their third manufacturing facility.

Dean describes several tactics his team uses to manage cash flow efficiently without cutting corners. When cash was tight, they offered customers a 1% discount for Net-10 payment (paying within 10 days instead of 30) to accelerate receivables. At the same time, they were careful not to delay payables to their own suppliers, "we've never really slowed up paying our suppliers, because I just think that's kind of dangerous... some companies try to stretch out their payables... but we didn't do that," Dean says. Paying suppliers on time helped Oxygen8 build trust and avoid supply disruptions, which is critical for a manufacturing business. The company also employs a prudential approval process for expenditures: depending on the amount, managers must submit a brief business case or ROI analysis before any significant spending is approved. As Dean describes it, good cash management, and being smart about expenditures is deeply ingrained in the company culture.

Going forward, Dean is weighing another equity raise to accelerate the growth even further, but this will be done judiciously. Notably, sustained profitability remains a core objective. Oxygen8's leadership even formalized an OKR (Objectives and Key Results) to "build the foundation for profitable growth" in 2024. This initiative involves tightening up internal processes, documentation, and systems (such as better ERP/MRP systems to manage materials) to enable scaling without chaos or quality issues. The mindset is that solid operational foundations will allow faster growth and protect margins.

By balancing extremely fast growth with financial rigor, Oxygen8 has achieved remarkable financial results. The company topped Deloitte's 2024 list of fastest-growing Canadian cleantech firms with a three-year revenue growth of 6,610%. Nevertheless, Dean maintains that focusing on fundamentals, not just financial metrics, is vital for long-term success,

If you focus on those [underlying] things – hire good people, take care of your customers, develop great products, build strong strategic partners – then all the right financial stuff happens… If you focus on [hitting purely financial] goals, you're focused on the wrong things.

This philosophy is reflected in Oxygen8's trajectory: the company has grown revenues and market share aggressively, but with careful cash management, minimal dilution, and a constant eye on profitability. Such financial discipline ensures Oxygen8 can control its destiny and continue growing sustainably in the years ahead.

Development and Training for Team and Partner Productivity

Fast growing companies that integrate advanced technology into their products typically face an ongoing challenge in hiring and training enough skilled employees to keep up with demand. James Dean attributes a large part of Oxygen8's success to the team and culture he's built, as evidenced by the low employee turnover and excellent employee engagement survey results. He leveraged his professional network to recruit strong talent early. Even so, onboarding a constant stream of new manufacturing technicians was a struggle. In the company's first few years, Oxygen8 relied on a "buddy system" for on-the-job training: new hires would shadow experienced technicians. But this approach had a critical downside – *"the problem with the buddy system is your most experienced guys are losing all their productivity when they are training new hires,"* Dean recounts. Improving employee training became a company priority.

Oxygen8's solution was to develop the "Oxygen8 Academy," a structured training and development program for employees (and eventually will also be for the company's sales reps and partners). In crafting the Academy, Oxygen8 drew heavily on its partnerships with suppliers. Dean highlights two key partners, Daikin and the German firm Viessmann, noting that both have been extremely open in sharing their employee training best practices and have served as inspiring models.

Daikin operates a large training campus outside of Houston for HVAC technicians, and Viessmann has its own technical academy in Germany. Dean says of visiting the Daikin training center, "It's almost like a university, where they have classroom training, hands-on training and digital training they're doing tests to confirm capabilities. That visit gave me kind of a vision of where we can get to over the next several years." For Oxygen8, product and supplier partnerships have benefits beyond technology or sales – they are also knowledge partners helping Oxygen8 mature its processes.

During the next few years, the Oxygen8 Academy will be rolled out in phases. The initial focus will be on manufacturing assembly technicians (those building the equipment on the shop floor) to ensure they are thoroughly trained and cross-trained in all assembly procedures. Standard operating procedures (SOPs) are being documented as part of this effort. Over time, the Academy concept will expand to cover the entire organization, and even external partners like the company's external sales rep network – those independent reps who are not direct employees but represent Oxygen8 in the field.

By offering formal training and certification accreditation to reps, the company ensures its channel partners have the knowledge to specify, sell, install and service products properly, which in turn improves end-customer satisfaction. This kind of comprehensive training program is rare for a company of Oxygen8's size and age, and it underscores Dean's conviction that investing in people is critical for sustained growth. Indeed, Oxygen8 tracks metrics like employee engagement annually as a key performance indicator, reflecting the central role of its workforce. The company also annually tracks customer engagement through a survey including a Net Promoter Score. Oxygen8 recently completed Voice of Customer interviews with their top Sales Rep Firms to help guide the company's product roadmap over the next 5 years.

Parallel to employee development, close supplier partnerships have been crucial to Oxygen8's operations and innovation. Aside from Daikin, whose heat pumps are integrated into Oxygen8 systems, the company sources specialized components like energy recovery cores and energy efficient ECM Fans and intelligent controls from advanced manufacturers. Maintaining good relationships with these suppliers is vital. Oxygen8's practice of timely payments and securing trade guarantees for suppliers has helped it avoid the supply chain snarls that often plague startups. This highlights a core belief at Oxygen8: success is a team spirit involving internal employees and external partners alike. By training its people well and collaborating deeply with suppliers, Oxygen8 creates an ecosystem of aligned stakeholders – all driving toward the company's mission of healthy, sustainable buildings. This collaborative, learning-oriented culture provides a strong foundation for scaling up efficiently.

Planning for Future Growth and Sustainable Impact

As a fast-growing cleantech company, Oxygen8 has ambitious goals for the next phase of its journey, centered on scaling its impact and market reach and powered by massive market demand for clean energy HVAC solutions. While James Dean doesn't fixate on exact revenue targets, he believes it is realistic to reach $200 to $250 million in revenues within the next few years. "There's lots of opportunity in our market to grow," Dean notes, given the push for retrofitting buildings and adopting modern approaches for ventilation, heating, cooling and dehumidification in North America.

To achieve these aspirations, Oxygen8 will focus on expanding its ventilation product line to serve larger buildings and new use cases. For example, in 2025 the company is rolling out units with higher airflow to tackle bigger commercial projects. At the same time, having achieved consistent profitability, Oxygen8 is ready to invest in R&D that will keep it on the cutting edge of product performance and being cost competitive. Dean wants to pursue advanced dehumidification solutions and high-performance materials as R&D targets, along with advanced manufacturing methods including robotics, AGVs (Automated Guided Vehicles), and integrating AI in its manufacturing operations. These innovations will help Oxygen8 stay ahead of evolving building codes and customer needs, much as European HVAC tech companies have done.

On the sales front, Dean sees major opportunities to win more business in current customer verticals that have substantial room for growth. Oxygen8 has established a positive reputation and client relationships in sectors ranging from schools and universities to offices, retail, restaurants, and multifamily residential construction. Oxygen8's position is that clean indoor air and energy efficiency are universal needs, so virtually any occupied building, in any market sector, represents a potential customer. The goal is to make Oxygen8 solutions ubiquitous in new construction and retrofit projects alike.

Internally, Oxygen8's growth plans are underpinned by increasingly efficient operations that can handle escalating expansion. The company's "foundation for profitable growth" initiative (implementing SOPs, better ERP systems, automation in manufacturing) was designed to enable the company to scale output without sacrificing quality or margin. Building a robust operational backbone will enable faster order fulfillment, supporting increased market demand.

Oxygen8 is gearing up for its next chapter – one in which it plays a major role in the North American cleantech and sustainable building movement. James Dean's plan is to continue the company's remarkable growth trajectory into the foreseeable future by staying true to his founding mission and ensuring outstanding quality and scalability on a foundation of hyper-efficient operations.

◆ ◆ ◆

The ability of Uwill, FlexCare, and Oxygen8 to scale while maintaining high quality, customer satisfaction, and profitability highlight operational efficiency as an essential element in every company's growth playbook. In each case, the founders approached operational design with the same intensity and creativity that some entrepreneurs reserve for product development or fundraising. The result? For all three companies, hyper-efficiency became the foundation upon which quality, team cohesion, customer satisfaction, and profitability could thrive at scale. Without this bedrock, even the most promising startups can buckle under the weight of their own momentum. With it, 100X entrepreneurs can become market leaders who set the pace for growth and quality based on both vision and operational excellence.

7
Transformational Outcomes with Financial Discipline

EVERY ENTREPRENEUR, NO MATTER how visionary or well-funded, ultimately faces the same unavoidable reality: financial discipline is not optional. Whether a founder is bootstrapping on a shoestring budget or flush with venture capital, aiming for 100X growth without a clear path to profitability is a dangerous illusion. The notion that growth alone guarantees success has led to the downfall of countless startups that burned through millions with no viable plan to earn it back. Seasoned 100X entrepreneurs understand that only disciplined financial management ensures long-term survival, strategic flexibility, and scalable impact.

For founders who reject external funding, profitability is the oxygen that sustains growth from day one. But even among venture-backed companies, financial discipline is a core competitive advantage. It allows startups to remain agile in lean times, make smarter bets, and confidently expand into new markets. Across the companies featured in this chapter—Upward Health, Awestruck, and WeCall—this commitment to disciplined financial execution has enabled profitable 100X growth and empowered each to pursue bold, transformational goals that would have been unattainable otherwise.

At Upward Health, the decision to manage risk-bearing health contracts—taking full responsibility for the outcomes of the most medically complex, high-cost patients in the U.S.—was only possible because of CEO Glen Moller's ability to negotiate high-value outcomes into care delivery contracts, backed up with companywide commitment to disciplined execution. Upward Health didn't just hope its integrated, in-home care model would work; it built the financial controls, outcome tracking, and shared company values to guarantee it. That enabled the company to deliver on its promise of lower costs and better health outcomes, scaling rapidly while achieving profitability.

Awestruck, a destination marketing agency, grew by 11,247% over three years without external funding. Founders Ryan Sprance and Dave Marcy knew from experience that financial discipline was essential for their startup to survive and thrive. From carefully structuring multi-year retainer contracts to eliminating underutilized office space, these entrepreneurs scaled with boundless creativity, ambitious goals, and tight control over spending. Their fanatical customer engagement delivered such outstanding results that early clients became loyal boosters, building a word-of-mouth customer acquisition flywheel. Financial discipline wasn't a barrier to growth—it became a component of their market differentiation.

WeCall's business model was built around positive unit economics from day one. David Maman only expanded the business after he validated that each new client engagement would be profitable, and each call would generate margin. That careful attention to every line item—every dollar spent, every call placed—enabled WeCall to scale to over $80 million in revenue without outside capital.

All the 100X entrepreneur stories in this book echo this same truth. Carbliss, the zero-carb canned cocktail startup, charted its path to profitability through a region-by-region sales model that kept costs low while igniting customer demand for broader distribution. Autosled's founders built early customer trust through service reliability and profitability on each shipment. Uwill used disciplined operational modeling underpinned by a scalable digital platform to ensure that every campus partnership contributed to the bottom line. Rarebreed Veterinary Partners kept a laser focus on clinic-level profitability to fuel its rapid roll-up and integration of veterinary practices.

The lesson across all these companies is unambiguous: financial discipline is essential for moving from momentum to sustainable, profitable growth. It's what gives founders the freedom to pursue an ambitious vision without compromising their companies' futures. In a world obsessed with top-line growth, these entrepreneurs prove that profitability is still the ultimate power move.

Upward Health

Upward Health emerged in 2018 from the core of BehaveCare, a struggling startup with a dismal revenue record and an uncertain future. That year, Glen

Moller, a seasoned executive renowned for turning around healthcare companies, took the helm. As CEO, Moller brought a bold vision to integrate physical, behavioral, and social care into a whole-person, in-home model and to
partner with insurers on value-based contracts. Over the next six years, he
executed a sweeping transformation. By 2025, Upward Health had evolved
into a profitable, mission-driven healthcare provider known for dramatically
improving outcomes in high-need populations while rapidly scaling its business across the United States.

In my conversation with Glen Moller, I looked forward to learning the
details of his strategy for accomplishing such a far-reaching transformation.
And eventually, Moller did share all those details. First though, he explained
the fundamentals he believes have made Upward Health so successful: the
values that inform the daily decisions of every staff member. Here's how
Moller describes the centrality of values at Upward Health,

*Let's start with the big picture of what we're doing here, what I think re-
ally makes Upward Health scalable. It's not AI, and even though we've
got a big tech unit, it's not tech. Our growth foundation is our culture
and values and mission. It is implementing the right idea, at the right
time. That's the special stuff behind this company. Of course, we give our
strategy and all the implementation decisions careful thought, but it's our
culture that enables us to succeed. I believe that the most important foundation for this whole company is faithfully, consistently, living our values.*

*We have defined six core values, and these values are built into every
single thing that we do around here. Values are a constant presence in
our meetings, our operational decisions, in performance reviews – everything. The values list is on the opening screen of every employee's computer, and hanging on the wall in every office. We hold virtual quarterly
town halls, and every quarter we cycle through one of the six values, de-
voting our meeting to open discussion about how we are doing on it. For
example, when we cover, **patients come first**, we invite patients to join
us and talk about their experience. We talk about learning, case studies from the field, and not pointing fingers at each other when we make
mistakes*

*To a large degree, I feel my gift to this company is making sure these
values really, actually, truly drive all the work and planning that's done*

at Upward Health. That doesn't mean just talking about our values – I have to show every day that I am personally living up to them. And if I can lead by that example, I think it's going to get passed on throughout the organization. I'm telling you this first thing because it's so essential to my own motivation and how I feel about this company.

At that point, Glen gets up from his desk and gives me an impromptu tour of Upward Health headquarters, pointing out all the places where the company's values are on display.

Come on, I'll give you a little tour…First of all, you can see our list of the six values on the wall right up here in the lobby, and on this wall here, and of course, in our conference rooms and offices.

Even though there's no way to recreate Moller's powerful, spontaneous values tour in this book, a full understanding of Upward Health's growth really does require reflecting on the role of the company's core values. So here they are:

We have six Core Values that we use to guide our work at Upward Health

We Serve
- *Patients come first. They are always our top priority. It is our privilege and honor to serve them.*

We Deliver
- *We love our clients. We do absolutely whatever it takes to be the best they ever worked with.*

We Collaborate
- *We stand or fall as a team, shoulder to shoulder. We work for each other daily, celebrating our diverse backgrounds, ideas, and experiences.*

We Learn
- *We can do hard things. If we stumble, we learn from it without assigning blame and become stronger.*

We Execute
- *We expect top performance. We set a high standard, and team members are rewarded based on quality of work and service to the team.*

We Promise
- *We have the highest integrity. We expect of ourselves always to do the right thing.*

The story of Upward Health from 2018 to 2025 illustrates how visionary leadership and disciplined execution can transform a floundering startup into a thriving enterprise. Glen Moller brought a clarity of purpose – improving the lives of society's most medically and socially complex patients – committed core values, and disciplined business growth strategies to the challenge of building a scalable and profitable company. By reimagining care delivery to be in-home and whole-person, Upward Health addressed an urgent, unfilled need in the U.S. healthcare system. By aligning its business model with patient outcomes and payer savings, it unlocked success that far surpassed expectations, as evidenced by its 30,000%+ revenue increase and position #6 among the Inc. 5000 List of the fastest growing companies in the U.S.

Each aspect of the company's strategy reinforced the other: the mission attracted highly committed staff and partners; the focus on outcomes earned payer trust and contracts; efficient operations kept costs down and quality up, fueling the value proposition; and smart fundraising provided the capital to expand rapidly without losing momentum. Upward Health's culture of empathy and resilience, championed by Moller, ensured that through it all, the team never lost sight of the why that motivates all their work.

Upward Health's trajectory has decisively validated a values-driven healthcare model that many thought unworkable. It is serving tens of thousands of high-need patients across numerous states, partnering with some of the biggest names in insurance, generating significant revenue and outcomes data, and maintaining a compassionate touch in each patient interaction. That said, the coming years will no doubt test Upward Health as it faces new competitors and evolving national healthcare funding policies. Nonetheless, the company's journey since 2018 has forged the strengths to adapt and lead. It has prepared as well as possible – financially, operationally, and culturally – to navigate whatever lies ahead in the Medicare and Medicaid funding landscape.

Starting With a Turnaround Strategy

This remarkable journey started with a mandate to turn around Upward Health's struggling predecessor. Moller doesn't mince words about the challenges he faced when he joined the original BehaveCare in 2018,

> I arrived at a very little company that had almost no revenue and almost no foundation for growth. There were around 30 employees, and only half of them stayed on to rebuild. It seemed clear to me that the company had been focused on the wrong thing. It wasn't offering any actual provider care; there were no doctors or nurse practitioners delivering health care. In fact, it had carefully decided not to do that. I was convinced that providing care, direct care by our own teams, was the central thing that we absolutely had to do. That rubbed a lot of people the wrong way at first, but we did it. Looking back, we could not have succeeded without making that change.
>
> Next, the investors that we brought on board in those early days was a fundamental turnaround pillar. First of all, we needed the money. And second, I truly thank God that we have investors who believe in our mission. I've learned over time that investor fit is mission critical, and it's so easy to get that fit wrong in the search for funding. Fortunately, by this point in my career I had figured out how to tell if an investor or a key hire was going to be a good fit for our mission and culture.
>
> Those were some of the turnaround components that we fashioned the company now known as Upward Health. It's been an incredible, awesome ride. Basically, from our decisions back in 2018 up to today, what we do as a company is provide in-home primary care for specifically targeted, very vulnerable, complex patients. That's our daily work. We don't have any bricks and mortar clinical locations. Our care teams go around and help people who need care. If those people don't currently have a home, we go to the bridge that they're under. We find them in the community. And we provide the care they need.

Upward Health embarked on its turnaround with a clear mission –– delivering multidisciplinary whole-person care to the most complex, underserved patients directly in their homes. Summed up as "Healthcare Comes Home®" this mission-driven approach became the centerpiece of the company's identity and strategy. Instead of relying on traditional clinic visits, Upward Health deployed physician-led care teams to visit patient homes, addressing not only medical issues but also behavioral health and social determinants like food or housing. Moller's bet was that this comprehensive model would yield better patient outcomes at lower cost, a value proposition that could attract payer partners and drive sustainable growth. The bet paid off. By focusing on improved outcomes and cost savings – and by directly taking on financial risk in contracting with health insurers – Upward Health was able to sign a series of major partnership deals, expand to new markets year after year, and multiply its revenue to levels of extreme growth, recording an astounding 30,000% growth from 2020 to 2023.

Today, Upward Health stands as one of America's fastest-growing private companies with a reputation for delivering compassionate care to high-risk Medicare and Medicaid patients. In 2025, Upward Health celebrated its third consecutive year among the top 10 companies on the *Inc 5000* list, ranking at number 4. The following sections analyze the key elements that underpinned this journey, including a focus on scalable improvements in patient health outcomes; a partnership-based sales strategy that landed health plan contracts and fueled geographic expansion; operational tactics and advances in predictive analytics that kept growth robust and cost-efficient; and the financial discipline behind fundraising and revenue acceleration.

Vision: Whole-Person Care at Home, at Scale

The core of Upward Health's strategy to fundamentally improve care for high-need patients starts with meeting them where they are, whether that is in their living rooms or in temporary shelter. Upward Health pivoted in 2018 from BehaveCare's narrow focus on behavioral health to a *"holistic, integrated home-based model"* that combines primary care, behavioral health services, and social support. This whole-person care approach was designed not only to treat illness but to remove barriers that kept vulnerable patients from getting well, a radically comprehensive strategy. Upward Health's teams geared up to treat chronic conditions and acute needs, provide mental health care, coordinate specialist visits, assist with medication, and even help with non-medical issues like nutrition, transportation, or housing support if those were impacting a patient's health. By addressing all these determinants of health, the company aimed to produce measurably better outcomes for a population that the traditional clinic-centric system often failed.

Crucially, the company developed innovative ways to deliver this comprehensive health care in a disciplined, scalable, and cost-effective way – a necessity for any startup hoping to survive. Upward Health adopted a "risk-bearing" business model: rather than billing fee-for-service, it partners with insurers and assumes responsibility for patients' health outcomes and costs. In practice, this means Upward Health enters value-based contracts where it gets paid to keep patients healthier and share in the savings from avoided hospital bills. This model aligns the company's incentives with those of payers and patients. It also forced Upward Health to build an engine for efficiency and scale – the company could only profit by improving health outcomes *and* reducing expenses. Moller's prior experience leading Medicare health plans and a risk-adjustment analytics firm informed this strategy. He understood how to manage capitated payment models and leverage data to target interventions that prevent expensive complications.

One of the early innovations was Upward Health's "Facilitated Virtual Care" program, which it launched soon after rebranding in 2019. This program marries in-home visits with telehealth technology to extend the reach of clinicians. For example, an Upward Health "Care Specialist" might visit a patient at home and, via a tablet, connect that patient with a remote Upward Health physician or psychiatrist for a consultation. This hybrid care delivery means patients get 24/7 access to care: same-day virtual appointments for urgent needs or mental health crises, supported by in-person follow-ups as needed. By integrating virtual care, Upward Health scaled its care coverage without having to station doctors in every locale. It also ensured timely interventions – a key success factor for treating complex patients who might deteriorate quickly without prompt care. Understanding that many high-risk patients find it difficult to get to a provider's office, or to wait weeks for an appointment, providers knew that bringing care to them (physically or virtually) was essential. This approach not only improved patient satisfaction; it also reduced costly emergency visits by addressing issues before they became crises.

Upward Health's decision to offer guaranteed results in its contracts reflected the company's "patient first" values and commitment to quality care; the decision was backed up by its operational efficiencies and ability to leverage patient data to create reliable outcome predictions. In contract negotiations, Moller's team was confident enough to "guarantee outcomes in both quality and cost of care" for their health plan customers. In other words, Upward Health put its fees at risk based on whether it could keep patients healthier while lowering the total cost of their care. Few startups would dare promise such results, and even fewer were equipped to consistently deliver the promised improvements for such a challenging cohort of patients. Early on, the guaranteed results contracts required a leap of faith – convincing investors and health plans that Upward Health's model could bend the cost curve. Over time, however, the company amassed evidence of its impact: patients under Upward's care had fewer hospitalizations and better chronic disease management, translating into significant cost savings. By 2022, for instance, Upward Health had improved patient outcomes so effectively that it was selected as one of just 22 organizations nationwide to participate in Medicare's new ACO REACH program focused on high-needs patients. This was a strong validation of the model – CMS (the federal Medicare agency) trusted Upward Health to coordinate care for some of Medicare's most complex beneficiaries in a pilot aimed at innovation.

The ability to deliver such impressive results on its outcome-based contracts called upon the skills of multidisciplinary care teams, facilitated virtual visits, data-guided interventions, and increasingly efficient, centralized operations. These capabilities strengthened the foundation for Upward Health's year-over-year growth. By 2025, the company's care model had yielded measurable improvements: high patient satisfaction (an industry-leading Net Promoter Score of 90) and better health outcomes that translated into lower costs. This proved to payers that scaling values-based, patient-centered care was not only possible; it was also profitable – a realization that underpinned a growing demand for Upward Health's services.

Sales and Expansion: Partnering for Cost-Efficient, Scalable Growth

A visionary healthcare model cannot make an impact without customer adoption, so a critical challenge for Upward Health was developing a scalable, cost-effective customer acquisition strategy. In practice, convincing health plans and other payers to entrust their members to Upward's care was a slow-moving and relationship-intensive process, especially in the company's early years.

Glen Moller's go-to-market strategy focused on partnering with managed care organizations (MCOs) – insurers covering Medicare, Medicaid, and dual-eligible populations – and convincing them that Upward Health could solve their toughest problem: the high cost and poor outcomes of their sickest members. Rather than trying to market directly to patients or build standalone clinics, Upward Health positioned itself as an extension of the health plan's care management, a specialized provider group that would take on the plan's most challenging patients. This B2B sales approach proved highly effective. Between 2020 and 2023, Upward Health signed contracts with a mix of national and regional health plans, entering at least one new state each year and expanding its services from coast to coast by 2023.

The geographic expansion strategy was both ambitious and disciplined. Rather than a scattershot approach, Upward Health often expanded in tandem with its clients. For example, after proving itself in one region, Upward Health would be invited by a national plan to enter another state where that plan operated. This client-following strategy helped Upward to expand to new regions with lower customer acquisition cost, since an existing partner's endorsement smoothed entry into new markets. By 2023, the company had employees in over 20 states, reflecting deals with both large national insurers and regional plans.

Throughout these expansions, Moller nurtured strong relationships with health plans, which he credits as the backbone of Upward Health's growth. The company became known for delivering on its promises to partners – improving their members' health outcomes and satisfaction. In a 2024 announcement, Moller noted that the company's three-year growth was "a testament to the strong relationships we have built with our health plan partners, including both national and regional managed care organizations". These relationships were strengthened by the company's transparency in data sharing and outcomes reporting, which gave payers confidence in the partnership. Additionally, Upward Health often employed a local workforce strategy; when entering a new region, it hired and trained healthcare workers from that area rather than parachuting in outsiders. By "hiring in and of the communities we now serve," as Moller put it, Upward Health demonstrated its commitment to local stakeholders and ensured that its care teams understood the community context of their patients.

Operational Excellence: Efficient Logistics and Predictive Analytics

Scaling a hands-on healthcare service to tens of thousands of patients in home settings is a massive operational challenge. Upward Health's execution on internal operations and logistics was a critical factor in turning rapid growth into sustainable success. Upward Health invested heavily in building a robust operational infrastructure that could maintain efficiency and care quality as the business expanded. One pillar of operational management is the use of data and technology to coordinate care. The company's increasing ability to leverage data about its patient populations is a competitive asset in the process of negotiating new contracts, and a crucial tool to boost the efficiency and effectiveness of care providers.

As Moller explains it,

The process of acquiring new patients starts with us approaching a health insurance company. Our offer is something like this – if the insurer will give us retrospective data on their patient population and care outcomes over the years, we will analyze that data to determine which individuals make sense for our program. Initially, Upward Health services will be more expensive, so we tell the insurer that we want to be sure there will be a significant financial ROI as well as patient care improvements when they sign up with us. We then take that data, and analyze it, using predictive modeling to model outcomes that we share back to the insurer or health plan. This outcomes model will help to persuade them that Upward Health will positively impact their patient population and their costs. Increasingly we're using machine learning and AI-based tools to improve our predictions. We also use these to speed up our data analysis.

Now that we are delivering care to tens of thousands of patients ourselves, and engaging with them to different degrees based on need, we're also starting to use these internal data and AI tools to help us predict what's coming at them next. We do that based on what we know about their past health issues, or what we see in the pharmaceutical record, or the latest info that's coming in from a recent interaction with our care team. It adds up to massive amounts of data that's coming into us daily from a lot of different sources, and we're trying to use AI to rapidly understand the data. We then share the insights and predictions right back to our field staff at the point of care. This provides them with more informed guidance about what they should prioritize in terms of care for that particular patient. So those are the key things that we're working on from a data management perspective.

In 2024, the company undertook a major overhaul of its data architecture, creating a unified data model to integrate information across clinical, behavioral, and social services. This unified platform gave care teams a comprehensive view of each patient's history and needs, and it powered accurate reporting of patient progress and outcomes. By centralizing data, Upward Health enabled its geographically dispersed staff to make informed decisions quickly. For example, a nurse in Arizona could see notes from a social worker in New York who previously helped the patient with housing, thereby ensuring continuity of care. The upgraded data systems also allowed the company to analyze trends and project future needs – essential for proactive care management of chronic conditions. Importantly, better data management translated into smoother logistics in the field: as Moller noted, these innovations "streamline field work, enabling our team to maximize impact while minimizing resource use". Leveraging data insights in practice translates into more efficient scheduling of home visits (grouping them by location to cut travel time) and the ability to adjust care intensity dynamically based on real-time patient risk indicators.

Upward Health also developed sophisticated care coordination protocols to manage the complexity of patient needs. In 2024, the company introduced a new *titration model* for addressing social determinants of health. This model helps the team identify and prioritize each patient's non-medical needs – such as food security, transportation, or social isolation – and titrate (adjust) the level of support accordingly. By implementing a "priority-driven model" for these interventions, Upward Health ensured that resources like community health workers or social services referrals were directed where and when they would make the most difference. For instance, if housing instability was a critical issue driving a patient's health crises, the care team would focus intensely on that determinant until it was resolved or under control.

This systematic approach helps prevent team members from being overwhelmed by the myriad issues each patient presents. It gives them a clear roadmap of which problem to tackle first. The result is more effective and faster interventions, improving patient outcomes while using staff time efficiently. It exemplifies how Upward Health manages its internal operations to improve performance and build scalability by developing repeatable processes and frameworks that transform what could be chaotic case management into a structured, high-impact workflow.

Another major aspect of operational execution was scaling the workforce without diluting quality. Upward Health grew from a small team to hundreds of employees by 2024, adding nearly 200 new staff in that year alone. To integrate so many new hires effectively, the company overhauled its training programs, anchoring new programs around the core value, "We Learn". It created comprehensive onboarding and ongoing education curricula tailored to each role, ensuring that nurses, care coordinators, physicians, and support staff all receive the training and preparation for Upward Health's innovative and integrated care model. Middle management training is also emphasized, reflecting the leadership recognition that as the organization grew, front-line managers (team leads, regional supervisors, etc.) needed development support to maintain consistency and morale across the company. By investing in education and development at all levels, Upward Health built a cadre of motivated leaders who could transmit the company's values and best practices to their teams. This was crucial for maintaining the culture of empathy and excellence as the headcount exploded. It also freed the executive team to focus on strategic issues, knowing that well-trained managers could handle day-to-day operations.

Adopting these strategies, Upward Health built a scalable infrastructure of technology, processes, and people that could deliver very personalized care in a cost-effective manner. The company turned the inherently challenging logistics of in-home, 24/7 multidisciplinary care into a comparative advantage. This operational strength allowed Upward Health to grow rapidly without collapsing under its own weight – a fate that many hyper-growth startups risk. By 2025, the company had demonstrated that it could integrate new markets and contracts smoothly, coordinate thousands of home visits and virtual visits, and uphold a high standard of care nationwide. Efficient internal operations translated to lower operating costs per patient even as clinical outcomes improved – the very equation that makes the business model work in a risk-sharing environment.

Financial Management: Fundraising, Revenue Growth, and Profitability

Upward Health's financial journey from 2018 to 2025 reflects a transition from a cash-strapped startup to a well-capitalized growth company with strong revenue streams. Thanks to disciplined management of financial resources, the company achieved a major milestone in 2024 – profitability back up by becoming cash flow positive. Glen Moller reflects on the importance of this achievement for his own priorities and the future growth and impact of Upward Health,

> *The more a CEO cares about the mission and impact of the business, the more pressure there is to bring in more capital and keep growing. Over the past six years, each time that we've been able to raise more has been a big inflection point for us. Whether the capital comes from a new investor, or from existing investors who are continuing to bet on you, that infusion of capital always feels good.*
>
> *An even bigger inflection point, that happened within the past year, is that Upward Health is now profitable. And besides being profitable, we are cash flow positive. In fact, now we have plenty of cash sitting in the bank to fund our work. It's great to feel that I don't have to distract myself with urgent fund-raising or worry about getting an infusion of money in the door. That milestone feels really big. It feels massive.*

Achieving profitability while on the path of extreme growth attests to Upward Health's carefully managed cash flow and capital structure. The risk-bearing model meant that the company sometimes had to invest upfront inpatient care and only reap financial rewards if outcomes were achieved. Raising outside funding enabled the company to invest in staff, technology, and provided working capital for executing on its value-based contracts (which can have slow reimbursement cycles). Importantly, despite aggressive growth spending, Upward Health had charted a clear path to profitability. Its unit economics improved as it scaled – each new contract added revenue that outweighed the incremental overhead, thanks to the efficiency of its care model. The company's proven ability to "lower the total cost of care" for plan partners meant Upward Health could command high fees and negotiate performance bonuses that improved its margins. By aligning its financial incentives with payers,

Upward Health essentially created a shared savings engine: if they saved the insurer money, they earned more. This dynamic helped Upward's revenue per patient rise over time as they proved greater value.

Financial discipline has been extremely important given Upward's environment – serving predominantly government-funded healthcare populations (Medicare and Medicaid) means margins can be thin and payments slow. Moller's team managed this by diversifying payers (mix of Medicare Advantage, state Medicaid agencies, and direct CMS programs) so that the company was not overly reliant on one revenue source. They also timed fundraising well: raising equity when growth prospects were strongest (2021 and 2024) and using debt tactically to fuel expansions without as much dilution.

Perhaps one of the most valuable early lessons was the importance of quantifying outcomes and building credibility. In the startup's first pilots, they had to prove that their intensive intervention made a difference. Upward Health invested in tracking metrics and sharing its results, which later became a cornerstone of their pitches. By the time of Series B, Heritage Group cited Upward's "track record of improving patient outcomes" as evidence of success. Achieving that track record meant learning in early trials what worked and what didn't – for example, discovering which interventions yielded the biggest reductions in hospitalizations and focusing on those. It also meant learning to tell the story with data – an ability that made conversations with skeptical CFOs at health plans much easier. Because they honed their outcome measurement early on, Upward Health could demonstrate that their model was not just transformational; it was financially sound. The company also learned to target the clients and patient populations that it could serve most effectively. It didn't waste time chasing unworkable models or unprofitable clients. Instead, it focused on what was proven to work: high-need patients, risk-based payer contracts, integrated care, and scalability through tech and process. This focus led to faster sales cycles and implementations.

It's consistent, well-documented track record meant that when Upward Health approached potential health plan clients, they came prepared with (a) an integrated service offering rather than a point solution, (b) a willingness to guarantee results financially, (c) a tech-enabled platform for scale, and (d) data proving their value in pilots. This has made their sales proposition highly attractive and allowed Upward to win and deliver on long-term contracts.

Navigating a Changing Medicare/Medicaid Landscape

As of 2025, Upward Health stands out in the healthcare industry with a set of key strengths that position it well to navigate the evolving Medicare and Medicaid funding landscape. One of its greatest strengths is a demonstrated ability to improve outcomes for high-cost patients while reducing overall costs – effectively cracking the code of value-based care for a challenging population. This is evidenced by strong data from the last few years: significant reductions in hospitalizations and ER visits among its patient cohorts (as reported by partners) and high patient satisfaction scores. Health plans and government programs face constant pressure to rein in spending on Medicare and Medicaid, especially as budgets tighten. Upward Health provides a proven solution to this problem. Its model delivers the kind of results that CMS and state Medicaid agencies need more than ever — better care at lower expense – which gives Upward leverage and credibility in policy discussions.

Another core strength is Upward Health's flexibility and adaptability in the face of policy and funding changes. The Medicare and Medicaid landscape can shift with new regulations, payment models, or political winds. Upward has repeatedly shown it can adapt: When states like Louisiana or California launched new value-based pilots or Medicaid waivers, Upward Health was nimble enough to secure contracts under those programs. This adaptability is a major asset as Medicare/Medicaid funding evolves – whether it's risk adjustment formula tweaks, new integrated care mandates, or shifts from fee-for-service to capitation, Upward Health is structurally and culturally equipped to adjust its model and keep delivering value. Smaller providers or tech vendors often struggle with such changes, but Upward's broad capability (being both a provider and a risk manager) means it is well-positioned to thrive under various funding schemes.

In 2025, Glen Moller was named an EY Entrepreneur of the Year® for New York, a recognition of his leadership and vision in transforming the company and redefining care for underserved populations. He founded the Shoulder to Shoulder Foundation (S2S), a nonprofit that provides one-time emergency relief to individuals and families in crisis. Where Upward Health's mandate leaves off, this charity steps in — offering direct support for eviction protection, heating, clothing, and housing needs. It's a natural extension of Glen's mission to serve the most vulnerable, and a way to address the urgent social challenges that impact health but fall outside traditional care models.

Building on its core values, Upward Health has demonstrated a powerful combination of proven impact, adaptable strategy, financial stability, and mission credibility. It has become a partner of choice for innovative healthcare payers and a respected voice in the push towards value-based care for complex populations. The foundation laid since 2018 means Upward Health is not only prepared to navigate challenges in Medicare/Medicaid funding, but to help shape the future of how those programs care for the most vulnerable. With its mission-driven compass and business discipline, Upward Health is poised to continue its upward trajectory, demonstrating that compassionate care and strong financial performance can go hand in hand in American healthcare.

Awestruck

Cofounders Dave Marcy and Ryan Sprance are excited to talk with us about their vision for Awestruck—and we are eager to learn more about how this destination marketing agency racked up a literally awesome three-year revenue rise of 11,247% — a feat that landed Awestruck in the #25 spot of the *Inc 5000* list of fastest growing companies for 2023.

The Awestruck story starts with lifelong friends embarking on a daring quest, as Marcy and Sprance set out to challenge the dominant marketing agencies and redefine the rules of engagement in a $2.3 trillion dollar industry. Instead of seeking outside investors, the pair proudly preserved their independence by bootstrapping Awestruck with the goal of being profitable from the start. But they didn't move forward alone – in fact, they recruited a skilled band of colleagues to forge a new path. Our conversation with these founders highlights the drama in Awestruck's rapid rise – after all, a mastery of storytelling is essential for every marketer's journey.

A Bond Built on Trust

Awestruck was born from the convergence of complementary talents and a shared vision. Ryan Sprance and David Marcy had been close friends for decades, each running their own marketing ventures. In late 2018, Marcy and a colleague at a prior company were working on a marketing project for a large resort. When that client needed social media expertise, Marcy brought in Sprance. This joint project was a resounding success, prompting the client to enlist their help to launch a new property, which also thrived. Recognizing both "an awesome opportunity...and the power of a built-in trusted relationship," Sprance and Marcy decided to embark together on a new venture. They launched Awestruck in 2019 to specialize in destination marketing.

The founders agreed that a laser focus on resort, hotel, casino, waterpark, and other tourism clients would differentiate Awestruck from generalist marketing agencies. Sprance and Marcy decided to share leadership in the new company as co-CEOs, and divided responsibilities based on their strengths, with Marcy driving sales and client acquisition and Sprance overseeing operations and execution. It was a partnership of equals, underpinned by complete trust in each other.

From the outset, their mission was to reinvent destination marketing to deliver outsize performance results in every engagement. The founders actively solicited feedback from early clients about what had been lacking in the services of other agencies. They learned that clients often felt that prior agencies didn't make their campaign a top priority, and didn't respond quickly to questions and issues. Clients had been frustrated by sparse agency communications and opaque progress reports.

Awestruck flipped that script by making deep engagement with their clients a company hallmark, integrating regular communication and availability into their service promise. Every account is treated like a partnership, with the agency team essentially on-call and embedded in the client's success. This high-touch approach stands out in an industry where many agencies limit client contact to formal check-ins. Awestruck's commitment to prioritize client success in every way possible differentiated its services and created a foundation for long-term relationships with satisfied clients.

Clients also wanted more transparency about campaign performance in terms they could easily use for decision making. They complained that prior agencies would send reports full of dense Excel spreadsheets that were hard to interpret. Awestruck responded by developing clear, user-friendly reporting dashboards and performance metrics that highlight business results for every marketing investment.

A commitment to transparency and putting client needs first extends to Awestruck's pricing model. In contrast to the many agencies that charge a base retainer plus a percentage of the client's ad spend, the founders decided to forgo any commissions on client advertising budgets. The flat-fee structure aligns Awestruck's incentives with the client and it earns clients' trust by removing a potential conflict of interest in ad budgeting.

Marcy and Sprance used this early client feedback to shape their strategy for customer acquisition and retention. It shaped the three core principles that underpin Awestruck's mission and the level of service it delivers. The first principle is Fanatical Client Engagement defined as becoming a "round the clock extension of your property's marketing team," and "being passionate executing your vision using our expertise."

Talent Strategy: Jaw -Dropping Expertise for Every Campaign

A cornerstone of Awestruck's success has been its people strategy – specifically, hiring professionals with deep experience in the travel, tourism, and resort industry. In fact, Jaw-Dropping Expertise is another of its three core principles, and part of the Awestruck promise is that "all of its account managers and directors are hospitality career professionals with high-level management and marketing pedigrees."

Marcy and Sprance are seasoned marketing experts, but neither founder came from a hospitality background. They knew from the outset that winning contracts and trust from clients in the destination travel sector would require hiring superstars fluent in the language of hotel and resort management, with credibility grounded in successful hospitality careers. Awestruck recruited former resort marketers, hotel sales directors, casino advertising managers, and top performers with similar profiles to build out their team. The commitment to onboarding deep expertise has paid huge dividends in establishing close relationships with their clients, as well as delivering consistent marketing campaign success. "Hiring top talent from the industry… has been very beneficial for us," Marcy notes. "Our team has been very good at teaching us the language of that space, and it's a huge reason that our campaigns are successful."

Many of Awestruck's senior leaders today first got to know Marcy and Sprance as early Awestruck clients. These individuals experienced Awestruck's work as customers, were impressed by the approach, and eventually decided to join them. This unusual pipeline from client to team member speaks to Awestruck's strong relationships and also guarantees an empathetic perspective within the agency. Awestruck's account managers and directors can say, "I've sat in your seat," to a resort's marketing team. When a hotel client says they are struggling to attract local diners to an on-property restaurant or to book mid-week stays off season, the Awestruck account director on the call has likely faced similar issues in their hospitality career. They can immediately relate and propose informed solutions, rather than merely relying on generic marketing playbooks. This insider insight makes it easy for clients to value Awestruck as experienced hospitality partners. It also boosts efficiency and results; little time is lost to a learning curve about industry basics, and campaigns are tailored with an intimate awareness of seasonality, guest demographics, and revenue drivers unique to travel businesses.

Today the company's leadership includes many executives from various hospitality and entertainment backgrounds, who bring the founders' vision to life in ways exceeding what Sprance and Marcy imagined five years ago. This leadership team not only delivers superior service but also constantly feeds back new ideas and insights from the field. In essence, Awestruck embedded the client perspective within its own ranks, which has been instrumental in crafting an agency experience markedly different from its competitors.

Another advantage of hiring "jaw-dropping expertise" was that Awestruck dramatically shortened the runway to establish itself as a leading specialist in destination marketing – a major advantage in customer acquisition and retention in a highly connected industry that prizes relationships as much as dedication and performance.

Revenue-Boosting Magic: A Referral Flywheel for Customer Acquisition and Retention

Awestruck's client base grew quickly from the very beginning, thanks to the founders' strategy of leveraging results and relationships. The agency's first revenues in 2019 came through the founders' professional networks and early projects, including follow-on projects with the resort property collaboration that inspired Sprance and Marcy to launch their startup. These initial wins established Awestruck as a credible up-and-coming agency that achieved stellar results for its clients. As Awestruck established a reputation for delivering successful new property launches and revenue boosts in a challenging travel market, the agency began fielding a steady stream of inbound inquiries and referrals. Resorts would recommend Awestruck to sister properties and hotel executives would refer the agency to their peers. Over time this word of mouth snowballed and became an acquisition flywheel, fueling Awestruck's growth without requiring paid advertising to attract new customers. Clearly, such rapid growth through word-of-mouth stems from extremely high customer satisfaction. Awestruck's commitment to fanatical client engagement, combined with their expert teams, and a touch of marketing magic from the founders, came together to inspire a level of enthusiastic client loyalty that is rare for any agency, and especially elusive for a new entrant.

The spread of COVID 19 less than a year into Awestruck's operations precipitated a drastic downturn for the U.S. destination travel and hospitality sector. Many agencies serving travel companies responded by pivoting away from hospitality to concentrate on other industries for the duration. Awestruck, however, doubled down on its destination marketing focus and found ways to grow even amid the crisis.

Sprance remembers this period as a test of their commitment to the industry that turned into an unexpected opportunity,

Being in destination marketing [during the pandemic] was tough ...many properties closed, but for us, it actually gave us opportunities that other agencies were not willing to explore, for example some branding projects, where we had to be on site regularly. We also worked with a couple of properties that were outdoor water parks in Texas. So even during the pandemic we kept working and had relatively fast growth— faster than any of us had planned.

Marcy adds,

The fact that we somehow managed to keep growing during the pandemic, that was kind of surreal for us. At the same time, we knew this was our moment to seize on new opportunities. Even while the industry had slowed down, we were talking to management companies, talking to properties, working to keep all of our client relationships fresh and ready to go when things came back. Then, as activity did come back in 2021, suddenly we were really taking off like a rocket ship. I think we could have missed out during that period if we hadn't had the right mindset about staying ahead of that growth.

Awestruck not only kept working for many of its existing clients; it even won new business during 2020 and 2021. Thanks to the groundwork laid during the slow pandemic period, the founders forged relationships with potential future clients, ensuring a healthy prospect and sales pipeline when travel rebounded. Their contrarian commitment paid off in an epic spurt of post-pandemic growth.

Awestruck's client roster and the demand from new prospects surged as travel destinations urgently ramped up their marketing to capture pent-up demand. The agency onboarded numerous resorts and attractions in 2021 and 2022, climbing from around $106,000 in 2019 to over just over $24 million in revenues by 2024. Even more impressive, the founders achieved this acceleration without needing to spend heavily on a conventional advertising or outbound sales budget.

Taking on the role of long-term strategic marketing partner underpins Awestruck's very high client retention rate, generating recurring revenue and referral-based acquisition. The agency's fanatical client service and tangible return on marketing campaigns inspire their clients to rely on the agency to provide marketing for additional properties and new project launches. This land-and-expand strategy, combined with a regular stream of customer referrals to new business prospects, means that future growth can be both deep (within accounts) and broad (across the industry).   At the current levels of customer retention rates, the portents are very favorable for Awestruck's rapid growth to continue in the years ahead. The magic behind the agency's customer acquisition and retention success doesn't involve any sleight of hand – it's sparked by the founders unwavering commitment to fanatical client engagement and to their innovative vision for the future of destination marketing.

Blazing New Trails

A defining element of Awestruck's value proposition is its emphasis on innovative marketing channels and technology. Early in its journey, the agency identified over-the-top (OTT) streaming media advertising as a largely untapped opportunity in hospitality marketing. While most hotels and resorts still relied on traditional digital marketing channels like paid search and social media advertising, Awestruck was convinced that creative ads and content delivered via streaming TV platforms would yield superior targeting and measurable results for destinations.

Awestruck emphasized this option in its mix of services, demonstrating the benefits of streaming media marketing whenever it seemed like the best fit for a campaign. They persuaded few forward-thinking clients to OTT pilot campaigns and those early adopters saw positive, game-changing returns. As a result, initial skepticism among clients gave way to widespread enthusiasm – today the majority of Awestruck's client portfolio uses the agency's OTT advertising products, boosting the impact and ROI from their marketing.

Awestruck even built its own OTT campaign management system, dubbed Ideal, when they couldn't find a third-party platform that met their standards. This system allows them to optimize streaming ad buys and performance tracking to a degree unmatched in the travel and hospitality sector. By developing new capabilities in-house and demonstrating the value to its clients, Awestruck has established itself as a leader on streaming media solutions in the destination marketing sector. This forward-looking approach is the foundation of the agency's third core principle, Unyielding Innovation. As part of its commitment to offer a one-stop, cutting edge solution, Awestruck operates a full in-house production studio that creates high-quality video and photography for its clients, eliminating the need to outsource creative work. Few competitors in the travel marketing space can match this blend of domain expertise, technological innovation, and white-glove client service, amplifying Awestruck's distinct value proposition.

Growth and Profitability with Disciplined Financial Management

From day one, Awestruck's founders built the business with financial discipline in mind, choosing to bootstrap growth and emphasize profitability over breakneck expansion. As Sprance reflects on the company's self-funded journey, he is proud to say, "We've never raised any money, we've been bootstrapped from the very beginning, and we've been profitable from the very beginning."

Awestruck's early profitability, even at modest scale, was possible because the founders kept overhead low and focused on securing retainer contracts that provided a predictable, steady cash flow. Every dollar earned was carefully reinvested into hiring, technology tools, and operational improvements that would support the next stage of growth. For example, Sprance recounts how they evaluated expenses like physical office space and decided to eliminate underutilized offices in 2023, saving about $80,000 annually, once they had confirmed that their team could function effectively with a work-from-home model. Decisions like this typify Awestruck's pragmatic financial management – constantly weighing costs against benefits, and trimming unnecessary expenses to sustain healthy margins. This approach has allowed Awestruck to scale rapidly without sacrificing profitability or the high quality of the services they deliver.

The founders deliberately structured client engagements as long-term retainer contracts, often with multi-year agreements. Retainers provide a predictable baseline of income each month, which in turn enables stable hiring and resource allocation. "Being a retainer model from the beginning on longer term contracts...allows us to staff appropriately," Sprance notes, since they know what work is secured ahead of time. This reduces the volatility often seen in agency finances and ensures Awestruck can meet its commitments without overextending.

On top of the retainer base, Awestruck generates revenues from product-based and performance-based revenue. For instance, Ideal, the agency's OTT advertising product, is sold with a markup. The same is true for other services Awestruck has added over time: data analytics tools, influencer marketing campaigns, and content production packages all are priced to include profit margins beyond the labor cost. This hybrid model has fueled revenue acceleration without needing exponential client growth. Awestruck has been successful at growing wallet share with existing clients by offering more value-added services. The result is a balanced portfolio of income streams that support both steady cash flow and higher-margin earnings. Combined with vigilant cost control, Awestruck's financial strategy has yielded a robust, sustainable growth engine.

The Road Ahead Goes Ever Onward – and Upward

Looking ahead, Awestruck's goals center on continued innovation, strategic expansion, and constantly enhancing the value it delivers to clients. Rather than pursuing growth for its own sake, the founders take a year-by-year, product-by-product approach to scaling their business.

Awestruck's first software product, a platform called Sugarcane, is a recent growth initiative designed to add value. Sugarcane is a creator marketplace that connects content creators and influencers with hotels, resorts, and restaurants that need fresh marketing content. The founders realized that their clients, who constantly need high-quality content, didn't have easy access to the vast community of creators who produce such content. In turn, those creatives who would love to post social stories featuring themselves in exciting travel destinations didn't have an efficient way to connect to specific resorts. Awestruck now offers Sugarcane as that needed connector on an SaaS platform.

The plan is for Sugarcane to streamline a process that Awestruck had previously handled manually for clients. The decision to build Sugarcane aligns with Awestruck's innovative spirit: instead of waiting for a third-party solution, they invested in creating their own. If Sugarcane achieves widespread adoption, it could serve designation properties industry-wide, and create a new revenue stream for Awestruck. In the long term, it positions Awestruck as a platform provider, potentially unlocking the scalability of software economics. This move into software is carefully considered – the problem space Sugarcane addresses is adjacent to the agency's current services, and the founders have the domain knowledge to execute it. It's a move that reflects Awestruck's growth philosophy: expand horizontally into related offerings that bolster the core mission of helping travel brands market themselves better.

From the start, the founders' vision for Awestruck has been to build a company that is sustainable, valuable, and rewarding for clients and for team members. Both founders prioritize a positive company culture that engages employees with a sense of purpose and fulfillment. They regularly check in with each other about the broader rewards of the work they are doing, determined to balance their growth strategies with a day to day lived experience that is personally fulfilling as well as financially rewarding. This perspective helps them avoid the burnout or mission drift that can come to overtake any company preoccupied with relentless expansion.

Sprance and Marcy's journey from the quest to reinvent destination marketing to managing an extreme growth enterprise is characterized by the courage to carve out their own path in a highly competitive industry. The vision of making Awestruck "the best possible company it can be" continues to expand as the founders see ever more innovative opportunities ahead. The next chapter of Awestruck's story is just beginning.

WeCall

WeCall Media, LLC (WeCall) scored the #17 spot on the 2023 *Inc 5000*'s list of fastest growing companies with a blazingly fast 10,993% rate of revenue growth in its first 3 years. Even more striking, founder David Maman achieved this milestone as a bootstrapped startup without any outside investors. How did he do it? It turns out that Maman's mission for WeCall was shaped by his earlier negative experience as the founder of a $20 million e-commerce venture.

David Maman kicks off our conversation with the still-poignant memories of struggling to make a profit with his online jewelry store – a struggle he attributes to the relentlessly high costs and low value of broad-based digital marketing.

> *I founded an e-commerce company prior to starting WeCall — an on-line jewelry company. We became pretty popular and even made it into a list of the top 500 e-commerce companies in the world. But we were wildly unprofitable most years. We barely broke even on $20 million of revenue in our peak year. We worked with digital marketing agencies to attract customers to our site, agencies that sold us on brand awareness, traffic, clicks and all that. Those promises never converted to profitable sales revenue, but we still paid cold, hard cash for all that marketing. It was very, very discouraging to be writing massive checks to Google, to Facebook, to all sorts of affiliate partners and working my butt off man-aging the e-commerce logistics and distribution work, then end up un-profitable most years. It wasn't sustainable, and sure enough, a couple of years later, I shuttered that business.*

What happens when an entrepreneur becomes so disillusioned with the cost of customer acquisition that he shuts down his online business? David Maman candidly says that his first reaction was to just give up on entrepreneurship. But then he learned about performance marketing from a close friend, and realized that starting a pay-per-call business would put him "at the other side of the table" in the digital marketing ecosystem. The prospect of running a company that would deliver qualified customer leads to brands and in turn would generate predictable, profitable revenues for the founder was appealing enough to rekindle his enthusiasm,

> *Frankly, after shutting down the ecommerce company, I lost my mojo as an entrepreneur. For a few years, I was just managing my own personal*

investments, looking for the next opportunity. But I had no real purpose – no clear idea about what kind of venture to start.

Then in 2019 I discovered performance marketing, or the pay-per-call model, meaning that my customers would pay me for generating qualified inbound calls. When my best friend joined this company named Ringba, which is a SaaS platform that handles call routing and call management for performance marketing companies, I learned how the model worked in practice, and it really resonated with me. I was fed up with how digital marketing agencies operated, and how the cost of marketing could quickly sink your business. I realized that being a performance marketing company is quite the opposite. You contract to achieve a clear target, a specific KPI with nowhere to hide. If you can hit that target at a cost that's lower than the price your customer will pay for qualified customer calls, then your company will be profitable. You just need to establish a well-managed value chain where the client is winning, you're winning, and you have created a scalable and sustainable business.

Embracing a Pay-Per-Call Business Model

Pay-per-call marketing is a radical shift from traditional agency models that charge for "branding" and "awareness" toward a performance-based approach. In this model, pay-per-call businesses contract with their clients to generate consumer-initiated inbound calls. The business takes on the cost of outreach to prospects, motivates them to make a call to learn more about their client's service, and routes these calls to their clients. In a typical service contract, the clients only pay when inbound calls surpass an agreed-upon duration, used to determine if the caller is a qualified lead.

The more he learned about flipping the script from traditional marketing where businesses pay regardless of results, to a pay-per-call model that directly connects marketing spend to qualified leads, the more enthusiastic Maman became. He embraced a new entrepreneurial mission —helping businesses achieve more predictable customer acquisition costs by starting a company based on specific metrics and clear-cut results.

Maman launched WeCall in 2019, optimistic that this type of business would reward his efforts and become reliably profitable over time. Rather than setting up any ambitious growth and revenue targets for WeCall at the start, Maman deliberately kept his focus on efficient execution of the straightforward but challenging strategy of consistently generating inbound consumer calls to clients at a lower cost than the clients had contracted to pay WeCall.

As Maman explains, that differential between the cost to WeCall for generating customer leads and the fees he collected from clients was the essential operational challenge. Ideally, his new business would consistently achieve a positive cash flow loop for every contract he signed,

> WeCall generates consumer-initiated inbound calls and we route them to our clients, on a pre-agreed performance basis. We get paid if a call surpasses an agreed upon duration. For example, a healthcare provider might pay us $50 for every inbound call that exceeds 90 seconds—giving them time to verify that the caller meets their criteria such as Medicare eligibility, age requirements, and geographic location.
>
> Basically, we›re in the lead generation business. We are profitable only if we can generate these qualified leads in a cost-effective manner. The heart and soul of our company is creating high quality leads at a consistent level that is cost effective. It's almost like arbitrage. If our operational cost is $40 to generate a lead, and we can sell it for $50 to our client, that's profitable. But if the cost is $40 and we can only sell it for $30 I›ll go out of business rather quickly. So, a key question is how do you establish that cost per call? It really is a byproduct of the client's acquisition target and it's very important to be able to get that figure right.

To ensure that WeCall stayed on the profitable side of this margin-management equation from the start, Maman established a handful essential metrics for business success. These metrics worked in tandem with his win-win philosophy of creating an equally measurable level of value for his company's clients to navigate the path to annual growth and profitability.

Metrics That Matter to WeCall

WeCall success hinges on meticulously tracking specific performance metrics that directly impact profitability. David Maman pays particular attention to several metrics, starting with how much it costs for his company to generate the inbound customer calls they have contracted to deliver to a client.

Cost of Generating Qualified Inbound Calls: It's essential to implement cost-effective strategies that reliably motivate the target groups to place inbound calls and measure the percentage of those calls that qualify for payment. A very brief hello and goodbye isn't enough. WeCall needs to generate calls that match up with the client-defined and contractually agreed parameters for a qualified lead. Typically, the payment threshold is measured by the length of time that a prospect stays on the phone after they are connected to the client's service center. This focus on cost-effective lead generation guides WeCall's advertising strategies and budgets, as well as its targeting parameters.

The next key metric is WeCall's success in attracting the most profitable clients.

Number of High-Value Clients: How much clients will pay for a qualified call is usually related to the projected life time value of their average customer. As a result, Maman notes that not all clients define quality leads in exactly the same way, and some potential clients are simply not a good match for WeCall,

> *Not all clients are the best clients for us to work with. Somebody who wants a Cadillac at the price of a Hyundai is not a good customer for WeCall. The clients we go after are the companies who have already clearly defined the value of attracting a customer.*

Typically, those clients come from industry sectors with consistently high customer lifetime value (CLV) opportunities, for example insurance and health care providers. Working directly with end clients rather than brokers or middlemen also creates better margin opportunities and enables higher-quality targeting. As Maman puts it, his company benefits by working with clients that are,

> *...at the top of the food chain, rather than brokers or people that are going to arbitrage your call. Strategic end user clients are the ones that will set up margin opportunities that allow for better targeting and filtering on our side to reach that ideal customer. I think our sales process is about creating synchronicity between WeCall and our clients by motivating a call from the consumers who are actually interested in their services. That's the definition of a quality, high-value lead.*

Strategic client selection means prioritizing direct relationships with end clients rather than intermediaries, and focusing on clients who value quality over simply seeking the lowest price. That selectivity supports WeCall's ability to maintain consistent profitability while expanding its revenues and client roster year after year.

Maintaining Operational Efficiency and Financial Discipline

In any high-volume, low-margin business, operational excellence is critical. This includes monitoring key performance indicators like earnings per call and maintaining efficient call routing systems. For companies handling tens of thousands of calls daily, even small inefficiencies can significantly impact profitability. Call routing and monetization represent a critical area for performance tracking.

Knowing this, Maman pays careful attention to key operational aspects of his company's overall efficiency to ensure cost-effective strategies for targeting prospects and converting them into qualified leads. With tens of thousands of calls routed daily, WeCall closely monitors "earnings per call" to ensure profitable operations and positive unit economics,

> *Waste can destroy a company, and efficiencies can really make your company. We're in a high volume, low margin type of business, the line between success and failure can be quite thin if you don't have the right operations and consistently measure and optimize every element that determines your unit economics at the cost per call/earnings per call level.*
>
> *For example, we know it costs us... $10 to generate a call, and we're selling a qualified inbound call for $20. We also know that only 50% of the inbound calls make it past that qualification buffer. So if the earning per call is $10 but if it costs me $10 to generate a call, then I'm just breaking even. Or even worse, let's say instead of paying you $20, that client actually only pays you $18. But there's another client who is also paying you $18 per call, and you realize that you can generate a 75% qualified rate for them. Well now you're making... $13.50 a call on that contract.*

This granular tracking of call costs, billable rates, and revenue per call enables WeCall to optimize their routing strategies and client mix to maximize profitability.

Consistent profitability in a low-margin business also requires careful operational management and expense control. It's not surprising that a critical aspect of WeCall's growth strategy has been disciplined cash flow management. Unlike many venture-backed startups that prioritize growth over profitability, Maman built his company with financial discipline from day one,

> *I was fortunate enough in the beginning to have a little bit of savings to launch the business, so I didn't have to raise any venture money. We started off as a two-man operation in 2019, and I just kept on doubling down. We were profitable from day one. To this day, we don't have any outside capital involved in the business.*
>
> *I also have a very much of a bend don't break philosophy as it relates to operations... Is this really a critical staff member? Is this really a critical expense? Can we do it without it? Are we going to see ROI from this individual?*

This disciplined approach to cash flow has enabled Maman to reinvest earnings strategically and selectively, while maintaining complete control in managing his company's direction.

Creating Client Value as a Core Growth Driver

Maman firmly believes that WeCall's success in performance marketing requires an unwavering focus on creating measurable value for its clients. His frustrations from paying for high-cost digital marketing and receiving low-quality customer acquisition results as an e-commerce business owner are still fresh in his mind. Becoming a player on the other side of the table in the marketing ecosystem has sharpened his insistence that value creation is the core driver of growth for his company.

WeCall's mission statement emphasizes **empathy, focus and excellence**, and promises that WeCall will "deeply understand our clients' unique goals and challenges" and "deliver outstanding results" by "driving cost-effective traffic that meets and exceeds our clients' acquisitions targets."

As Maman succinctly puts it: "If you always create value for your clients and they can see profitable outcomes, then why wouldn't they continue to scale with us?"

He elaborates on how the WeCall mission statement has guided his company's growth over time,

> *We started off just working with home services clients, and then we expanded into insurance services and health insurance services and focused on just becoming better at what we do every year. There was never a goal outside of just creating value. And that's really the core of our business, is that value grows, and it will continue to grow so long as we stay committed to our mission statement which is basically a marketing philosophy of empathy, focus and excellence.*
>
> *For me, empathy means that we will deeply understand our clients' unique goals and challenges, ensuring we address their specific needs better than any other agency. Focusing to deliver outstanding results, we will concentrate our efforts on driving cost effective traffic that meets and exceeds our clients' acquisition targets, avoiding distractions that do not contribute to sustainable growth. We believe that excellence is non-negotiable. By consistently delivering top tier performance, we will ensure a positive return on investment for our clients. We achieve this by maintaining a relentless commitment to quality, innovation, and client satisfaction.*
>
> *So that's who we are. I believe our job is to focus on creating value, and then everything else will work itself out.*

While pay-per-call marketing offers compelling advantages for select clients, particularly those in sectors with high customer lifetime value, the business model itself also faces challenges. The performance marketing sector operates in a regulated environment, particularly when dealing with industries like healthcare, insurance, and financial services that handle sensitive customer information and privacy restrictions. Companies may have to navigate the complex compliance requirements impacting their clients, while maintaining efficiency. With increasing consumer privacy regulations worldwide, performance marketers may also have to follow stricter guidelines about the collection, storage, and security of international consumer data and maintain transparent practices in how they generate and route calls.

Balancing quantity with quality presents an ongoing challenge. When some companies in the industry lean on their staff to generate more and more calls to meet quotas, there's a risk of pursuing volume at the expense of lead quality, casting a shadow on the whole performance marketing sector. Maman believes that the WeCall mission and its emphasis on creating value is the best foundation for dealing with any new regulatory challenges, "Grow at your own pace… do the right thing and create value. Make sure you're creating value for somebody, because value grows… and you will always have a buyer for value."

Leveraging Technology and AI for High-Growth Performance

Like other high growth companies, WeCall analyzes its data and uses AI to fine-tune and optimize internal operations. Maman sees significant potential in customer-facing AI applications, though he maintains a measured approach, "I think we're at the beginning of AI and … really just scratching the surface on how it's going to help us".

WeCall is introducing applications like conversational AI chat bots and conversational outbound dialing that could further enhance his company's lead generation capabilities. As AI capabilities continue to evolve, Maman will consider implementing lifelike avatars and interactive dialogs, predicting that, "We could create a lot of short form video content where we'll use an AI avatar… and that avatar may be reading a script to you on Facebook or TikTok." These technologies could make the WeCall model even more efficient.

The pay-per-call performance business model David Maman's entrepreneurial spirit with its emphasis on measurable marketing results and a clear, two-sided value proposition. From Maman's perspective, pay-per-call performance marketing represents a long overdue shift toward accountability in an industry historically plagued by vague metrics and uncertain returns. He launched WeCall in 2019 determined to deliver value to clients and earn enough to support himself in the process. WeCall's growth trajectory and profitability have far exceeded these modest startup goals. The company's success to date resoundingly validates Maman's conviction that performance marketing was the right fit for his entrepreneurial skills, and a sector where lean operations and results-driven strategies would pay off,

I started WeCall with a goal of just trying to get back into being an entrepreneur and hoping to make around $10,000 a month to support myself. Well, that first year we made a profit and I think we generated close to a million in revenues. Then by 2020 our revenue was around $10

million, and $25 million the next year. Revenues have kept going up from there, until now we are an $80 million business. I think that gives you an idea of the sort of percentage growth that's possible.

WeCall continues to expand into additional high-value verticals, adding home services, auto insurance, life insurance, and pet insurance to its client services portfolio. The company also made its first acquisition in 2025, acquiring Slikk Mobile, a programmatic media company that strengthens its in-house technology and media buying power.

WeCall's 100X growth illustrates the potential of performance marketing services when executed with a disciplined focus on creating measurable value for both service providers and clients. In an increasingly competitive marketplace, the performance-based model seems poised to claim an ever-larger share of marketing spend.

◆ ◆ ◆

Financial discipline may not be the flashiest part of a startup's story, but it is always an essential element because extreme growth cannot outpace financial reality forever. In this chapter, Upward Health, Awestruck, and WeCall each demonstrate how financial rigor creates the breathing room for scalability and transformation. Whether it's Upward Health's ability to guarantee outcomes and assume downside risk for vulnerable patient populations, Awestruck's commitment to deliver world-class marketing on a sustainable budget, or WeCall's insistence on profitable margins for every client call, the throughline is unmistakable: disciplined financial management is the enabler of sustainable growth.

These three founders prove that transformational impact, market leadership, and profitability can go hand-in-hand. By applying precise metrics, making hard decisions early, and reinvesting wisely, they built companies that are leading their industries in innovation, service, and staying power.

8

Is Your Company Ready to Scale?

YOUR BUSINESS IS WORKING. Customers are buying, your team is busy, and revenue is ticking up, month after month. You've proven there's demand, and you're building something real.

But it's slow.

You're wondering if it's time to step on the gas. You see competitors raising money, expanding into new markets, or investing heavily in marketing—and you think, "Should we be doing that too? Are we ready to scale?"

Here's the hard truth: scaling is not possible unless you have your act together. Scaling magnifies what's already happening in your business. If your systems are sloppy, scaling makes them chaotic. If your customer acquisition is expensive, scaling drains your cash faster. If your market isn't big enough, scaling will run you into a wall. Doing it wrong can even destroy your business. It's one of the biggest reasons businesses stall out or fail altogether.

Growth and scaling are not the same thing. Growth means you're adding customers, building revenue, and expanding your team at a steady, manageable pace. It's incremental.

Successful scaling requires your operations to handle 5x, 10x, or even 100x more demand without breaking down. It's tough. Better start by asking yourself, "Is my business ready to grow exponentially while maintaining quality, profitability, and sanity?"

In this chapter, we'll walk through five fundamental questions that every entrepreneur needs to answer to assess their readiness to scale:

ONE: Have you validated strong, addressable market demand from target customers?
Do you have a clear path for reaching 100,000 or millions more, efficiently and sustainably?

TWO: Are your customer acquisition and retention processes cost-effective and efficient?
Can you bring in customers at a reasonable cost and keep them coming back without relying on heroic efforts from your team?

THREE: Do your company's unit economics drive profitability and positive cash flow?
Is each new customer making you money, or are you subsidizing growth with hope?

FOUR: Can your operational systems and processes handle exponential demand?
Can you maintain quality while meeting 100X demand, or will your team burn out trying to keep up?

FIVE: Are you leveraging data and AI to drive customer value and internal operational efficiency?
How is data and AI used to work smarter, serve customers better, and make your team more efficient?

These aren't academic questions. They provide a practical framework for every executive to evaluate their company's readiness to scale successfully.

This chapter is your mirror. It will help you see where you're strong, where you're exposed, and what you need to shore up before you scale. It's your chance to slow down, so you can go faster later with confidence. If you're serious about scaling, these five questions will be your roadmap. They will help you build a business that isn't just bigger—but better, stronger, and more resilient for the next stage of your journey.

Ready to find out if you're truly positioned to scale? Let's dive in.

Have You Validated Strong Market Demand with Key Customers Who Represent a Large Addressable Market?

You already know people want what you're selling—at least, some people. You've built a steady base of customers, your team is delivering, and revenue is moving in the right direction. The real question now isn't whether your business works. It's whether your business can scale to grow faster and work better.

This is a critical distinction. Many businesses get stuck because they confuse initial demand with scalable demand. They've proven there is interest within a small circle of early adopters but haven't tested whether that demand extends to a broader market they can reach efficiently. Scaling means you can find and serve thousands—or millions—more customers without your costs exploding or your operations collapsing. Scaling means your business can handle much, much more demand, and do it profitably.

Why Validating Scalable Demand Matters

Scaling amplifies your business model—warts and all. If your product only appeals to a niche, efforts to attract different types of customers will drain your cash and energy without meaningful returns. If your pricing or delivery models can't hold up at volume, scaling will magnify those weaknesses. Validating scalable demand means you aren't guessing about growth potential—you have a clear roadmap for future growth based on evidence.

To validate scalable demand, you need to test whether enough customers will pay your price, stay loyal, and refer others in a way that keeps acquisition costs manageable and lifetime value high. You have developed a replicable process that can support aggressive growth.

BEST PRACTICE: CharterUP

CharterUP founder Armir Harris didn't assume the charter bus industry would embrace his vision; he tested it. Starting in Atlanta, he piloted CharterUP's platform with a small but meaningful group of operators and customers, confirming that real-time booking, transparency, and reliability were pain points felt across the market. This pilot gave Harris confidence that the problems CharterUP solved in one city were widespread, validating national expansion—and ultimately propelling it to over 111,000% growth.

How to Validate Scalable Demand in Your Business

The first step is to define your Ideal Customer Profile (ICP) clearly. This isn't about general demographics; it's about identifying who your best customers are—the ones who buy repeatedly, refer others, and value what you're offering at the price you need for a healthy business. Look for patterns in who sticks around and why, and build a clear profile of the customers you need to grow your business.

Next, you need to test your offering in new segments or geographies before rolling out at scale. Too many businesses assume that what works in one city or niche will translate seamlessly elsewhere. Run low-risk pilots in different regions or with new customer segments, tracking whether these customers convert and stick around. Analyze sell-through rates, repeat purchase rates, and customer feedback to understand whether demand is real beyond your initial bubble.

Retention and repeat purchases are your best signals of scalable demand. A customer who buys once is good; a customer who buys again is gold. If your customers return without heavy re-engagement efforts, it's a strong sign that your product or service delivers real value. Likewise, pay attention to organic referrals—customers telling friends or sharing on social media without incentives is a powerful indicator that you have something people want and will advocate for.

You also need to validate pricing and willingness to pay. Discounts can drive sales, but they can also mask whether your customers truly value your product at your target price. Test your pricing to confirm that customers are willing to pay enough to sustain healthy margins, even when you scale and can't offer constant promotions.

Finally, track your customer acquisition costs (CAC) and ensure they align with your customer lifetime value (LTV). If acquiring a customer costs too much, scaling will only amplify your losses. Ensure your acquisition channels can deliver customers cost-effectively and that those customers stick around long enough to justify the cost of acquiring them.

BEST PRACTICE: OLIPOP

Ben Goodwin and David Lester learned the difference between a niche product and mass market demand the hard way. Their first healthy soda venture, Obi, proved that health-focused buyers would try a new wellness drink, but growth potential was limited. With OLIPOP, they prioritized taste while retaining health benefits, positioning the company to compete head-to-head with mainstream soda brands. They tested demand at independent stores, watched restock orders, and tracked repeat buyers to confirm that OLIPOP's appeal extended to everyday soda drinkers looking for a healthier option.

Red Flags That Indicate You're Not Ready to Scale

If your sales depend heavily on your personal involvement—networking, founder-led selling, or relationships you've built—scaling will be difficult. You need to prove that customers will buy without your direct intervention. If your retention drops when you enter new markets or test new customer segments, that's a signal that your product's appeal may not translate widely. If you notice your acquisition costs rising while your LTV remains flat, you may be trying to force demand where it doesn't exist naturally. Unclear or untested assumptions about your market size (TAM) are another warning sign. A large theoretical market doesn't mean you can capture it efficiently, especially if you haven't validated demand through pilots and measured actual conversion rates in those segments. Finally, if your customers require heavy customization or hand-holding to close a sale or stay engaged, scaling will strain your team and your resources. These dependencies indicate that your product or service needs refinement before you can efficiently serve many more customers at once.

People, Process, and Tech to Support Validation

To validate scalable demand, you need to build a culture of learning within your team. Encourage your team to approach growth with curiosity, testing, and iteration rather than assumptions. Make space for collecting and analyzing customer feedback regularly, and create clear channels for that feedback to influence your sales, marketing, and product decisions.

On the process side, establish a structured testing cadence for new markets, customer segments, and channels. This could include running pilot programs, A/B testing pricing and offers, and systematically measuring results to inform your decisions.

The right tech stack will help you track and interpret your validation efforts. A CRM system can help you monitor conversion rates, lead sources, and customer retention patterns. Analytics platforms can reveal which channels bring in the highest-quality leads, and simple survey tools can help you gather direct customer insights. These tools should give you clear visibility into what's working, what isn't, and where to adjust.

By aligning your people, processes, and technology around validation, you can move beyond gut feelings and into data-driven readiness, building the confidence you need to scale without regrets.

BEST PRACTICE: MUD\WTR

MUD\WTR founder Shane Heath knew that creating a coffee alternative would scale only if he convinced people to switch their morning ritual. He built a compelling online presence with personality, hand packaged his mushroom-based brew, and launched. Shane watched orders grow from a trickle to hundreds per week. He asked early customers why they bought and if they would repurchase, discovering that many felt better, were reducing caffeine, and were eager to share MUD\WTR with friends. This methodical, customer-driven validation allowed Shane to confirm scalable demand before moving to a profitable subscription model and eventually onto the shelves of Target and Sprouts.

Bringing It All Together

CharterUP, OLIPOP, and MUD\WTR founders took the time to test, measure, and learn, ensuring that demand was real and scalable before investing heavily in growth. They built multiple distribution channels, with systems that allowed them to find and serve more customers while keeping costs under control and maintaining product quality.

If you want to scale successfully, you need to know—not just hope—that the market is ready for you. By validating scalable demand now, you build the foundation for exponential growth without burning cash, stretching your team, or damaging your brand.

In the next section, we'll look at how to capture that demand efficiently through cost-effective customer acquisition and retention systems that ensure your business grows with quality, not just speed.

Have You Created Effective Processes for Cost-Effective and Efficient Customer Acquisition and Retention?

You're not in the "any customer at any cost" phase anymore. You've built a working business, and customers are coming in. But if you want to scale exponentially, you need to acquire customers even more efficiently—and keep them coming back. This is where many businesses get stuck. They try to scale what worked in the early days—referrals, founder-led sales, ad spend without clarity—and find that their customer acquisition costs (CAC) skyrocket while retention drops, burning cash and morale.

Scaling isn't just about getting more customers. It's about getting them at a cost you can sustain while ensuring they stay and grow with you.

Why Efficient Acquisition and Retention Are Non-Negotiable

Your growth flywheel depends on two levers: Acquisition that is repeatable and cost-effective. Retention that extends customer lifetime value (LTV).

Without both, you're pouring water into a leaky bucket. If your CAC is too high, scaling drains your cash faster than you can replenish it. If your retention is low, you'll need to keep spending to replace every customer you lose. Winning CAC and LTV combinations include subscription models for B2C products and recurring revenue for B2B products and services. A retention flywheel that generates repeat business makes it possible to grow faster and at a lower cost. Companies that scale well focus on refining their customer journey—from the first touchpoint to onboarding to long-term engagement—so that acquiring and retaining customers becomes smoother, cheaper, and more effective as they grow.

BEST PRACTICE: Odeko

Odeko founder Dane Atkinson discovered that early adopters didn't love his AI-based predictive inventory software, even though it worked flawlessly. Café owners were skeptical about buying a solution that didn't address their real inventory pain points. Listening closely to his customers, Atkinson pivoted Odeko into a logistics and supply chain partner, consolidating deliveries and handling the entire restocking process. The shift transformed Odeko into an essential operational partner for coffee shops, reducing the cost and the pain of inventory management.

This customer-centric pivot created an acquisition and retention flywheel that propelled the company's revenue from near zero to $150M+.

How to Build Cost-Effective Acquisition Processes

Cost-effective acquisition requires understanding who your ideal customer is, what they value most, and what messages resonate with them.

Start by mapping your customer journey to understand how people find you, what drives them to convert, and what objections slow them down. Look for patterns: Which channels bring in your highest LTV customers? Which sales efforts convert at the lowest cost? Don't try to scale using channels that are untested or expensive until you've proven that they deliver profitable customers. Focus on repeatable processes like targeted outbound efforts, content marketing that drives organic leads, and partnerships that create warm introductions at a lower cost than cold ads.

Invest in systems that support this. A CRM helps you track conversions, sources, and pipeline health. Marketing automation tools let you nurture leads without heavy manual effort. If you're relying on founder-led sales, start documenting your pitch and outreach process so others can replicate what works.

BEST PRACTICE: Autosled

David and Dan Sperau turned frustration with auto transport inefficiencies into a digital platform that could scale through self-service options and clear two-sided value. Rather than spending heavily on broad marketing campaigns, Autosled offered free trials and no-risk pay-per-use terms to dealerships, removing barriers to adoption and making it easy for skeptical customers to try the platform. As dealers experienced Autosled's benefits—faster, transparent vehicle shipping and easier tracking—they became loyal customers and spread the word within the tight-knit auto dealer community. One important feature of Autosled's platform enabled easy "self booking" which allows car dealers to quickly and easily place an order. On the transporter side, Autosled's fast payment system attracted drivers to the platform, ensuring supply matched demand without heavy marketing expenses.

This grassroots, customer-first approach enabled Autosled to scale to thousands of customers and transporters with positive unit economics and operational efficiency from day one.

Retention: The Critical Growth Multiplier

Retention is where profitability and scale intersect. A long-time repeat customer not only continues to pay you; they often buy more over time and refer others. Retention starts with onboarding. Customers need to see value quickly and understand how to use your product or service effectively. Clear communication, easy setup, and proactive support reduce churn early. Ongoing engagement keeps customers connected. Regular check-ins, helpful content, and personalized recommendations show that you care about their success. Listen to customer feedback, and adapt your offerings to meet evolving needs. Retention isn't just a customer service function; it's a growth function. Reducing churn improves your LTV, making your CAC investments more efficient and creating space for sustainable scaling.

BEST PRACTICE: FlexCare Infusion Centers

FlexCare cofounders Aaron Smith and Callie Turk built a fast-scaling healthcare business by improving the patient experience while reducing care provider paperwork. By designing clinics that were convenient, comfortable, and patient-centric, FlexCare dramatically reduced the stress of drug infusion treatments. Their approach to referrals—essential in healthcare—was also retention-focused. By making it easy for physicians to refer patients and managing paperwork and insurance on behalf of patients, FlexCare gained the trust of care providers, who became consistent partners in patient acquisition through referrals.

FlexCare's excellent service retained patients and also moved them to share positive experiences with others. This flywheel of exceptional service, high patient retention, and provider trust enabled FlexCare to scale from a single clinic to a national leader while controlling acquisition costs and maximizing LTV.

Red Flags That Indicate You're Not Ready to Scale Acquisition

If your CAC is increasing while your LTV remains flat, your growth isn't sustainable. This suggests you're either targeting the wrong customers, your pricing isn't aligned with your costs, or your onboarding and retention processes are weak. If your growth is driven entirely by discounts or promotions, you're not creating durable customer relationships. Customers who come for the discount often leave when it ends. If you rely heavily on founder-led sales or a single channel, scaling will strain your team and resources. You need repeatable, documented processes others can execute. Finally, if your retention rates are low, scaling will only increase churn and customer acquisition costs, making it difficult to build a profitable growth engine.

People, Process, and Tech to Support Scalable Acquisition and Retention

Your people are your frontline for acquisition and retention. As you scale, invest in building a sales and customer success team that aligns with your culture and mission. Train them not just on your product but on your customer's problems and how your offering solves them. Your processes should document how you acquire customers, onboard them, and keep them engaged. This creates consistency and makes it easier to train new team members and maintain quality as you grow.

Together, people, processes, and technology will allow you to acquire customers efficiently and retain them effectively, creating a scalable engine for growth.

Bringing It All Together

Odeko, Autosled, and FlexCare built systems that made customer acquisition cost-effective and retention reliable. They focused on creating genuine value for customers, simplifying adoption, and ensuring customers stayed for the long term. They listened, adapted, and built systems to reduce manual work while increasing customer satisfaction.

If you want to scale efficiently, you need to treat acquisition and retention as a system, not a series of one-off wins. Refine your acquisition channels, reduce friction in the buying process, and build retention strategies that turn customers into fans. By doing this work, you create a business that doesn't just grow—it grows profitably, sustainably, and with customers who want to stay with you as you scale.

Do You Have Positive Unit Economics That Will Drive Profitability and Positive Cash Flow?

Most small businesses reach a point where more sales alone won't fix the underlying issues. If you're losing money on each sale, scaling up just means you lose money faster. If your margins are too thin or your operations are too costly, adding more customers strains your cash flow instead of strengthening it. That's why healthy unit economics are non-negotiable if you want to scale.

Unit economics are your ground-level view of how your business actually makes money, customer by customer and transaction by transaction. They answer questions like:

- Does each sale contribute profit after direct costs?
- How long does it take to recoup customer acquisition costs?
- What is the lifetime value of your customer compared to the cost to acquire them?

These fundamentals aren't just financial metrics—they're a diagnostic tool for your business's readiness to handle exponential growth without collapsing under its own weight.

Why Positive Unit Economics Matter for Scale

Scaling with poor unit economics is like running faster while carrying a heavy backpack. You might move for a while, but you'll burn out your cash, your team, and your energy before you reach your goals.

Businesses ready to scale ensure that:

- Each new customer is profitable (or becomes profitable quickly).
- Their cost to deliver the product or service is sustainable.

- Growth doesn't require perpetual external funding to cover operational losses.

In this way, positive unit economics are your green light to scale. They indicate your business can grow while generating cash to fuel that growth, reducing dependency on outside funding and giving you control over your scaling journey.

BEST PRACTICE: CSN Stores

Niraj Shah and Steve Conine built CSN Stores—later Wayfair—on a foundation of disciplined unit economics. From their very first site, RacksAndStands.com, they meticulously tracked advertising costs, keyword performance, and conversion rates, ensuring profitability on every sale. Unlike many early e-commerce ventures chasing traffic at any cost, CSN focused on positive margins from day one. Their vendor-direct fulfillment model further strengthened unit economics. By drop-shipping most products directly from suppliers, they avoided the massive inventory costs that sank many competitors. Proprietary software integrated supplier data in real time, reducing errors and increasing efficiency, while volume-based supplier discounts boosted margins.

By 2006, CSN surpassed $100 million in sales—without a dollar of venture capital. Their disciplined, data-driven approach proved that scaling wasn't about blitz growth but about ensuring each transaction strengthened the business. This foundation paved the way for Wayfair's eventual multi-billion-dollar success.

How to Assess and Improve Your Unit Economics

Start by calculating your gross margin on your product or service. Are you consistently generating a healthy percentage after direct costs? If not, analyze pricing, sourcing, and delivery methods to find ways to improve it. Next, look at your CAC (Customer Acquisition Cost) to LTV (Lifetime Value) ratio. A healthy benchmark for many industries is an LTV at least 3x your CAC, ensuring the money spent to acquire a customer pays off over the relationship. Review your CAC payback period—the time it takes to earn back your customer acquisition costs from the customer's purchases. The shorter this period, the more cash-efficient your business becomes, reducing the need for external funding to fuel growth.

Evaluate your operational leverage. Can you increase revenue without increasing costs at the same rate? If every new customer requires a proportional increase in labor or fulfillment costs, your model may need refinement before scaling. Finally, analyze churn. High churn erodes LTV and can ruin unit economics even if acquisition costs are low. Improving retention often has the highest ROI for improving unit economics.

BEST PRACTICE: ButcherBox

ButcherBox founder Mike Salguero bootstrapped his company with a commitment to capital efficiency and profitability. From the start, ButcherBox adopted a subscription-based model that generated recurring revenue, reducing the volatility of one-time purchases. Instead of keeping operations in house (which would increase costs and complexity), ButcherBox outsourced every possible aspect of the supply chain for sourcing and shipping grassfed beef from farm to table. Salguero's philosophy was clear: each box shipped should be profitable, focusing on dollars per box shipped rather than vanity metrics like topline revenue. This focus on unit economics enabled ButcherBox to grow to over $400 million in annual revenue without raising venture capital, managing cash flow to fund growth.

ButcherBox's asset-light model, outsourcing production and distribution while maintaining quality control, kept overhead low and allowed for operational flexibility. Salguero's disciplined, data-driven approach to pricing, customer acquisition, and fulfillment enabled ButcherBox to scale based on improving unit economics in tandem with increasing sales volume.

Red Flags That Indicate You're Not Ready to Scale
Sign that you need to fix your unit economics before scaling include:

- Negative or razor-thin gross margins: If you lose money on each sale, scaling will magnify losses.

- High CAC relative to LTV: When your cost to acquire customers is more than what they spend, your model is broken
- High churn: If it takes a year to recover your acquisition costs but your average customer churns in six months, you're losing money on every customer.
- No operational leverage: If scaling revenue requires scaling costs at the same rate, you won't gain margin improvements with growth.
- Dependence on constant discounts: If sales rely heavily on promotions to convert, your margins are likely too thin.

People, Process, and Tech to Support Unit Economic Discipline

To emphasize the importance of financial discipline, especially in sales and marketing, align incentives and company culture with profitable growth, not just top-line sales. Your processes should include regular reviews of pricing strategies, supplier negotiations, and operational efficiencies to ensure gross margins remain healthy as you grow.

Your systems should provide:

- Real-time dashboards tracking customer acquisition costs, lifetime value, churn, and margins.
- Inventory and fulfillment systems that help reduce waste and optimize costs.
- Analytics tools to identify which products, customers, or channels contribute most to profitability.

By aligning your team, processes, and technology with a focus on healthy unit economics, you can build a business ready to handle growth without compromising financial stability.

BEST PRACTICE: WeCall

David Maman built WeCall on a simple but powerful principle: every customer contract had to be profitable from day one. After experiencing years of unprofitable growth in a previous e-commerce venture, Maman embraced the pay-per-call performance marketing model, where clients pay only for qualified inbound calls. WeCall's unit economics are crystal clear: if it costs $40 to generate a call and a client pays $50 for it, the business thrives; if the cost exceeds the payout, it fails. To stay on the right side of that equation, Maman tracks metrics like earnings per call, qualification rates, and client lifetime value, focusing on industries like healthcare and insurance with strong margins.

This disciplined approach kept WeCall profitable from its first year, scaling to $80M in revenue without outside capital—proof that healthy unit economics fuel sustainable growth.

Bringing It All Together

CSN Stores, ButcherBox and WeCall prove that it's possible to scale rapidly while maintaining healthy unit economics and cash flow discipline. They didn't grow by chasing vanity metrics; they grew by ensuring that each customer added value to the business.

If you want to scale confidently, take the time now to ensure your unit economics are solid:

- Know your numbers.
- Identify where you're leaking value.
- Fix inefficiencies before investing heavily in growth.

Healthy unit economics give you the freedom to scale without fear, ensuring that as your customer base grows, so does your profitability and your ability to reinvest in the next stage of your journey

Have You Created Operational Systems and Processes That Can Handle Exponential Demand?

Many businesses think scaling is about adding more customers or launching into new markets. But if your operations aren't ready, growth exposes and amplifies every hidden weakness, turning success into stress. You can't build a skyscraper on sand, and you can't scale sustainably without systems. If you want to grow exponentially, you need operational systems and processes that don't just support your business—they power it forward. The right systems let you deliver faster, with higher quality, and at lower cost, creating a competitive advantage that compounds as you grow.

Why Operational Systems Matter for Scaling

At a small scale, messy spreadsheets, founder heroics, and verbal instructions can keep the lights on. But as your customer base grows, these shortcuts become bottlenecks. Operational systems transform chaos into consistency, helping you:

- Free up your team to focus on high-value work.
- Create predictable, repeatable processes that ensure quality.
- Scale efficiently without linear cost increases.
- Gain real-time data to drive decisions and improvements.

The difference between businesses that scale well and those that stall often comes down to how well they build and maintain these systems.

BEST PRACTICE: Upward Health

At Upward Health, CEO Glen Moller transformed a struggling healthcare startup into one of America's fastest-growing private companies by building operational systems that made scalable, in-home, whole-person care possible. Upward Health invested early in a unified data platform, predictive analytics, and standardized case management protocols while maintaining flexibility to adapt to each patient's needs. They developed field logistics systems that optimized care team routing and scheduling, allowing teams to serve high-need patients in their homes efficiently while maintaining high standards of care.

These operational systems fueled Upward Health's exponential growth, allowing it to meet ambitious payer contracts while delivering better outcomes, proving that strong operations can turn a mission-driven healthcare model into a scalable, profitable enterprise.

Building Operational Systems for Scale

Start by mapping your core processes. Identify what drives value in your business and break it down into clear steps. For some, it's customer onboarding; for others, it's product fulfillment or delivery of a service. Mapping these processes helps reveal inefficiencies, bottlenecks, and areas ripe for automation.

Once mapped, standardize and document these processes so that any team member can follow them. This reduces errors, makes training easier, and ensures consistency as you grow. Next, look for opportunities to automate repetitive tasks such as scheduling, billing, reporting, or customer follow-ups. Automation frees your team to focus on higher-value work that requires human judgment. Finally, build data and feedback loops into your operations. Use dashboards to track key metrics like turnaround times, error rates, customer satisfaction, and team productivity. Use these insights to adjust and improve continuously.

BEST PRACTICE: Uwill

Michael London built Uwill's student mental health platform to serve millions of students across hundreds of institutions while maintaining high service standards. The company developed algorithms to connect students with skilled therapists within minutes, implemented real-time triage systems to handle crises in under 30 seconds, and customized data dashboards to monitor service delivery and client satisfaction across its expanding network. These systems allowed Uwill to respond to demand spikes while maintaining high quality services, proving that operational systems can be the backbone of rapid, effective, and sustainable growth.

Red Flags That Indicate You're Not Ready to Scale Operationally

If your business feels like it's always in chaos mode, with team members constantly fighting fires, it's a sign your processes aren't scalable. Constant emergencies drain energy, distract leadership, and create burnout, making it impossible to handle more customers without quality slipping. If quality drops when volume increases, that's a clear indicator that your operations are stretched too thin. Whether it's longer delivery times, more customer complaints, or higher error rates, scaling will only magnify these issues if they're not fixed.

If onboarding new customers or employees is slow and inconsistent, it's a sign your processes depend on individual heroes rather than systems. A scalable business can integrate new customers or team members smoothly, without overwhelming the team or sacrificing customer experience. If you're overly reliant on key individuals—often the founder—for critical tasks, scaling will quickly hit a ceiling. When too much knowledge is locked in one person's head, the business becomes fragile, and any absence can cause operations to stall.

If you lack clear visibility into operational performance, making decisions feels like guessing. Without tracking key metrics, you won't know what's working, what needs fixing, or where to invest resources for improvement. If your business still relies heavily on manual processes, you risk delays, errors, and inconsistent customer experiences as demand increases. Manual processes can't scale efficiently, and your competitors who automate will outpace you on speed and cost. If any of these signs sound familiar, it's a clear signal to pause and invest in operational systems before adding fuel to your growth engine.

People, Process, and Tech to Build Operational Readiness
People: Build a team that understands the value of consistent processes. Empower managers to improve workflows and train their teams, creating a culture where everyone contributes to operational excellence. Process: Create clear, documented processes for key activities while leaving room for flexibility where it matters. This balance between structure and adaptability is essential for scaling without losing agility. Tech: Use technology to multiply your team's effectiveness. Project management tools help track workflows. CRM systems manage customer interactions systematically. Automation tools can handle repetitive tasks, and data dashboards keep you informed in real-time, enabling proactive management. Together, the right people, processes, and technology form a foundation that allows your business to grow with confidence, efficiency, and consistency.

BEST PRACTICE: Harness

Harness founder Jyoti Bansal knew from his $3.7 billion AppDynamics exit that scaling isn't just about great products—it's about operational systems that enable innovation and growth. When he launched Harness in 2017 to streamline software delivery, he rejected traditional structures in favor of a "startups within a startup" model. Each product—whether focused on delivery, cost management, or security—operated like its own startup with separate P&L accountability, growth goals, and metrics. This prevented resource drain, created clear accountability, and kept Harness agile as it scaled to 15 product lines.

Harness also embedded data-driven systems across the company, using dashboards to track KPIs and early AI tools to automate testing and deployment validation. These efficiencies freed engineers to focus on innovation while ensuring reliable delivery. The result: Harness surpassed $250 million in ARR while staying nimble, proving that operational discipline is the engine of sustainable scale.

Bringing It All Together

Upward Health, Uwill and Harness prove that operational systems are not a "nice to have" but a strategic imperative for scaling. These systems allowed them to deliver exceptional quality and customer experience even as they grew rapidly, turning operations into a competitive advantage. If you want to outperform your competition as you scale, start now by building the systems that will allow your business to grow without sacrificing quality or profitability. When your operations run smoothly, growth isn't something you fear—it's something your business is ready to handle.

In the next section, we will explore how to leverage proprietary data and AI to further accelerate your competitive edge as you scale.

Are You Leveraging Proprietary Data and AI to Drive Customer Value and Internal Operational Efficiency?

At a certain point in your growth journey, doing more of what's working isn't enough. To scale effectively, you need to work smarter, not just harder—and that means using data and AI to power decisions, streamline operations, and enhance customer value. The best businesses aren't just selling products or services; they're collecting and leveraging proprietary data that competitors don't have, turning it into actionable insights to improve customer experience, reduce costs, and fuel growth.

AI isn't a replacement for your team's expertise or intuition. Instead, it acts as a force multiplier, helping you analyze patterns, predict customer needs, and automate repetitive tasks so your people can focus on what matters most.

Why Data and AI Matter for Scaling

Maximizing the visibility and value of internal data and AI-based systems allow you to:

- See what's working and what isn't—faster and more accurately.
- Personalize customer experiences at scale.
- Identify inefficiencies and fix them before they become crises.
- Predict customer behavior, allowing proactive service and inventory management.
- Free up your team's time by automating repetitive, low-value tasks.

While many small businesses think data and AI are only for tech giants, the reality is that strategically using your data is often the difference between a company that scales well and one that stalls.

BEST PRACTICE: Rarebreed Veterinary Partners

Dan Espinal built Rarebreed Veterinary Partners into one of the fastest-growing veterinary networks in America by treating data and AI as strategic assets. From the outset, Espinal invested heavily in building an integrated data platform he called the Rarebreed Operating System. This infrastructure unified data across 130+ clinics, enabling real-time insights into everything from patient care to staffing efficiency. Rarebreed uses AI to make data actionable at the clinic level. Managers can query performance metrics in plain language—asking why revenue dipped last month, for example—and receive immediate, data-driven answers with suggested interventions. AI also automates back-office workflows like onboarding and scheduling, reducing overhead while freeing staff to focus on patient care.

By marrying technology with a people-first culture, Rarebreed transformed messy, fragmented veterinary data into a powerful growth engine, proving that data and AI can elevate both operational efficiency and customer value.

How to Leverage Data and AI in Your Business

Start with the Data You Already Have
Every business generates valuable data: customer purchases, website behavior, service usage, and operational workflows. Start by organizing this data to identify patterns: Which products have the highest repeat purchase rates? Which customer segments generate the most profit? Where are delays occurring in your processes?

Build Feedback Loops
Use data to inform decisions, measure outcomes, and refine your approach. For example, track customer onboarding times, delivery success rates, and support ticket resolution times. Share these insights with your team and empower them to adjust processes accordingly.

Use AI Where It Adds Immediate Value
You don't need to build proprietary AI models on day one. Start with accessible AI tools:

- Automate routine administrative tasks.
- Use AI-powered forecasting tools to improve demand planning.
- Implement chatbots for handling common customer support queries.
- Test AI-based personalization tools to recommend products or services to customers.

BEST PRACTICE: Carbliss

Adam and Amanda Kroener scaled a great tasting, carb free cocktail into one of America's fastest-growing alcoholic beverage brands. Leveraging internal data was a core part of their success. Carbliss focused on depletions (actual sales to consumers) rather than shipments to distributors, ensuring they weren't fooled by inflated numbers. They tracked reorders as a true sign of product demand, monitored granular cost metrics down to the cent for each ingredient, and used this data to refine pricing and purchasing decisions.

On the AI front, Carbliss adopted a "test and learn" approach. Rather than blindly jumping into AI, they experimented with using AI for forecasting and operational analysis, comparing outputs with traditional methods while retaining human oversight. This practical, disciplined approach ensured AI added value without creating new risks.

As Carbliss's experience shows, AI should supplement, not replace, human decision-making. Use it for learning, experimenting, and efficiency, while maintaining human judgment for critical business decisions.

Red Flags That You're Missing Data and AI Leverage

If you are making decisions based purely on gut feeling or historical habits without real-time data insights, you are likely leaving opportunities on the table. When your business grows, these blind spots can turn into expensive mistakes. If you find yourself reacting to problems rather than predicting and preventing them, you're missing the predictive power data and AI can provide. For example, if customer churn surprises you or stockouts catch you off guard, it's time to use data to get ahead of these issues. If your team is drowning in repetitive tasks that could be automated, such as manual data entry or routine customer follow-ups, you're using human time inefficiently—time that could be redirected toward strategic initiatives or customer relationships. If you don't know which products, services, or customers are your most profitable, you're missing the clarity you need to focus your resources where they will drive the most growth.

These red flags indicate it's time to take a hard look at how you're using (or not using) your data.

People, Process, and Tech for Data and AI Readiness

People: Cultivate a culture that values data-driven decisions. Train your team to interpret dashboards and metrics and to ask questions that drive continuous improvement. Process: Build structured ways to collect, review, and act on data. Establish weekly or monthly review rhythms to analyze key metrics with your team. Tech: Use accessible tools before building custom AI:

- Business dashboards for real-time insights.
- CRM systems to track customer behavior and history.

- AI-enhanced forecasting tools for sales and inventory planning.
- Marketing automation with AI capabilities for personalization and segmentation.

Start small, prove value, and expand your data and AI capabilities as your business scales.

BEST PRACTICE: Crisp

Crisp cofounder Are Traasdahl built Crisp on the belief that solving food waste required a modern data infrastructure. Traditional food supply chains ran on outdated, fragmented systems, making it nearly impossible to track demand accurately. Crisp changed that by creating a cloud-based platform that ingests and harmonizes real-time retail and distributor data. Traasdahl prioritized data under management as Crisp's "hero metric," knowing that the more data flowing through its system, the more valuable the platform would become. Crisp used AI-driven analytics to forecast demand, identify phantom inventory, and optimize product distribution, helping retailers and suppliers reduce waste while improving profitability.

By embedding with early partners like Walmart and Target and proving strong ROI, Crisp scaled to serve over 6,000 customers, processing hundreds of millions of data points. Its disciplined, data-first approach shows how AI and proprietary data can fuel both growth and global impact.

Bringing It All Together

Rarebreed, Carbliss and Crisp illustrate that leveraging data and AI is not about jumping on hype—it's about building a smarter, more efficient, customer-focused business that can handle growth with confidence.

Used well, data and AI give you:

- The clarity to know what's working.
- The foresight to prevent issues before they become costly problems.
- The ability to personalize at scale, delighting customers while maintaining efficiency.

As you continue your growth journey, let data and AI become your partners in scaling—enabling your team to work smarter, your customers to feel seen and valued, and your business to grow without the chaos that often accompanies rapid expansion.

Conclusion: Scaling with Confidence and Discipline

Scaling your business isn't about simply pushing harder on what's already working. It's about building a company that can handle 10X demand without breaking, where growth compounds rather than creates chaos, and where each customer strengthens your foundation instead of weakening it.

In this chapter, we explored five questions that every entrepreneur should ask before scaling. These questions are not academic; they are a practical readiness test. As you've seen through the stories of companies that have grown rapidly, founders who scale successfully take the time to test, refine, and strengthen their business models before stepping on the gas.

Scaling before you're ready can drain cash, demoralize teams, and damage your customer relationships. Scaling with readiness, on the other hand, can transform your business into a durable, profitable, and industry-leading company.

What does readiness look like?

- You know your best customers and can find more like them efficiently.
- Your sales and retention systems run predictably without constant heroic effort.
- Your unit economics are healthy, so growth improves your financial position, not drains it.
- Your operational systems can handle volume without sacrificing quality or culture.
- Your data and AI capabilities help you see clearly, move faster, and serve customers better.

If you find gaps as you answer these questions, that's not a failure—it's an opportunity to focus your efforts where they will have the greatest impact before you scale. Scaling is a choice, not a requirement. But when you choose to scale, choose to do it confidently, backed by the discipline and systems you've built. The path to 100X growth is not a mystery. It is a series of deliberate steps, executed with intention, validated by data, and guided by a commitment to building a business that lasts.

Appendix

Insights from the *Inc 5000* and Deloitte *Fast 500* Leaderboard

As part of our research for **The 100X Entrepreneur**, we analyzed the top companies on the *Inc 5000* and Deloitte *Technology Fast 500* lists from 2022, 2023 and 2024. We gathered data on the 135 companies that grew by at least 10,000% in a period of 3 years to identify what these extreme growth companies had in common – and to select many of the founders featured in this book.

This Appendix presents highlights from 100X growth companies on these lists in quantitative terms and analyzes some of the patterns that we discovered. We know that this data (and the lists themselves) are just one lens among the many needed to understand the strategies that empower companies to grow consistently and profitably over time, as well as to scale rapidly in a defined period. That's why we decided to center this book on the 100X founders who shared their experience, growth strategies, and lessons learned with us.

That said, we also love data. Sometimes the data tells its own story, and analyzing the trends, the outliers, and some surprising stats gives us a better understanding of what kinds of companies manage to achieve 100X growth. If you're an entrepreneur wondering how your own company stacks up—or what kind of environment seems to foster extreme growth—we hope you enjoy this Appendix. Think of it as a map of where the fastest-growing companies come from, and what they look like when they arrive.

Geography of 100X Growth: State-by-State Observations

When you look at where the fastest-growing companies in the country are based, the results aren't exactly shocking—at first. California, New York, Texas, and Florida all have strong showings, just like you'd expect. But dig into the numbers a little deeper, and you'll start to see some surprising patterns.

California Leads in Raw Numbers, But Not Per Capita

California dominates in total count, with 29 companies—over 20% of the total list. That's not exactly shocking given California's population of nearly 39 million and its long-standing reputation as the home of Silicon Valley. What's more interesting, though, is that even with its size, California still overperforms on a per-capita basis. There's one 100X company for every ~1.34 million people in the state.

Compare that to Texas, which has 9 companies and a larger population (over 30 million). That works out to one per ~3.4 million Texans—respectable, but not quite the same concentration as California.

Utah and Kansas: Small States, Big Density

The real overachievers in this dataset are smaller states with a dense concentration of high-growth companies. Utah stands out in a big way. With just over 3.4 million people, it still produced 6 companies—more than Illinois, Florida, and Georgia. That's one 100X company for every 570,000 people, the best ratio in the entire dataset.

Kansas is another standout. With 3 companies from a population of under 3 million, it's punching well above its weight. That's roughly one 100X company for every 979,000 residents—better per capita than New York, Florida, or Georgia.

These are states that don't usually top the "tech hub" lists, but clearly something interesting is happening there—whether it's tax policy, startup ecosystems, or just scrappy founders making things work outside the coasts.

Strong Showings from the Northeast and Mid-Atlantic

Massachusetts continues to be a strong performer, with 6 companies and a population of just 7 million. That's one per ~1.17 million people—very strong. New York also impresses, with 14 companies and one per ~1.4 million. These results support what we'd expect from established innovation corridors like Boston and NYC.

New Jersey also makes a solid appearance with 4 companies. Meanwhile, Maryland, Connecticut, and Virginia show modest but respectable results.

A Note on Canada

There were also a few entries from Canada: British Columbia (BC) and Ontario (ON). Ontario had 3 companies out of nearly 15 million people. BC also had 3, but from a population of just 5.3 million—putting it in the same performance bracket as top U.S. states.

This geographic lens shows that while traditional hubs still dominate in absolute numbers, several smaller states are producing 100X companies at an impressive rate. That confirms opportunity isn't limited to the coasts—ambitious entrepreneurs are building rocket ships in unexpected places.

100X Growth by Industry

When it comes to 100X growth, not all industries are created equal. Some sectors show up again and again on our list—while others are barely represented. Here's how the fastest-growing companies shake out by industry.

Software Still Dominates

No surprise, but the data is striking: software companies dominate the lists, with 25 of the 135 companies—nearly **one in** five—coming from this category. That's a strong showing, and it tracks with what we'd expect. Software companies have scalability advantages, including high margins, relatively low capital requirements, and often operate on subscription-based models that lend themselves well to rapid revenue growth.

Whether it's SaaS, developer tools, or B2B platforms, software continues to be a prime engine for massive scale.

A Broadly Defined Health Care Sector is Rising Fast

Coming in second is Health Care, with 20 companies. That number covers a wide range of subcategories—from health tech and biotech to services, devices, and diagnostics. It's worth noting that healthcare-related businesses often deal with long sales cycles, regulation, and capital intensity—so seeing so many grow 100X is notable.

This could reflect macro trends like increased demand, digital transformation in medicine, and investment in health innovation during the COVID-19 years.

Life Sciences and Financial Services Tie for Third

Life Sciences and Financial Services are tied at 12 companies each. These are high-stakes industries where complexity is the norm—and growth often follows innovation or regulatory shifts.

In financial services, this includes everything from fintech disruptors to niche investment platforms. In life sciences, we're talking about everything from clinical trials to novel therapeutics. Again, high barriers to entry—but massive upside when the timing is right.

Consumer-Facing Categories Hold Their Own

Surprisingly, Consumer Products landed 9 companies on the list. These aren't just digital darlings—they're selling physical goods, and still scaling fast. That's hard to do in a world where logistics, margins, and customer acquisition can eat you alive. This group likely includes DTC brands, health and wellness products, and other breakout consumer hits.

Food & Beverage also posted 8 companies, showing there's still room for explosive growth even in what might seem like mature markets—especially when combined with a strong brand or distribution play.

Retail and **Travel & Hospitality**, on the other hand, barely registered—with only 3 and 2 companies respectively. These sectors are still recovering from the pandemic and often grow at slower, more capital-intensive rates.

Sectors That Surprised (Both High and Low)

- **Logistics & Transportation** (5 companies): With supply chains in the spotlight over the past few years, it's no shock to see this category doing well. But it's interesting to see it rival categories like HR and Construction.
- **Construction** (4 companies): Another surprise. Growth in this sector may be tied to modular building, green construction tech, or B2B service models—not just hammer-and-nail outfits.
- **Human Resources** (6 companies): The HR tech and staffing space continues to grow, especially with the rise of remote work.
- **Crypto & Blockchain**, **Security**, and **Digital Media** all had minimal representation (1–3 companies each). While you might expect crypto to pop off the charts post-2021, this could reflect volatility, the impact of regulation, or just timing in the listing cycles.

And then there are the one-offs: **Insurance, Real Estate, Commercial Products, IT Services**—all with a single company each. It's not impossible to scale in these industries—they just didn't produce many 100X companies in the snapshot our dataset represents.

It's clear that industries don't scale at the same pace. Some sectors may be due for breakout moments in future cycles. But if you're looking for sectors where companies are hitting 100X growth today, this data points the way.

Is There a Company Life Cycle Sweet Spot for 100X Growth?

One of the biggest myths about hypergrowth is that it typically happens early in a startup lifecycle – often in the first 3 years. While there's some truth to that idea—early-stage companies can grow fast—the data paints a more nuanced picture.

We looked at the age of each company at the time it made the list, meaning the number of years between when it was founded and when it achieved 100X growth. Here's what we found from 134 companies where age was available.

Most Hypergrowth Companies Are 4–6 Years Old

If there's a "sweet spot" for 100X growth, it's actually between 4 and 6 years old. That's when most of the companies in this dataset hit escape velocity.

- 5 years is the most common age by far, with 49 companies (36.5% of the list).
- 6 years comes next, with 21 companies.
- 4 years after launch trails behind with 18 companies.

Put together, companies aged 4–6 years account for more than two-thirds (66%) of all 100X growth companies in the dataset.

This makes intuitive sense. It often takes a couple of years to build a product, find product-market fit, raise early funding, and start generating real traction. Year 4 to 6 is when things seem to click—and, in some cases, skyrocket.

Growth After Year 7 Drops Off, But Doesn't Disappear

After the six-year mark, the percentage of extreme growth companies goes down —but they don't go to zero.

- 7–10 years old: Still relatively common, with 14 companies at age 7, and 5 companies at age 10.

- 10+ years: A long tail of outliers exists—13 companies hit 100X growth when they were between 12 and 36 years old.

In other words, while the *typical* hypergrowth company is five years old, there's still room for later-stage breakout growth. Maybe the company pivoted, found a new market, or got a shot of capital that changed everything. Whatever the reason, it proves that hitting it big isn't only a young startup game.

So, while the image of the three-person startup going viral overnight is romantic, the reality is more grounded: most companies that grow 100X aren't newborns—they're 4 to 6 years into the journey, with enough time to build a product, a team, and a scalable model.

The takeaway? You usually need a few years to get your foundation in place before you can really scale.

Behind the Numbers: Capital, Revenue, and Team Size at 100X Scale

You might imagine that 100X growth leads to a lean, ultra-efficient machine—or maybe a bloated, VC-fueled rocket ship. The truth is, it's a bit of both. Once we dug into the detailed data on **capital raised**, **revenue earned**, and **employee headcount**, a few fascinating trends emerged.

Let's break it down.

Capital Raised: The Gap Between Average and Reality

The average amount raised by these hypergrowth companies was a jaw-dropping $333 million. But that's only part of the story.

The median amount raised was much lower—around $118 million—and the standard deviation was huge, suggesting a wide spread. Some companies raised under $10 million and still cracked 100X growth. Others raised billions.

The takeaway: You don't need $300 million to grow 100X, but it certainly helps. Capital is a catalyst—but it's not the only one.

Revenue: Strong Correlation with Headcount, Not Funding

The average revenue among these companies was $288 million, but again, the spread was massive—ranging from $2.2 million to over $3.1 billion.

What's interesting is the strong correlation between revenue and employee size. The bigger the team, the more revenue these companies tend to generate. That's not surprising—but it's a good reminder that 100X growth usually comes with major headcount growth.

On the other hand, the correlation between capital raised and revenue was relatively weak. In plain terms: just because you raised a lot doesn't mean you earned a lot. Throwing money at growth doesn't guarantee results.

Employee Count: Scaling Up Fast

On average, these companies had 509 employees at their peak growth moment. But again, this average can be misleading. Actual headcount ranged from just 24 people to over 5,800.

The companies that reached the highest revenues per employee tended to be software or tech-enabled services. In contrast, companies in healthcare, manufacturing, or logistics had much larger teams relative to their revenue—suggesting more labor-intensive operations.

Efficiency: Revenue per Employee

Let's talk about efficiency. The average revenue per employee across all companies was $660,000—a very healthy number.

But this figure also varied wildly:

- Some companies made less than $100,000 per employee, suggesting high labor costs or lower-margin models.
- Others cleared $1 million+ per employee, pointing to strong pricing power or product leverage (think SaaS or fintech).

Interestingly, there was little correlation between capital raised and revenue per employee —implying that efficiency isn't something you can buy.

Key Takeaways:

- Raising capital helps, but it's not everything: The companies that raised the most weren't always the most efficient or profitable.
- Revenue scales with team size: Big growth = big hiring. Many successful 100X companies built large organizations quickly.
- Efficiency is uneven: Revenue per employee varied significantly—some

companies were lean machines, others were people-heavy and operationally complex.

- You can achieve 100X with a small team: A few outliers managed to scale to hundreds of millions in revenue with under 100 employees.

What does this mean for entrepreneurs? There's no single template. Some companies sprinted with minimal capital. Others scaled with heavy funding and headcount. What they have in common is not **how** they got there—but that they **got there**, using whatever leverage they had.

Founders, Capital, and the Human Element of 100X Growth

When we think about hypergrowth companies, we often start with metrics: growth percentages, millions raised, employees hired. But those numbers all begin with one decision: a founder deciding to start something.

By adding detailed data on founder experience, gender, growth rates, capital raised, revenue, and team size, we're able to get a clearer picture of *who* builds 100X companies—and how those human factors correlate with the outcomes we typically focus on.

Here's what the data reveals.

Who's Leading These 100X Companies?

From a demographic and experience perspective:

- 63% of founders were first-timers.
- 37% were serial entrepreneurs.
- 15% of founders were female, across industries like health services, food & beverage, retail, security, and software.

These proportions align with general industry patterns—but with subtle and important distinctions when we look at how those founders performed across dimensions like revenue, efficiency, and fundraising.

Founder Experience: A Head Start—But Not a Prerequisite

There's a perception that repeat founders always outperform. The data shows a more nuanced story.

- First-time founders had an average 3-year growth rate of 46,687%.
- Repeat founders averaged slightly lower at 38,809%.

Surprisingly, first-time founders showed stronger correlation with ultra-high revenue-per-employee ratios—suggesting a potential leaner, faster execution style. These founders often grew high growth companies without massive teams, and in some cases, without major capital.

First-time founders were significantly less likely to raise large amounts of venture investment. Conversely, repeat founders had more consistent access to capital, which likely helped in capital-intensive sectors like fintech and life sciences.

Takeaway: Experience gives you access—but it's no guarantee. First-time founders, especially in software and consumer sectors, still cracked the 100X threshold with remarkable frequency.

Gender: Still a Big Gap—But Impressive Performance from Female Founders

Among all the founders analyzed:

- 85% were male
- 15% were female

While male founders dominated numerically, female-led companies were responsible for some of the most capital-efficient growth in the dataset.

For instance:

- One female founder in health care grew 146,319% with just $20M raised—reaching $1.13B in revenue with 450 employees.
- Another, in the food & beverage space, turned $1M of capital into a $14.6M business.
- A retail founder achieved $40M+ in revenue on a lean team of 20.

What's clear is this: female founders are underrepresented but not underperforming. When capital and opportunity align, they deliver strong returns.

Final Word: Behind Every Stat Is a Strategy

The founders behind 100X growth stories don't all look the same. They're not all serial entrepreneurs or Silicon Valley unicorn builders. Some bootstrapped. Some raised a small amount of capital and ran lean.

The ultimate takeaway? There are multiple paths to achieve scalability and extreme growth. Choose the one that matches your own vision and strengths, and build your company using the essential elements recommended by every100X entrepreneur in this book.

Acknowledgements

First, our heartfelt appreciation to the entrepreneurs who so generously took time to meet with us, answer our many questions, share their successes and challenges, and review the 100X stories we wrote for this book. Without their time, insights, and reflections on the experience of scaling their companies, *The 100X Entrepreneur,* quite literally, would not have been possible.

In order of where their stories appear in this book, a giant THANK YOU to Niraj Shah and Steve Conine (CSN Stores/Wayfair); Mike Salguero (ButcherBox); Armir Harris (CharterUP); Ben Goodwin (OLIPOP); Shane Heath, (MUD/WTR); Adam and Amanda Kroener (Carbliss); John Williamson (Songfinch); Dane Atkinson (Odeko); Yoseph West (Relay); David Sperau (Autosled); Jyoti Bansal (Harness); Are Traasdahl (Crisp); Dan Espinal (Rarebreed Veterinary Partners); Luke Tomaszewski (ProxyPics); Michael London (Uwill); Aaron Smith and Callie Turk (FlexCare Infusion Centers); James Dean (Oxygen8); Glen Moller (Upward Health); Dave Marcy and Ryan Sprance (Awestruck); and Dave Maman (WeCall).

Our appreciation comes with recognition that due to page limit constraints and editorial timelines, this book could only cover selective aspects of each company's growth story, and acknowledgement that any errors in sharing these stories are the responsibility of the authors.

In our research for this book, including recording, transcribing, and analyzing founder interviews, outlining and formatting our content, we have leveraged generative AI tools including those provided by Otter.ai, Zoom, Gemini, Anthropic, OpenAI, and Grammarly. These tools did not substitute for our human work of idea generation, critical analysis, writing, and editing. That said, first-hand experience with AI deepened our appreciation of the role that AI applications play in today's fastest growing business.

Thanks to Kelly Yu, our invaluable research assistant, for aggregating data on the top-ranked companies on the *Inc 5000*, Deloitte Fast 500, and other high-growth company lists, and for compiling the initial materials that informed our 100X entrepreneur interviews. Many thanks also to Brenda Riddell at Graphic Details for *The 100X Entrepreneur* cover design. Finally, special appreciation to all the entrepreneurship students, guest speakers, colleagues, and clients whose business planning questions, startup strategies, and shared experiences of challenges and success helped inspire us to write this book.

Mary J. Cronin & David A. Reske
The100XEntrepreneur.com
2025

Sources

Chapter 1

Niraj Shah (CSN Stores/Wayfair), unpublished interview with M. J. Cronin, March 25, 2025.

Steve Conine (CSN Stores/Wayfair), unpublished interview with M. J. Cronin, April 2, 2025.

Kathy Hovis, "Wayfair founders share story of company's rise," *Cornell Chronicle*, April 23, 2018

About Wayfair, "20 Years of Home," Wayfair Company Timeline, 2022

Lagorio-Chafkin, Christine. "Meet the Guy Who Wants to Mail You a Box of Meat Every Month." *Inc.*, September 9, 2015.

Mike Salguero (ButcherBox), unpublished interview with M. J. Cronin, March 31, 2025.

Poulden, Amory. "ButcherBox: How They Reached $600M in Annual Revenue with No VC Funding." *Medium*, July 12, 2025.

Moore, Kaleigh, and Web Smith. "Member Practical: ButcherBox's Growth Arbitrage." *2PM*, January 28, 2021.

Chapter 2

Armir Harris, " CharterUP (Our Team profile)," *CharterUP website*, accessed May 2025.

Armir Harris (CharterUP), unpublished interview with M. J. Cronin, November 10, 2024.

Christine Lagorio-Chafkin, "He Fled a Civil War at Age 8. Now He's Driving One of the Fastest-Growing Companies in America," *Inc. Magazine*, September 2023

CharterUP Blog, "CharterUP Hits $1 Billion Platform Volume: How Our Network Powers Group Travel," January 27, 2025

Chapter 3

Ben Goodwin (OLIPOP), unpublished interview with M.J. Cronin, December 5, 2024

Chhabra, Esha. "Olipop Merges Profit and Purpose With $200 Million in Sales and a New B Corp Certification." *Forbes*, November 21, 2023.

Kats, Rimma. "How the Pandemic Pushed Olipop into the D2C Space (And How an SMS Message Led to $15,000 in 15 Minutes)." *Insider Intelligence/ eMarketer*, March 4, 2021.

Mendler, Adam. "Believe In Yourself and Your Idea To Make It Happen: Interview with Ben Goodwin, Co-Founder and CEO of OLIPOP." *AdamMendler.com Blog*, 2023

Planet Money Staff. "The Battle for Grocery Store Shelf Space, and the Rise of Olipop (Niche Brands)." *NPR – The Indicator*, January 25, 2024.

Yahoo Finance. "How Prebiotic Soda Olipop Leveraged Social Media to Grow from a $100,000 Investment to a $1.85 Billion Brand on Shelves at Walmart, Target, and Whole Foods." *Yahoo Finance*, May 1, 2025.

Zhang, Crystal. "2023 Best Marketers: Olipop's Influencer Marketing and Social Media Plays Are Paying Off." *Advertising Age*, December 11, 2023.

Shane Health MUD/WTR), unpublished interview with D.A. Reske, October 31, 2024

Shane Heath. *MUD\WTR Founder's Story.* MUD\WTR website, accessed November 2024

Amrita Khalid. "How This founder Made His Startup a No Burnout Zone," *Inc. Magazine,* May 12, 2021

Adam Kroener (Carbliss), unpublished interview with M.J. Cronin, October 24, 2024

"This Husband-Wife Duo Is Changing the Face of Wellness Spirits," *Life & Style*, Sep. 25, 2023

"Entrepreneurs to Watch: Amanda and Adam Kroener – Carbliss," *BizTimes Milwaukee*, May 2025

John Williamson (Songfinch), unpublished interview with M.J. Cronin, November 5, 2024

Rebecca Deczynski, "What's a Custom Music Platform Anyway? Chicago Startup Songfinch Has the $36 Million Answer," *Inc. Magazine*, Sept. 2023

Chapter 4

Dane Atkinson (Odeko), unpublished interview with M.J. Cronin, January 22, 2025

Turner Novak, From Zero to $150 Million Revenue in Two Years with Odeko Founder and CEO, Dane Atkinson. *The Split*, April 15, 2024

Yoseph West (Relay), unpublished interview with M.J. Cronin, January 24, 2025

Atkinson, David. "How Relay Grew 6X in One Year While Keeping Its Free Business Banking Model." *Fintech Today*, June 20, 2024.

Bain Capital Ventures. "Why We're Doubling Down on Relay." *Medium (Bain Capital Ventures Blog)*, May 7, 2024.

Bensinger, Greg. "Small Business Banking Goes Digital." *The Wall Street Journal*, July 21, 2023.

Curry, Kristen. "Relay's Cash Flow Clarity: A Solution for SMB Pain Points." *TechCrunch*, May 10, 2023.

David Sperau (Autosled), unpublished interview with D.A. Reske, October 29, 2024

AutoRemarketing. "Autosled leads auto industry on Inc.'s list of fastest-growing private companies," August 13, 2024

Jyoti Bansal (Harness), unpublished interview with M.J. Cronin and D.A. Reske, February 7, 2025.

TechCrunch. "Harness valuation hits $3.7B." *TechCrunch*, April 26, 2022.

Contrary Research. "Report: Harness Business Breakdown & Founding Story." Accessed January 2025.

Edward Targett, "Harness CEO Jyoti Bansal on 'startups within startups'." *The Stack*, January 2, 2025.

Chapter 5

Are Traasdahl (Crisp), unpublished interview with M.J. Cronin, January 8, 2025.

SupplyChain Digital, "How Crisp Helps Nestlé USA Boost Visibility and Efficiency," October 28, 2024.

AlleyWatch, "Crisp Adds $17M to Bring Data Connectivity and Insights to All Facets of the CPG Supply Chain," October 2024

Jordan Crook, "Crisp convinces more investors that it will rid the world of empty grocery store shelves," *TechCrunch*, February 2, 2022.

Crisp website. "About & Mission," *Gocrisp.com* accessed March 15, 2025.

Dan Espinal (Rarebreed Veterinary Partners), unpublished interview with M. J. Cronin, December 4, 2024.

William Hall. "Breeding innovation: Rarebreed grows out of Maine's animal-health hub." *Mainebiz*, March 4, 2024.

Jack Salter. "Rarebreed Veterinary Partners: Reimagining the Veterinary Experience." *Healthcare Outlook*, March 12, 2023.

Rarebreed Veterinary Partners. "Rarebreed Veterinary Partners Acquires Vet's Best Friend Group in Landmark Veterinary Deal." News release, June 30, 2022.

Luke Tomaszewski (ProxyPics), unpublished interview with M. J. Cronin, December 11, 2024.

Appraisal Buzz Staff. "ProxyPics Partners with Freddie Mac to Simplify Refinance Mortgages in the Digital Age." *Appraisal Buzz*, July 18, 2022.

Ben Sherry. "3 Ways Inc. 5000 Companies Are Using AI." *Inc. Magazine*, August 14, 2024.

ProxyPics "About Us – How It Started." ProxyPics website, Accessed July 10, 2025.

Chapter 6

Michael London (Uwill), unpublished interview with M. J. Cronin, December 12, 2024

Hillary Chabot, "Technology Meets Compassion: Uwill Founder Brings Mental Wellness Solutions to College Students," *Babson Thought & Action*, January 8, 2025.

Chloe Aiello. "How This Mental Health Startup's Mission Helped Generate Millions in Sales," *Inc. Magazine,* Jan 17, 2024

Aaron Smith (FlexCare Infusion Centers), unpublished interview with D.A. Reske, December 12, 2024

Sarosh Lateef, "Episode 21: Starting an Infusion Center with Aaron and Callie, FlexCare Infusion Center," *WeInfuse Podcast* (transcript), July 24, 2019.

Claire Rychlewski et al., "Scoop: Optum agrees to acquire FlexCare Infusion," *Axios Pro: Health Tech Deals*, Jan. 15, 2025

James Dean (Oxygen8), unpublished interview with M. J. Cronin, December 16, 2024

Innovate BC. "Innovate BC and NRC IRAP invest in British Columbia businesses through BC Fast Pilot Program," Feb 16, 2022

Chapter 7

Glen Moller (Upward Health), unpublished interview with M. J. Cronin, January 14, 2025

Joyce Famakinwa. "How 3 Home-Based Care Companies Jump-Started Their Growth," *Home Health Care News*, August 25, 2023

Karen Turner. "Shining a light on Canada's 2024 cleantech innovators" EDC. ca October 29, 2024

Dave Marcy & Ryan Sprance (Awestruck) unpublished interview with D. A. Reske, November 22, 2024.

"How a Destination Marketing Company Soared to No. 25 on the Inc. 5000." *Inc.Magazine*, November 3, 2023

David Maman (WeCall) unpublished interview with D. A. Reske, November 1, 2024

Symone Graham. "How Charlotte ad agency WeCall Media snagged a top spot on Inc. 5000 list of fastest-growing private companies," *Charlotte Business Journal*, Aug 22, 2023

www.ingramcontent.com/pod-product-compliance
Lightning Source LLC
Chambersburg PA
CBHW060334200326
41519CB00011BA/1938